COUNTRY
COMPETITIVENESS

COUNTRY COMPETITIVENESS

Technology and the Organizing of Work

Edited by

BRUCE KOGUT

New York   Oxford
OXFORD UNIVERSITY PRESS
1993

Oxford University Press

Oxford   New York   Toronto
Delhi   Bombay   Calcutta   Madras   Karachi
Kuala Lumpur   Singapore   Hong Kong   Tokyo
Nairobi   Dar es Salaam   Cape Town
Melbourne   Auckland   Madrid

and associated companies in
Berlin   Ibadan

Published by Oxford University Press, Inc.,
200 Madison Avenue, New York, New York 10016

Oxford is a registered trademark of Oxford University Press

Library of Congress Cataloging-in-Publication Data
Country competitiveness :
technology and the organizing of work /
edited by Bruce Kogut.
p.   cm.   Includes bibliographical references and index.
ISBN 0-19-507277-4
1. Competition—Case studies.   2. Competition, International—Case studies.
3. Industrial management—Case studies.
I. Kogut, Bruce Mitchel.
HD41.C68   1993   338'.064—dc20   92-22897

2 4 6 8 9 7 5 3 1

Printed in the United States of America
on acid-free paper

Acknowledgments

A published volume is as remarkable for what is in it as for what is left out. Of the list of things not obvious in the final publication—the papers that never arrived, those that did not ultimately fit, the discussion left unrecorded because of the slugging of a nearby jackhammer—it is the efforts of colleagues and friends who abetted this enterprise that most deserve recognition.

The participants at the conference from which this book is largely drawn generated an intellectually stimulating environment when they met in Brussels in June 1990 at the facilities housing the European Institute for Advanced Studies in Management (EIASM). It was a fun and intense two days, which ended with acts of desperation to avoid the effects of an imminent rail strike. There was a wide mix of disciplines and nationalities, the papers were engaging, and the atmosphere was intimate. Participation by contributors and those attending was active. Program participants included Edward H. Bowman, Michael Brocklehurst, Claudio Casadio-Tarabusi, Diana De Pay, Enrico Deiaco, Fabtenne Fecher, Peter Friederick, Allan Mas Gjerding, Hans Glimmel, Richard Goodman, Agnes Haak, Franco Malerba, Mark Rainer, Piero Migliarese, Walter W. Powell, Hagge Rilegard, Bengt Sandkull, Erica Schoenberger, Allen Scott, Helart Soldner, Fred Steward, Jan Stuip, Danny Van Den Bulcke, Alain Verbeke, and Beverly Winterscheio.

The success of those days was due to assistance from Professor Ned Bowman of the Wharton School; Professor Daniel van den Bulcke, now of the University of Antwerp; and Ms. Gerry van Dyck. I would like to thank the Reginald H. Jones Center of the Wharton School; the Center for International Management and Development at the University of Antwerp; the National Fund for Scientific Research in Belgium; and EIASM for their generous financial assistance. Professors Bowman and van den Bulcke were responsible for building a positive intellectual tone in the proceedings. And those who have witnessed an EIASM meeting before know the irreplaceable role played by Ms. van Dyck and her very able staff. A grant from the German Marshall Fund was instrumental in giving me the time to analyze country competition in relation to variations in how work is organized differently among nations and to prepare the conference from which this book stems.

There are regrets. I had hoped to have included the perspective of economic geography and the economics of innovation. Due either to publications committed elsewhere, or the press of other obligations, we fell short in this regard. But the participation of Erica Schoenberger, Diana de Pay, and Allen Scott was an important contribution, teaching us a lot about time, space, and use of slide projectors.

I was fortunate in having such agreeable colleagues as contributors, and I would like to thank them for their cooperation.

Philadelphia   B. K.
June 1992

Contents

III Diffusion of New Ways of Organizing

IV Concluding Notes

Contributors

Florence Charue
Center of Management Research
Ecole Polytechnique, Paris

Giovanni Dosi
Department of Economics
University of Rome

John H. Dunning
Department of Economics
University of Reading

W. Mark Fruin
University of British Columbia

Gary Herrigel
Department of Political Science
University of Chicago

Horst Kern
Department of Sociology
University of Goettingen

Bruce Kogut
The Wharton School
University of Pennsylvania

James R. Lincoln
Haas School of Business
University of California at Berkeley

Marc Maurice
Laboratory of Economics and
   Organization
University of Aix-en-Provence

Michael Schumann
Department of Sociology
University of Goettingen

Christophe Midler
Center of Management Research
Ecole Polytechnique, Paris

Toshihiro Nishiguchi
Wharton School
University of Pennsylvania

David Parkinson
The Wharton School
University of Pennsylvania

Arndt Sorge
Department of Sociology
Humboldt University

Jürgens Ulrich
Science Center, Berlin

Juliette Webster
Research Center for Social Services
Edinburgh University

Eleanor Westney
Sloan School of Management
Massachusetts Institute of Technology

D. Hugh Whittaker
Faculty of Oriental Studies
University of Cambridge

COUNTRY
COMPETITIVENESS

Introduction

BRUCE KOGUT

Determinants of Economic Leadership

The history of the industrial world reveals striking cycles in economic leadership among countries. The first great industrial empire was the British. At the turn of this century, the United States was recognized as the preeminent economic power in the world. And, there is solid evidence to believe that current economic leadership is increasingly shared by Japan.

This book is premised on the simple observation that changes in economic leadership are marked by radical changes in the principles by which work is organized. The economic epochs of England, the United States, and Japan witnessed the introduction and diffusion of new methods of organizing economic activities. England introduced a radical break with previous practices by organizing workers in factories under the principle of the division of labor. By the end of the nineteenth century, factories in the relatively young United States were attracting foreign visitors who were seeking to understand the organization underlying a system of mass production. In our own time, the organizing principles of Japanese production are only slowly and gradually being identified and understood.

The chapters in this book analyze country patterns in the organizing of work. They vary in their focus, a few providing detailed description of the impact of new methods in a few locations; others analyzing the organization of work as embedded in a wider web of institutional relationships; and several offering a historical comparison of countries. Despite this diversity, the chapters present the common theme that country location matters, that organizing practices are difficult to change, and that historical patterns persist.

To place these contributions into perspective, consider alternative explanations as to why certain countries gain economic leadership. A conventional approach has been to seek the answer in how well countries use their supplies of labor and capital. Since Robert Solow (1970) showed that the vast proportion of American economic growth cannot be attributed to either capital or labor inputs, the usual suspects, to paraphrase the inspector in *Casablanca,* have been rounded up and tested. While the mystery appears to diminish with the addition of new factors (e.g., expenditures for research and education), these tests have failed to identify a component that greatly adds to the explanation.[1] What we have is an assemblage of causes, whose composition provides no unifying explanation.[2]

Because of the difficulties in identifying an economic cause in the sense of factor inputs, many analysts have turned to looking more rigorously at institutional determinants. One school of thought stresses the impasse among political groups. In an ambitious formulation, Olson (1982) points to the decline of countries through the ossification of the economic structure due to conflict among interest groups, none of which is broad or powerful enough to embrace and represent the welfare of the country. The analyses by Thurow (1982) and Ouchi (1984) of the American decline also point to stagnation caused by adversarial relations among interest groups.

There is no doubt much to be recommended in this approach. But the approach of Olson is subtly content free and strangely ahistorical in its implications, as if the secret is but to let market forces determine the correct prices and institutions. Yet, while interest groups—unions, firms, or governments—may have an understanding of the politics of how to cut the pie, it is completely another matter whether they have a sense of how to better organize the economy. Whereas Ouchi is persuaded of the value of the Japanese corporatist model, what exactly should be borrowed from Japan? And why is this borrowing so difficult to carry out? These questions are difficult to answer because there is so little known regarding how work is organized differently across countries and which practices, even when identified, should be transferred.

Consider the case of the reconstruction of Eastern Europe, which poses so clearly the issue of what practices should be recommended. The primary focus has been on deregulating these economies by removing price controls, floating the currency in international markets, and designing capital markets to establish the value of privatized firms (e.g., see Lipton and Sachs, 1990). These policies are directed, and rightly so given the catastrophic consequences of faulty relative prices, toward generating better *information* regarding the costs of production and the preferences of consumers.

Yet, it is hard to imagine that simply improving information in a market setting will move these economies into levels of productivity commensurate with the West. Part of the problem is that restructuring also entails the loss of information. When suppliers become bankrupt, or their production is exported, the purchasing firm is suddenly in the position of not knowing where to turn. There is no readily available information on alternative suppliers, the prices and quality of their products, and reliability of their delivery.

The dilemma of these East European firms calls into sharp relief the importance of the social environment, and the strength of the overall economic network, to the performance of individual enterprises. It is convenient to conclude that failure in this period of transition is an indication of inefficiency. We cannot rule out, however, that the source of these failures lies in the weakening of the economic network of suppliers and buyers, as well as with the wider institutions of finance and government counsel, rather than in the relative long-term inefficiency of a particular firm.[3]

But information is only one part of the story. Should we believe that if only these enterprises should know the right prices, then suddenly they would achieve comparable rates of productivity to the West? To use an American term, what would still be lacking is the *know-how* of product development, production, marketing, and services.[4] Equip a factory in East Europe with the most modern machinery and install the most advanced information systems available, and productivity will still lag behind that of the West. If the issue were simply one of information and technology, then why is there such disparity in performance even among developed countries?

It is the very ambiguity of the concept of know-how that returns us to our original problems with identifying the practices responsible for the superior performance of some firms. The introduction of new production methods by Toyota in the 1950s and 1960s was an innovation in the know-how by which mass production of automobiles was organized. Its slow evolution and diffusion in Japan suggests the difficulties by which Toyota, as well as its Japanese competitors, understood the implications. (See Chapter 11 by Fruin and Nishiguchi in this volume.) But consider the problem from the perspective of non-Japanese competitors, trying to decide which practice idiosyncratic to Japan is responsible for superior performance. The differences among countries regarding how finance is organized; workers are hired, paid, and promoted; and technology is developed are so many that identification of the best practice is especially troublesome across borders. (I explain this point in more detail in Kogut, 1991.)

Adoption of these practices is even more impaired because they are embedded in a system or, to use a parlance growing in popularity, in a larger network. In an instructive study, Robert Cole (1985) looked at the adoption of quality circles in Sweden, the United States, and Japan. He concluded that the inability of American firms to adopt this practice was due to the absence of supporting institutions. These findings reflect the important point that the feasibility of the adoption of best practices by a firm is strongly linked to the system-wide characteristics of its regional and national environments.

It is a short step, inductively, from this point to the stronger claim of national principles for the organizing of work and technology. While the claim of national principles of organizing work is hardly new (see Alfred Marshall's *Industry and Trade* [1921]) it is a surprisingly difficult one to pin down and define. A central difficulty is that there is a tendency for countries to experience both periods of differentiation and convergence in their practices of work. It is, thus, misleading to study national differences without an understanding of the history of these practices and the social context of their development.

One of the important lessons of the 1980s is that organizing principles have been too narrowly studied in the context of manufacturing. Taylorism, in fact, was in many ways supplanted by the growth of systems of mass production and the discipline imposed by the regularity of the assembly line. In the office place, Taylorist ideas were widely adopted through such innovations as secretarial pools. Functional specialization also is an outstanding characteristic of the development of corporate research laboratories.

Broadly seen, national organizing principles pertain to how the shopfloor and the workplace, the corporation, and the institutions between and supporting individual firms are organized. It is because the resources of a firm are linked to the greater economy that competitiveness must be understood, partly, as a question of the productivity of its resident country. But, more subtly, it is because the country of origin of a firm has impressed a set of operating rules—for example, how to manufacture, to manage people, to do research—on the firm that even when it is a multinational corporation, it carries this organizational baggage.

Structure of the Book

This book consists of essays written to analyze the organizing principles of work in different countries and their implications for performance. There has been no attempt to impose a common framework on these chapters. This decision was motivated by the recognition that no such unanimity can or should exist regarding such a complex set of principles. Yet, because the authors are mostly industrial sociologists with varying emphasis on technology and society, the chapters do evoke common themes and methodologies.

The structure of the book is divided along the lines of three types of studies. The thematic combination of national systems of work and the impact of new methods of organization provide the background to the studies in Part I, but becomes the central leitmotif in the subsequent two parts. In Part I, the empirical studies concern primarily country patterns and national comparisons. Part II consists of studies analyzing the adoption of new technologies and practices. Finally, Part III looks more closely at the process of diffusion, both within and across countries. It is a striking testimony to the nature of international competition that the division of the book into these three parts breaks down in particulars. For all the chapters discuss the diffusion of new practices and the responses of firms to these organizational challenges. It is impossible to take a snapshot view of firms in industrialized countries without analyzing the powerful pressures for change in their organizations of work due to international competition.

Despite the thematic similarity, the chapters differ vary widely in their orientations, from careful micro-observations on the introduction of new technologies into plants of two French automobile firms, to comparisons of industries within the same countries, to contrasts between entire countries. This variety in levels of analysis should work to the reader's advantage by providing multiple perspectives on specific country practices from the workplace to the larger societal institutions.[5] These multiple perspectives are also facilitated by the focus on only five countries: France, Germany,* Japan, the United Kingdom, and the United States.

The chapters by Gary Herrigel (Chap. 1) and Eleanor Westney (Chap. 2) share an emphasis on the importance of understanding the firm-level practices in the context of the wider social institutions. Herrigel shows how the notion of *flexible specialization*—a term coined by Piore and Sabel (1984) to characterize modern production and organizing practices—requires the support of public and private institutions within the region of Baden Württemberg in Germany. He describes a

---

*All references to Germany mean West Germany (Federal Republic of Germany) prior to 1990, unless East Germany (German Democratic Republic) is specified.

political and economic order by which know-how is shared among small- to medium-size firms as a way of sharing risk. An interesting development in the region is the policy by the larger firms, such as the auto part and electronics firm Bosch, to spin off subsidiaries into independent operations and to rely on many suppliers, which also serve other firms. In this sense, the policy of Bosch resembles the federated suppliers to Toyota, as described in Chapter 12.

Westney applies the lens of institutional theory to analyze a similar topic: how the capabilities—in this sense, technological—of Japanese firms are structured by the pull between corporate and societal scientific institutions. In the brief summary of studies on Japanese research and development activities, Westney debunks several misperceptions regarding the organization of scientific and engineering work in Japan. She notes that while in the United States corporate scientists are more pulled toward professional norms, Japanese scientists and engineers view their careers within the corporation.[6] Yet, at the same time, Japanese engineers evidence a higher rate of participation in professional societies. Personal reputation in a profession is viewed as a way of enhancing company prestige.

These observations are confirmed in the contribution by James Lincoln (Chap. 3), who summarizes the major findings of his research comparing U. S. and Japanese manufacturing firms. Lincoln notes that changes in the organization of work appears to be greater in the United States, an observation he makes in support of the endurance of Japanese practices, but which can also be interpreted as a statement on the necessity of the United States to adopt these practices. Lincoln details exhaustively the many differences in the organization of work, internal labor markets, and industrial relations between the two countries. In one comparison, he notes that whereas both Japan and the United States score similarly on the degree to which authority is formally centralized, actual decision making is far more decentralized in Japanese factories. This finding, that best practice is linked to greater autonomy and self-regulation in the workplace, is echoed in many of the other studies.

The final chapter in Part I is by Arndt Sorge and Marc Maurice (Chap. 4), who compare the machine-tool industry in France and Germany. The analysis by Westney of the organization of American and Japanese research underscores how many ways countries may develop by which to organize what some would argue are "functionally equivalent" activities. Like Westney, Sorge and Maurice reject this view of functional equivalence. They seek to demonstrate that in France and Germany, there exist distinct "societal effects" that constrained and predisposed the reaction of their firms to the crisis of the mid- and late-1970s. In their analysis, they pay careful attention to the effect of demand on the kinds of products firms deliver to qualify the interpretation that the differences in the organization of work are simply derived from differences in what consumers want. The crux of their argument rests on their evidence that French producers were, in fact, better positioned to respond to changes in the market. In contrast to German firms, they failed to do so due to larger "discontinuities in the structure of its firms, between firms, and between institutions at large." This conclusion coincides with Herrigel's examination of the social underpinnings to the German machine-tool industry.

Part II turns directly to studies of the experiences in different countries in adopting new technologies and organizing principles. In Chapter 5, Horst Kern and Michael Schumann summarize succinctly the major trends in three German industries since the publication of their renowned study of the end of the division of labor. Their book, entitled *Das Ende der Arbeitsteilung* (the End of the Division of Labor) and which has not been translated into English, represented a major shift in German industrial-sociological thinking from pessimism to positive evaluation of the introduction of more automated and flexible manufacturing systems in Germany. Their chapter underlines the importance of the availability of skilled German labor, while at the same time noting the increasing international division of labor that is causing greater emphasis to be placed on outsourcing (i.e., purchasing parts or services from outside the firm) and on research and development activities.

The critical aspect of the skill level of workers is underscored in Ulrich Jürgens's comparison of three automobile companies in the United States and Germany and their plants in these countries, as well as in the United Kingdom (Chap. 6). Jürgens does not blink an eye, as he outlines how Japan and Germany present models of best practice in the manufacturing of automobiles; the United States model of mass production is briefly described for its historical value. His description of the difficulty of introducing new technologies into the U. S. plants due to the shortage of labor skills is sobering, especially in light of the improvement in the United Kingdom due to its labor training programs inaugurated in the early 1980s. Jürgens's comparison of the Japanese and German models presents the fascinating question of which one is better suited for introduction into other Western countries. To a certain extent, this question is answered in his comments on the transfer by American automobile firms of German techniques into their British plants.

Ronald Dore (1986) has posed an intriguing question about why Japanese corporations, despite being rigidly constrained in their ability to lay off workers or to shift production overseas, appear to achieve higher rates of flexibility. In Chapter 7, summarizing his remarkable study of paired British and Japanese factories, Whittaker reveals one source of flexibility by analyzing how firms differed in their solutions to the introduction of the operation and programming of computer numerically controlled (CNC) machinery. Whittaker, in effect, is looking at the customer side of the industries that Herrigel, Sorge and Maurice, and Kern and Schumann all analyzed. Computer numerically controlled machines provide the capability to respond more flexibly to changes in market conditions. A principal problem is whether to let the traditional operator of the machinery also now undertake the task of programming. In Japan, the operator tends to be also the programmer. This policy is feasible because, despite the seniority system, younger workers are used, with the more senior workers being retired early or delegated to other tasks. In the United Kingdom, the solution has been to maintain the distinction between skilled and unskilled workers; older workers are kept as operators, with programming tasks being carried out by a skilled engineer. Yet, while Japan and the United Kingdom appear nominally to have found functionally equivalent solutions, Whittaker argues that the Japanese system is likely to favor greater innovation over time.

Juliette Webster's chapter represents the conflict between the introduction of new information technologies and the existing organization (Chap. 8). Though the sites of installation are manufacturing firms, her study is of the user side to essentially a service industry. With a new wave of Japanese practices spreading across industrialized countries, British firms need to integrate these new methods with the mixture of indigenous and assimilated American methods. Her studies show that these systems are encountering substantial difficulty because the information and data are not available and because there is no resident know-how regarding the management and organization of these systems. Her results have an archaeological quality as she peels off the sediments of Japanese, American, and indigenous influences.

Chapter 9 by Christophe Midler and Florence Charue compares the process of technological change in two French firms. By this contrast, they are able to capture the important variation of organizing practices within the same country. Both Peugeot and Renault, the two French car manufacturers, began to experiment with new flexible manufacturing technologies by the early 1980s. Surprisingly, only in 1987 did engineers and plant managers compare their developments against Japanese examples. Both companies slowly recognized the radical implications for redesigning the organization of work. Renault, as a nationalized firm, stayed more within the conventional norms of the distinction between skilled and unskilled workers. Peugeot has increasingly moved toward a German model of eliminating unskilled jobs and relying more heavily on technicians who have earned the appropriate educational credentials. In both cases, Midler and Charue note, the process of change was influenced by the existing organizational conception of work. As a result, the pattern of change exhibits certain "irreversible" characteristics; not all avenues of development are open.

The final section of the book, Part III, focuses on the diffusion of practices within and across countries. As seen in many of the chapters, the impact of new technologies such as flexible manufacturing systems is often contrasted against Taylorist principles, no matter if the country under discussion is Germany, Japan, the United States, or any other developed country. The international diffusion of Taylorist principles of organization has resulted in the irony that the different country experiences with the introduction of new technologies is often analyzed against a common benchmark of these earlier principles. The ideas of Taylor, who was an American consultant at the turn of the century, spread throughout Europe, as well as to Japan, by the 1920s. They were, of course, modified and adapted to local conditions. In the chapter by David Parkinson and myself (Chap. 10), we argue that the acceptance of Taylorism and the later expansion of the multidivisional structure of American corporations were influenced the indigenous societal conditions. Given the class antagonism in Britain, it is not surprising that Taylorism was not widely adopted at the shopfloor, but the multidivisional structure—which affects only the white-collar workers—spread quickly and widely among the United Kingdom's largest corporations. These conclusions are stark reminders that the existing structure of labor relations and organization—or what Herrigel calls the "political ordering"—delineates the possibilities for the adoption of best practices.

John Dunning's chapter shows clearly how the international expansion of firms is driven by the organizing principles learned in their home environments (Chap. 11). Dunning applies an economic taxonomy of advantages specific to countries to compare the organizational traits that American firms brought to the United Kingdom in the 1950s and that Japanese firms are currently transferring along with their new subsidiaries established in the 1970s and 1980s.[7] Because he again surveyed the American subsidiaries in the 1980s, his data allow an interesting look into period effects (1950 vs. 1980), as well as country differences. Dunning finds that the competence gap between American and British firms was greatly narrowed by the 1980s, resulting in considerable delegation to the United Kingdom and other European subsidiaries. The Japanese subsidiaries, however, were tightly controlled in three regards: a large proportion of components were sourced from Japan, production control and accounting were tightly implemented according to standards set at headquarters, and the top managers and finance officers tend to be Japanese expatriates. Dunning's conclusions that the organizing principles of subsidiaries reflects strongly the country of origin underscores the important role of foreign investment in diffusing techniques across borders.

Mark Fruin and Toshihoro Nishiguchi address their concerns to analyzing the evolution of the Toyota Production System in Chapter 12. Their historical account shows that this system is still very much in development, and its diffusion even within Japan is incomplete and in the process of adaptation and reinterpretation. Their explanation also questions a body of literature that has tried to understand the design of organizations by analyzing the incentive properties that exist to temper the selfish behavior of individuals. Without discarding this approach, they argue that a more fruitful way to understand the Toyota Production System is by focusing on its dynamic of continual learning and sharing of the benefits of this learning in the context of long-term and cooperative relationships. This chapter is an interesting reminder that while the diffusion of Japanese organizing principles is underway internationally, these principles are still evolving within Japan itself.

The final chapter of the book is an interpretative essay by Giovanni Dosi and myself (Chap. 13). We stress the importance of the historical roots of "national specificities" and link this process to the work in evolutionary economics and sociology. A central observation in our analysis is the dynamic linkage (or coevolution) between technologies and organizing principles. This linkage, which is a theme throughout the book, is not deterministic in the sense of a matching of a type of technology to a type of organization, but nevertheless is bounded by critical elements that are difficult to forecast and to identify. Our approach permits the possibility of change and evolution, but in the context of historically rooted social systems.

Conclusions

The essays in this book are mostly positive in their approach; only a few hazard normative implications. But there is an implication in these chapters that is, in many ways, shocking. Only four of the authors to this book are U. S. citizens; the rest are citizens of Canada, European countries, and Japan. In none of these chapters was the American model of organization discussed other than for its historical value or for the sake of comparison.

Hegel wrote that the owl of Minerva flies at dusk; wisdom is only earned when it is too late. It is too late for the United States to regain its position of the exemplar of best practice in the world. Yet, many of the practices described in the pages in this book appear to be out of the reach for the United States, even if it wishes only to share this leadership. The repeated theme of the importance of skilled workers with relative autonomy over a wide variety of tasks has been found to rest significantly upon the quality of education, the existence of programs of apprenticeship and worker qualifications, and the elimination of occupational distinctions. The United States is sorely lacking in these concepts.

But the problem does not seem to be only the American system of worker training and education. As this book goes to press, the American economy is reeling from layoffs at major U. S. corporations in their American plants. At the same time, some of these firms are expanding production in plants located in lower wage environments, while some of their competitors are opening new plants in the United States. There is a clear irony in this pattern. And the implications are ominous for these corporations, as the benefits of these low-cost offshore platforms diminish due to rising wages or to the improved productivity and quality of more automated systems.

The challenge is the mastery of new systems of technologies, along with the concomitant development of organizing principles. The progress made by American corporations in this regard is unquestionable. By their rich detail, the essays in this book suggest why this progress is not enough. The recommendation is not to adopt either the German or Japanese model as solutions. The insight of these essays is that there is no single model. There is a need to consider programs of social experimentation, and business firms cannot do it alone.

Notes

1. For one recent and admirable attempt to explain away this residual, see Maddison (1982).

2. An excellent critique of this approach is given in Nelson (1981).

3. This point cannot be pursued here, other than to note that it is consistent with the treatment of a different question by Winter (1964).

4. For a discussion of information and know-how as constituting the knowledge of the firm, see Kogut and Zander (1992).

5. Moreover, six of the twelve empirical studies concern the automobile and machine-tool industries. This industry commonality is not surprising, given the emphasis on Germany and Japan in the book.

6. In this sense, the analysis of Westney parallels the work of the Aix-school (see Chap. 4 for a description), whereby labor markets among countries differ, such as the stress in Germany on professional qualifications and in France on seniority in the organization; this difference leads to a greater importance of a market for labor with mobility in Germany and of internal labor markets (i.e., promotion within the firm) in France. Japan, Westney suggests, appears to combine the two, at least regarding scientific employees.

7. Dunning is well-positioned to make this comparison, having written the foremost study on earlier American investment in Britain and a pioneer book on recent Japanese investment. See Dunning (1958, 1986).

References

Cole, Robert. 1985. "The Macropolitics of Organizational Change: A Comparative Analysis of the Spread of Small-Group Activities," *Administrative Science Quarterly* **30**:560–85.

Dore, Ronald. 1986. *Flexible Rigidities. Industrial Policy and Structural Adjustment in the Japanese Economy 1970–1980.* Palo Alto: Stanford University Press.

Dunning, J. 1958. *American Investment in British Manufacturing Industry.* London: George Allen and Unwin.

Dunning, J. 1986. *Japanese Participation in British Industry: Trojan Horse or Catalyst for Growth?* Dover, N.H.: Croom Helm.

Kogut, Bruce. 1991. "Country Capabilities and the Permeability of Borders," *Strategic Management Journal* **12**:33–47.

Kogut, Bruce, and Udo Zander (1992). "Knowledge of the Firm, Combinative Capabilities, and the Replication of Technology," *Organization Science* **3**(3):383–97.

Lipton, David, and Jeffrey Sachs. 1990. "Creating a Market Economy in Eastern Europe: The Case of Poland," *Brookings Papers on Economic Activity* **1**:75–147.

Maddison, Angus. 1982. *Phases of Capitalist Development.* Oxford: Oxford University Press.

Marshall, Alfred. 1921. *Industry & Trade, A Study of Industrial Technique and Business Organization; and of their Influences on the Conditions of Various Classes & Nations,* London: Macmillan.

Nelson, R. R. 1981. "Research on Productivity Growth and Differences," *Journal of Economic Literature* **19**:1029–64.

Olson, Mancur. 1982. *The Rise and Decline of Nations.* New Haven and London: Yale University Press.

Ouchi, W. M. 1984. *The M-Form Society: How American Teamwork Can Recapture the Competitive Edge.* Reading, Mass.: Addison-Wesley.

Piore, M., and C. Sabel. 1984. *The Second Industrial Divide.* New York: Free Press.

Solow, Robert M. 1970. *Growth Theory.* The Radcliffe Lectures, delivered in the University of Warwick. New York and Oxford: Oxford University Press.

Thurow, Lester C. 1982. *The Zero-Sum Society.* New York: Penguin Books.

Winter, S. G. 1964. "Economic 'Natural Selection' and the Theory of the Firm," *Yale Economic Essays* **4**:225–72.

I

ORGANIZING OF WORK AND TECHNOLOGY: COMPARISONS OF COUNTRY PATTERNS

1

Large Firms, Small Firms, and the Governance of Flexible Specialization: The Case of Baden Württemberg and Socialized Risk

GARY HERRIGEL

The southwest German province of Baden Württemberg has been known for a long time as the home of giant and hugely successful multinational firms, such as car manufacturer Daimler Benz and auto parts supplier Robert Bosch. But in the last several years attention has focused on the dense networks of very successful small and medium-size manufacturing enterprises in the region. The fascination with these producers stems from their capacity to flourish in a highly competitive manufacturing environment characterized by rapid technological change and rising development costs.

This chapter analyses the relationship between the system of dynamic smaller and medium-size producers and large firms within the political economy of Baden Württemberg. It presents a broadly historical and institutional account of the reasons behind the success of small and medium-size producers and points to the institutional contours and governance mechanisms that define and regulate relations between large and small firms. The point of this essay is that the coexistence of large and small firms in Baden Württemberg presupposes a clear set of institutional arrangements, both in the government and in society, that bring order to their mutual relations. Such extrafirm arrangements are the key to the competitiveness of both large and small firms. Moreover, they are subject to continual redefinition and adjustment as both large and small producers make efforts to adapt to changes in their competitive environment. Industrial adjustment in Baden Württemberg is a broadly political process of continually redefining industrial order.

I begin by describing the less well-known dimension of economic life in Baden Württemberg: the small and medium-size firm system. My premise is that the success of these firms rests in a decentralized system of risk spreading that can really only be understood at the interfirm (regional) level of analysis. I go on to sketch out where that system came from historically. In doing so I also describe the way in which large firms grew out of the system and devote some attention to the problem of the relationship between large firm systems and the decentralized small and medium-size firm industrial systems in the historical period prior to the current one.

Finally, I focus on the changing relationship between large and small firm systems in the present. My argument is that as large firms seek to enhance their own flexibility in the current world market environment, they embark on processes of decentralization that result in increasingly intense interpenetration with small and medium-size producers. This process is transforming and displacing many old problems that have been characteristic of large firm–small firm relations in the past, such as power imbalances in contracting and extraregional capital mobility. At the same time, the process of mutual convergence is creating new problems of system governance that, at least as of now, have no clear solution. The emergence of a new system of production relations in the region, in other words, has given rise to an important set of political debates about how to govern it.

Decentralized Production Among Small and Medium-size Firms

Most accounts of Baden Württemberg have emphasized that the small and medium-size producers in this region utilize an interesting combination of organizational and interorganizational principles—contract, authority, trust, networks—to create a dynamically innovative (and prosperous) industrial system. To understand the success of producers, one cannot take either solely the firm or the industry as the unit of analysis. Rather, one has to understand the interfirm dynamic at work at the level of the region as a whole. Key dimensions of production and its administration are decentralized and, quite literally, centerless within the industrial region.[1]

In Baden Württemberg, 99.4 percent of manufacturing establishments[2] and 57.9 percent of manufacturing employment[3] is accounted for by firms employing between 50 and 1,000 employees.[2] There are two central characteristics of these contemporary small and medium-size companies: they are highly flexible and they are very specialized. Their special feature is that they have been extraordinarily successful at applying and utilizing new technologies in traditional areas of manufacturing, such as machinery, electronics, automobile components, textiles, and fine mechanical and optical equipment. The key to their success is the ability to rapidly produce high quality, specialized products, with very short product cycles while simultaneously reducing the cost gap between a standard product and a specialized, custom tailored one. It is possible to say of these producers in Baden Württemberg that they produce an almost infinite array of special industrial products in virtually infinite variety.[3] These characteristics have been fortuitously matched with changing international market conditions that are characterized by more intense competition, rapid technological change, short product cycles, and climbing development costs.

How has it been possible for so many small and medium-size firms to successfully combine specialization with flexibility? My argument is that their success is based on a system that socializes risk across a broad array of public and private organizations. Small firms do not have to bear the entire burden developing new technologies; finding new markets; training skilled engineers and workers; and raising capital. Many of the costs of specialization are shared by or embedded in a deep network of organizations and practices in the political economy.

Organizations

EDUCATIONAL INSTITUTIONS

Baden Württemberg has the largest and most extensive network of universities and training centers in Germany. A three-way division in the educational system exists. First, and at the top, there are the technical universities, such as those in Stuttgart and Karlsruhe. These universities have international reputations for excellence in technological research. Small and medium-size enterprises have some direct contact with the research laboratories in these universities, mostly in the form of contract research. But the relative amount of contract research done at universities by any firms in Germany is fairly small: less than 3 percent of all research contracted out by German firms goes to universities. What the universities do, however, is train doctoral and masters candidates who often go into jobs (with their technological skills in tow) in the surrounding industry.

Second, and in the middle, are Fachhochschulen, or community colleges. These institutes play a much more important role for the small and medium-size enterprises. Often located in the communities in which the enterprises are active, Fachhochschulen provide training, consulting advice, and small amounts of applied contract research for firms. Linkages with the surrounding economy are both formal and informal. Formally, every student that receives an engineering degree from a Fachhochschule must complete a program that involves considerable on-site experience in industrial enterprises. Often small and medium-size firms will sponsor a student's thesis in their own factory because it deals with a specific technological problem of importance to the firm. Professors are instructed to encourage these sorts of contacts and make it their business to cultivate broad contacts in the local industry. Exchange between the Fachhochschule and the economy about technology is built into this educational process at little monetary cost to the firm.

Informal exchanges are at least as important in the process of technology transfer as the formal ones. Often the owners of small enterprises will have been educated at the local Fachhochschule and maintain social and professional ties with people in the faculty, former students, alumni, and so on. For example, most of the firms in the German textile machinery industry, a large proportion of which is located in Baden Württemberg, have connections with the Fachhochschule "Textiltechnicum" in Reutlingen that are constituted and maintained by ties between graduates of the schools and important professors on the faculty. Fachhochschulen in this way act as a local technological resource for the small firms that is extremely important in the process of technology transfer.

The third level of training institution is the Berufsschule, or the vocational training schools. Germany's dual system of vocational education is world renowned for its ability to produce extremely talented skilled workers. Students receive intensive classroom training that is systematically supplemented by practical training in factories and workshops. Younger workers are trained in the most advanced microelectronic manufacturing technologies and are required to receive training in CNC (computer numerically controlled) programming.

The point about each of these educational institutions is that they provide services for small and medium-size enterprises that the firms would otherwise have to provide for themselves. Paradoxically, this is more important the further away one moves from abstract high science toward practical industrial and shop floor problems.

TRADE ASSOCIATIONS AND CHAMBERS OF COMMERCE

Business associations are very important in the system. Trade associations, such as the Verein Deutscher Maschinen- und Anlagenbau (VDMA), or the Zentral Verband Deutscher Elktro-Industrie (ZVEI), represent particular sectors of industry, while the chambers of commerce represent all enterprises in the economy at a local and regional level. Other important non-sector-specific associations that are important to small and medium-size firms are the VDI (Verein Deutscher Ingenieure) the association of German engineers; and the RKW (Rationalisierungs Kuratorium der deutschen Wirtschaft), an institution that concerns itself with the technological and organizational problems of small and medium-size enterprises nationwide.

Together, associations of this type provide three important services for small firms. First, they all provide different varieties of market information: statistics, reports on special regional or technological markets, export information, and the like. In this they differ little from trade associations anywhere. Second, associations appraise firms of the different varieties of local regional and federal technological development programs that are available. They act as indispensable mediators of information between industry and the state.[4]

Third associations, especially sectoral associations such as the VDMA or the ZVEI, coordinate relationships among firms in particular industries. The VDMA, for example, actively coordinates cooperative, so-called precompetitive research projects for member firms. Sometimes the research problem is suggested by a group of firms themselves; other times the VDMA, or one of its subsidiary associations, suggests a project to its members. The association then goes to the appropriate research institute or university and arranges and manages the project. The participating firms pay half the cost of the research, the rest, typically, is paid by the Ministry of Economics in the federal government. The VDMA negotiates all relationships between its members and the state.

In general, the trade associations pay attention to the university and research institute structure in a region. If the region lacks the relevant technological capacity, the associations lobby to have it filled. In the mid-1970s, for example, the VDMA successfully lobbied for the creation of a special research chair and institute for printing technology in Darmstadt, halfway between the significant regional centers of printing machinery production in North Rhine Westafalia and Baden Württemberg.

Another perhaps more significant role of the trade association in coordinating the relationships between small and medium-size firms is in the area of specialization and technical standards. Industrial technologies are often distinguished from one another through a process of technical standard setting. Continuous change in technology involves continuous change in the relevant standards in products. Rapid change causing product boundaries to overlap can lead to devastating forms of competition—especially among flexible producers—if not somehow checked or coordinated. In the industries in which small and medium-size producers are most dominant, such as the machinery industry, the coordination of competition in the process of technological change takes place within the standard-setting bodies of the trade association. The VDMA has a special committee, known as the Normen-Ausschuss, in which all member firms are active participants.

Standard setting by member firms, with the trade association as a forum, coordinates specialization and ensures that competition remains healthy and beneficial.[5] This practice of using collusion to further the competitive character of the industry is a general feature of most highly flexible regional agglomerations.[6] Observers (and competitors) from an Anglo-american economic culture, who tend to view economic practice as binarily divided between cooperation (typically reduced to collusion) and competition, invariably find their stable intermingling difficult to grasp.

BANKS

Small and medium-size producers in Baden Württemberg have little trouble getting capital for their projects, yet they do not engage to a significant extent with the large universal banks that are classically associated with industry in Germany. They have traditionally turned to local banks—either the state-owned Sparkassen, or the cooperatively operated Volksbanken. During the period of industrialization, these banks were created by local industrialists and craftsman to pool their funds and gain access to the national credit markets. To a large extent today, they continue to be important sources of capital for smaller and medium-size industrial firms. Heads of local firms often sit on the boards of these banks, so the banks themselves are well attuned to the technological and financial situation of small producers. The presence of knowledgeable local entrepreneurs on the board also provides an important policing function that engenders an incentive for good industrial practice: banks know how to evaluate the technical and business potential of projects and can provide important suggestions concerning how they should be reformulated or restructured.

THE REGIONAL GOVERNMENT

The role of the regional government in the success of smaller and medium-size producers in the Baden Württemberg economy has received considerable publicity. While it has been important, one should be careful not to exaggerate its role. The programs of the state in many ways duplicate the services that are provided by the institutions already mentioned, such as providing technical information, knowledge, and capital. The provincial government Economics Ministry provides direct subsidies to firms for specific technical development projects. The Landesgewerbeamt plays the important role of coordinating the infrastructure of institutional resources available to firms: education, state-sponsored consulting on technology, export promotion, trade fairs, and so on.

An important new institution, formally private, but in fact entirely owned by the government of Baden Württemberg, is the Steinbeis Foundation. The primary role of this organization is to match the technological needs of small and medium-size producers with the technological specialties of Fachhochschulen—and even specific faculty members—within the Baden Württemberg region.

The Steinbeis Foundation's role, like that of the other institutions of the state, partially duplicates services that are already performed by other institutions in the economy, such as the chambers of commerce and the sectoral trade associations. It is an important role, nevertheless, in the sense that most resilient systems of political economic organization benefit from redundancy. The institutions are concerned with spreading the risk that firms are confronted with. The more that risk can be dispersed across institutions, the greater flexibility the individual participants have.

A similar logic of redundancy is at work with technology subsidy programs provided by the Baden Württemberg government. The state makes a relatively small amount of money available to small and medium-size enterprises (1.1 billion DM in 1984) and then distributes the money through more than sixty different special subsidy programs. Firms obviously cannot rely on the state to keep them competitive when the state is engaged monetarily in such an insignificant way. Nor can the state reasonably claim that its programs are responsible for the successful adjustment of small and medium-size firms in the economy (though at times the government has made hyperbolic statements in this direction). In fact, small and medium-size firms receive financial and technical input from a broad variety of sources, each individually quite small, but taken together amounting to a considerable opportunity for firms with good ideas in need of investment funds. Redundancy in this form obviously serves as a form of insurance for firms. But it also is a kind of incentive. In putting together financing deals or research projects, firms must make their ideas more precise to persuade enough of the different agencies to actually support them.

Redundancy is the key summary characteristic of the institutional infrastructure in which the decentralized system of production in Baden Württemberg is embedded. The fragmented, overlapping, and seemingly redundant character of the public and private institutional network in Baden Württemberg is, paradoxically, the most efficient way to provide services to decentralized production.

Practices

COLLABORATIVE SUBCONTRACTING

Collaborative subcontracting is a relatively new practice among small and medium-size firms in Baden Württemberg, but it has been integral to their current success. Given the volatility of the current environment with rapid technological change, short product cycles, and increasing development costs, subcontracting is a way to reduce the level of fixed costs that any single firm must carry. But, importantly, it also allows firms to enjoy the benefits of the technological know-how and experience of their suppliers. Most firms think of subcontracting as a strategic act of partnership in which two parties enter into mutual and equal exchange of know-how and service. Systematic collaborative subcontracting depends on, but also creates, a broad, decentralized pool of know-how in the region that is in principle accessible to all who are active in it.

Collaborative subcontracting is a practice that socializes risk at the same time that it pools resources. At the limit, the practice of subcontracting completely eliminates hierarchies between firms. That is, a system in which there are clearly identifiable end product producers who are distinct from pure subcontractors no longer exists. Instead, an unending series of relationships between constantly innovating firms, a decentralized system, takes its place. The decentralized system in Baden Württemberg has not gone this far yet, but there are areas within the region, such as the Black Forest, or the Hohenzollern regions around Tüttlingen and Sigmaringen, that approach it.

OPENNESS

Firms within the decentralized system of production in Baden Württemberg are all acutely aware of the limitations of their own in-house know-how. They realize that to retain their autonomy and independence within the system, they must accept their dependence on the system itself. Firms continually seek to enhance what they know through contact with subcontractors, customers, banks, the state, Fachhochschulen, and so on. Firms know that the only way that they will be able to survive is by continuously bringing in know-how, enhancing their ability to keep up technologically, and ultimately offering a continuous array of new products.

It is worth mentioning that since everyone has an interest in the continuous reproduction of the system of exchanges at all levels, the system itself begins to engender trusting behavior among firms. This trust follows from the character of the exchange. In many cases the exchange of know-how between firms cannot be explicitly specified—what gets transferred is often ineffable or discovered only in retrospect. A price can be assigned to a product, which can then be exchanged through the system of contracts that are protected by law. But the ineffable exchanges cannot be priced in any practical way, nor can they be conveniently defined in contract form.[7] This amorphousness does not make them any less crucial for the profitability of the firm, however. The existence of trust between producers, therefore, is important functionally for the healthy reproduction of the system. Among small and medium-size producers in Baden Württemberg, opportunism is limited as much by mutually held conceptions of honor and trust as it is by the policing qualities of law and contract.

SELF-POLICING TROUGH FEAR

The practice of diligent worry among small and medium-size producers stems from the same set of concerns that encourage them to be open to new information. Firms realize that their future independence is completely dependent on their ability to continually come up with a marketable new product or service. This awareness makes them open to information from outside the firm, but it also causes them to be constantly attentive to weaknesses in the broader system. As it were, fear is one way that the system polices itself. Firms and trade association members worry that the amount of information in the system concerning certain new technologies is insufficient, so they seek to devise ways to amend the system (make contacts with firms abroad that are experienced with the technology or the market in question, acquire monies and services from supporting institutions, bring in experts, etc.). In that many firms and many members of the surrounding institutions do this, there is, inevitably, redundancy, but there is also change and adaptation. These dynamics are the strength of the system.

Highlights

The four organizations and three practices just discussed together describe reasonably well the dynamic system of small and medium-size manufacturers in Baden Württemberg as it exists today. Of all that has been said, two characteristics of this risk socializing system should be featured. First, the firm is not the central unit of analysis in the operation of the system. That is, to understand the way that small firms succeed in Baden Württemberg, one cannot simply look at the balance sheets of the firms themselves. Rather, one has to view the system as a whole. It is much greater than the sum of its parts.

Second, the analytical point just made is literally true, in most cases, about the actual products that firms produce. That is, the products of any given Baden Württemberg firm are typically the outcome of a long string of decentralized, subcontracting relations; know-how transfers; research projects; state promotion schemes; and so on. The boundary line between firm, industry, and society in the production and administration of goods is virtually impossible to define precisely.

Origins of the System and the Role of Large Firms

The account given of the decentralized system of small and medium-size producers in Baden Württemberg will inevitably have provoked two questions in the minds of skeptical readers (or, perhaps more precisely, of anyone who knows anything about Baden Württemberg): Where did the system come from? and What about the large firms? I contend that the answers to both of these questions are linked together in the economic history of the region.

The regions now contained within the state of Baden Württemberg have always been populated by large numbers of specialized small and medium-size firms. The extrafirm institutions described in the previous section (Fachhochschulen, vocational training, cooperative banks, Landesgewerbeamt, etc.) all emerged in the nineteenth century (though the role of some, such as the trade associations, did not take their present shape until the twentieth century). The story of industrialization in southwestern Germany is yet to be adequately written, but the few studies that exist show that there was a great political effort throughout the nineteenth century to shape the emergence of industry in a way that preserved its small and medium-size, decentralized character.[8]

Baden Württembergers today tend to attribute the special character of their economy to the absence of raw materials and a special cultural propensity to tinker within the population. I would emphasize instead the character of inheritance in agriculture (partible inheritance) and the way that this practice shaped the emergence of the labor market. Partible inheritance allowed large numbers of people to own land, but it resulted, ultimately, in highly fragmented and less productive holdings. To help these people get by, centuries ago the regional government began to encourage industrialization. The state engaged directly in, or sponsored the activities of a merchant in, the putting out of industrial work to small holders in the countryside. The mercantilistic-directed putting-out system enabled people to stay on the land and engage in small-scale industrial work as by- employments. The more the system succeeded, the more difficult it became to change it and collect the dispersed laborers to place them in factories.

Over time, the decentralized producers in the putting out system became as important to the government as the government became to them. The prosperity of both, and ultimately the entire political and economic character and stability of the region, depended on the perpetuation of the decentralized system. When the British entered world markets with their factory produced wares at the beginning of the nineteenth century, Badeners and Württembergers (such as Ferdinand Steinbeis, after whom the foundation is named, who headed the first technology promotion agency in the Kingdom of Württemberg) struggled to find ways to make their decentralized system adapt to the machine age. The system of specialized production that combines technological sophistication with flexibility and the risk spreading organizations and practices previously described is what they came up with.

Up until early in the twentieth century, this political economic system of decentralized industry in southwestern Germany was virtually free of large firms. Only in the periods leading up to the two world wars (when the central government in Berlin fostered the growth of large firms for defense needs) and then dramatically after the Second World War (when the European Economic Community created a set of market conditions that permitted mass production) did large firms begin to become a significant part of the political economic landscape in Baden Württemberg.

The most significant change came after World War II when the new environment encouraged local firms to break out of the system of decentralization and begin mass producing. The automobile and automobile components industries in Baden Württemberg grew extremely rapidly in this period, and the leading firms were clearly following mass production strategies. The significance of the shift can be see in the fact that by the beginning of the 1980s, nearly a seventh of the regional economy's total product was related in some way to the automobile industry (Muenzenmaier 1984). Firms in other industries broke out of the decentralized system as well, especially in electronics, fine mechanical and optical equipment, and textiles and apparel.

During these middle decades of the twentieth century, the distinctive feature of the emergence of a large-firm sector was that the large mass-producing firms began to make important changes in the role that firms, as institutions that organize production, played in the regional political economy. In order to stabilize their sources of supply and to protect the proprietary character of their products, large mass-producing firms began to internalize most of the functions provided by the organizations in the decentralized economy and abandon many of the practices that had been so important in making the decentralized system work.[9]

Their desire to control these functions internally, rather than leave them to the traditional extrafirm institutions, was related to their character as mass producers. Because in those pre-microelectronics days they produced standardized products in large quantities on relatively inflexible machinery, the large firms were extremely vulnerable to rapid changes in their markets. To prevent the emergence of competitors that would cause them to make expensive changes in their plant and equipment ahead of schedule, they internalized product development and paid careful attention to limit the dissemination of technological know-how. To protect themselves from unwanted disruptions of supply, they internalized much of production. The result was the emergence of a new system of industrial organization that existed outside of the old system of decentralized production. The new system was firm based and focused on centralized control of resources. It drew the boundary lines between firms, industries, and society quite clearly, and it energetically resisted any forms of intrusion, by the state or other organizations, in the way that private firms exercised control over production. This tradition of liberal hostility to the role of government and secondary associations in the governance of production and its administration continues to be a key dividing line between large and small firms.[10]

Despite the fact that the principles of organization that governed these powerful new mass-producing firms shared little with those that governed the preexisting decentralized system of production, the latter system was not forced out of existence by the growth of large firms. The small and medium-size firm system survived as a niche within the mass production system of post-war German Fordism. There are, I believe, three reasons for this.

1. Many industries in the region never moved into mass production. This nonoccurrence is particularly true of capital goods producing industries, such as machine tools, because the growth of mass-production firms created a demand for special purpose capital goods that could not be mass produced. Large firms attempted to make their production processes as efficient as possible by automating them. And they called upon machine-tool producers and others to construct the often one-of-a-kind mechanical contraptions needed for automation. The result was that such firms remained relatively small and continued to rely on the principles of organization and practice, as well as the extrafirm institutions, that had characterized the earlier decentralized system.

2. Despite their efforts to internalize production and product development as much as they could, mass-production firms, especially in Baden Württemberg, used many suppliers, primarily because the economy was rich with them. Concern about the stability of supply was not as great in an economy densely populated with potential supplier firms because if one firm was unable to deliver an order, it was always possible to turn to one or several others.

Another, more systemic, reason for the tendency of large firms to use suppliers has to do with the relationship of mass-producing firms' investment strategies to the business cycle. The worst possible cost situation a mass-producing firm can have is when its very expensive production machinery has to lie idle. To avoid the amortization expenses it would incur from such a situation, firms generally tried to set their own production capacity somewhere below what the market would bear in a period of upturn. This way its production could be relatively continuous even if demand in the market, with the business cycle, was moving up and down. During peak periods, then, mass-producing firms tended to try to expand their capacity through the use of subcontractors. Baden Württemberg, being rich in potential sub-contractors, tended to draw significant business of this kind to it, not only from endogenous mass producers, but from mass producers from other (more northern) regions of Germany where the base of subcontractors was not as plentiful.[11]

It is important to emphasize that this practice of subcontracting differs quite substantially from the collaborative subcontracting practices currently character-istic of exchanges among small and medium-size firms mentioned previously. These firms use subcontractors as sources of know-how and manufacturing exper-tise that they themselves do not have. In the mass-production system, subcontrac-tors were simply employed on short-term contracts to supplement the already exist-ing capacity of the core firm. In particular, due to the importance of protecting the proprietary character of the firm's product, virtually all subcontracts were given out for manufacture only. Development and design was performed by the subcontract-ing firm and supplied to the subcontractor.

3. The third reason why the emergence of the mass-production system did not eliminate the older decentralized system and its institutions is that the period of time when mass production as a strategy was clearly superior to all others was rel-atively brief. Conditions favoring flexible small and medium-size producers began to appear again as early as the mid 1970s. In 1975, Baden Württemberg passed a Mittelstandsförderungsgesetz (Law for the Promotion of the Industrial Middle Classes) that was designed to revive the traditions of state small and medium-size industry technology transfer. In 1978, the government established a special export promotion agency for small and medium-size producers in Baden Württemberg. The Steinbeis Foundation was created in 1981. These changes were signs that the substructure of small and medium-size firms in Baden Württemberg was coming back to life. The more volatile and uncertain the technological and market envi-ronment became, the better the position of the flexible and specialized Baden Würt-temberg firms became.

Large Firms and Decentralized Small and Medium-size Production in Contemporary Baden Württemberg

The current situation in the world economy has created a whole new set of prob-lems concerning the relationship between large firms and the small and medium-size enterprises in Baden Württemberg. As for the smaller specialized firms, the competitive environment for large firms was also tremendously altered over the course of the 1980s by new developments in technology, increased international competition, shrinking product cycles, and rising development costs.[12] Large cor-porations today, just as small firms, are driven to change their product palettes more frequently and apply new technologies to their products or in production about which they have little prior knowledge or experience. They find, invariably, that they are compelled to look to outside specialists to help them keep abreast of tech-nology and stay competitive in their markets.

Automobile companies, for example, now find that they must integrate micro-electronics and advanced plastic technologies into their products within a product cycle time that is only a third as long as it was in the heyday of mass production. To accomplish this updating, the major German producers—Daimler Benz, BMW, VW—are each experimenting with subcontracting and collaborative manufacturing practices. BMW, for example, now purchases between 50 and 75 percent of its production costs; 80 percent of its purchased parts involve some form of collaboration with its supplier. Moreover, in interviews it became clear that the firm is prepared to subcontract the production of virtually any part of the automobile if it drains the firm of valuable resources for development and can be done more cheaply outside. Several managers in purchasing revealed that the company was even debating giving the production of trademark engine components such as cylinder heads over to outsiders.[13]

The experience of the automobile industry is being reproduced across firms and industries in Baden Württemberg. Levels of vertical integration within large firms are falling dramatically and the number of collaborative subcontracting arrangements is increasing rapidly (Cooke and Morgan 1990). The result is that large firms are not only beginning to interpenetrate with the smaller producers through the establishment of collaborative and subcontracting relationships, they are increasingly adopting principles of organization and practices typical of the small and medium-size firm system.[14]

This process of interpenetration or "mutual convergence"[15] between the two systems of production is interesting for the problems of governance to which it does and does not give rise. On the one hand, the spread of decentralizing production practices among large firms is tending to make obsolete many problems that traditionally had been associated with large firm–small firm relations in the period of old-style mass production. Fears of strategic power imbalances in contracting and of the consequences of large firms' capital mobility, for example, once considered to be a threat to small firms and regional systems, now appear to be increasingly misplaced. On the other hand, the mutual convergence of the two systems has given rise to a series of other problems of governance (especially regarding the proper role of the government in the regional economy) that if not resolved could prove potentially destabilizing to the system of decentralized production in Baden Württemberg.

In the following discussion of the problems eliminated and generated, it should be clear that the argument attempts to draw out a coherent model of clear tendencies within the region and in no way intends to imply that specific examples of older and contradictory practices cannot be found.

Problems Eliminated

POWER IMBALANCES IN CONTRACTING

At the core of the current adjustment situation, in both large and small firms, is the phenomenon of collaborative subcontracting. The old decentralized system among small and medium-size firms with its important extrafirm institutions and the two practices of openness and fear always involved extensive subcontracting. Such dispersion in production, as explained at the beginning of this chapter, is a way to

reduce risks and pool resources. The shift to subcontracting and collaborative manufacturing on the part of large firms involves not simply an intensification of existing practices as it does for small firms, but a dramatic departure from past practice.
The shift is an indication of the fact that large producers can no longer control their
environment the way that they used to do. This fact has completely redefined the
relations of power within the contracting environment between small and large
firms.

In the old environment, large firms typically engaged in mass production. Product cycles were relatively long, and development costs as a result were less of a strategic problem. Mass-producing firms controlled the evolution of technology in their
markets. In this situation, large firms always used suppliers from a position of
strength: they were used to supplement capacity during upturns or simply for the
supply of standardized, low value added goods (e.g., standard screws or flanges). For
their part, the old style suppliers were weak and vulnerable. They contributed nothing to the development of technology in the large firm, usually engaged in short
term contracts, and competed fiercely with other suppliers for their sales.

Such unequal relations were a direct result of the large firms' desire and capacity
to control the development of its technology. Indeed, truly important technologies
and development work were produced in-house where the firm could ensure that
know-how would not seep out of the firm to competitors. Significant engagement
with suppliers in a way that involved the transfer of know-how was considered dan-
gerous because the supplier could potentially use the know-how against the firm:
give it to a competitor or use it itself to become a competitor. A firm engaged in
mass production with a very long product cycle was not interested in leaving itself
open to such risks. The desire and the capacity to control the evolution of technology in a mass production environment militated against collaborative relations
with suppliers.[16]

Now, since the new environment makes it virtually impossible to keep abreast
of, much less control, all aspects of newer product technology (regardless of a firm's
desire to do so), large producers find it prudent to draw on outside specialists for
significant portions of production, development, or both. Specialist suppliers are
consulted as sources of know-how and expertise. Both the large firm and the specialist supplier transfer know-how to each other to ensure that they quickly arrive
at an adequate solution to the contractor's needs. In the new environment, control
is no longer the primary strategic concern in subcontracting: arm's-length relations
give way to intimacy; control over technology, to openness and cooperation.

Finally, once the large producer has determined that it cannot control the evolution of all of the technologies that are necessary to remain competitive in its business, there is an incentive to spread subcontracting relations with specialists as
widely as possible. The absence of control means that the producer must be able to
react in unforeseeable ways to the market. A broad range of relations increases the
available pool of know-how for the producer. Large firms with many specialist subcontractors can keep abreast of new developments in technology without having to
invest their own capital and attention in developing it all. This strategic orientation
is fundamental to the traditional system of relationships that has long existed
among smaller firms in Baden Württemberg.

A paradigmatic case for how large firms are changing in this way in Baden

Württemberg is the Robert Bosch Corporation.[17] The firm has adopted a strategy of transferring its own know-how in certain technologies to outside firms to free resources to product development in other areas it considers more strategic. By transferring certain operations to suppliers, however, Bosch is by no means capitulating on the development of technology in those areas. On the contrary, because the technology in the businesses in which Bosch competes (specialized auto parts, microelectronics, consumer electronics, specialized machinery) is continuously changing, it is not possible for Bosch to define precisely which specific technologist will (need to) produce in the future. It seeks, therefore, to remain abreast of developments in as many areas as possible. It does so by cultivating a broad array of intimate relations with subcontractors, and, logically enough, not exclusively in Baden Württemberg, but throughout Germany, Europe, and the world. Such supplier-collaborators provide Bosch with information about developments in their specialties, and Bosch in turn, provides the specialists with know-how in areas relevant to the specialists (Sabel et al. 1989). The benefits for Bosch are clear, but the benefits to the region of its linkage through Bosch to a worldwide network of technological information is often underappreciated.[18]

This system of decentralized know-how transfer can only work if no single firm controls the process of exchange. Thus, Bosch attempts to prevent subcontractors from becoming dependent on Bosch for business. The company goal is that any given subcontractor should conduct only approximately 20 percent of its business with Bosch. The rest the subcontractor must find from other producers and the experience it gains from this diverse work, Bosch's reasoning goes, provides a valuable store of potentially useful know-how and expertise for Bosch. Here it is clear that Bosch has discovered the principle of openness that is at work in the industrial district that surrounds it.

Conversations with people in other larger firms in Baden Württemberg, such as IBM, Hewlett Packard and even Daimler Benz, reveal that they are pursuing subcontracting strategies resembling Bosch's.[19] Given this occurrence it is entirely possible that the extension of subcontracting by the large firms will blend (though certainly not effortlessly, see the discussion of problems generated) into the actively expanding networks of subcontracting relationships among small and medium-size supplier firms, particularly if the Bosch model is pushed to its logical conclusion. On this view, the massive internal resources and stores of know-how of the large firm—research and development laboratories, easy access to high-level university research teams and resources, contact with technological specialists world wide, and the like—would enter the decentralized system of exchange as one more redundant input of know-how and institutional capacity in the system of decentralized production.

LARGE FIRMS AND CAPITAL MOBILITY

These changes in the power relations between small and large firms with respect to subcontracting in the new environment have been paralleled by (and, partially, have given rise to) changes in the balance of power between large producers and the regional economy as a whole. In the classic age of dependent and vulnerable subcontractors and dominant mass-producing large firms, the economic and industrial health of a region was dependent on the continuing willingness of large firms to invest there. If a large firm, such as Bosch or Daimler Benz, were to decide to shift all of its production of a given product out of the region, the dependent suppliers would have no alternative strategy for production. Lacking in know-how and vulnerable to begin with, the supplier firms would be faced with the choice of bankruptcy or following the large producer out of the region. Regional governments, unwilling to suffer the consequences of either option, as a result typically went to great lengths to provide large firms with incentives to keep production in the locality.[20]

In the new environment, both the capacity of large firms to make credible their threat to leave, and the capacity of small and medium-size producers to survive without them have changed. And, as a result, the room for autonomous maneuvering for the regional government has increased. Large firms have trouble making credible threats to shift production entirely out of a region such as Baden Württemberg, which is densely populated by highly specialized and flexible small and medium-size producers, because they are uncertain enough about the future evolution of technology and markets that they are unwilling to completely abandon the resources of know-how that the smaller specialist firms make available. The capacity of large producers to remain competitive in a technological environment that they cannot control depends on their being able to cultivate and maintain access to a decentralized network of technological information. This situation does not preclude efforts on the part of large firms to globalize: just as they have an interest in cultivating access to information locally, so do they in cultivating access to information in markets in other regions. Their interest, now, in an environment without control over the evolution of technology, is in the acquisition and transfer of information, regardless of its location. The only point is that interest elsewhere does not involve neglect at home.[21]

For the same reasons, small specialist firms, embedded in dense decentralized networks, do not feel threatened by efforts on the part of large firms to establish global operations. They not only know that the local large producer relies on them for technological expertise, they also benefit from investment in the region on the part of foreign multinationals seeking to gain access to the resources that are located within the region. So it is not at all surprising, for example, that all opinion polls of small and medium-size producers in Baden Württemberg, conducted by trade associations, chambers of commerce, and the regional government, show universal enthusiasm for the completion of the European Economic Community's common market in 1992.

For its part, the regional government in Baden Württemberg has learned quickly how to take advantage of this situation, both for the benefit of producers in the region and to strengthen its own position. It undertakes trade expeditions throughout the world, particularly to market areas where Baden Württemberg producers are weakly represented, such as the Pacific Rim and Eastern Europe. It subsidizes trade shows in these markets, assists in the arrangement of joint ventures, and institutes formal programs of technology transfer. At the same time at home in Baden Württemberg, the regional government has reserved large tracts of scarce development space, zoned for industrial use, in the densely populated region exclusively for Far Eastern investors. The local government has grasped the paradox that the more globalization it can encourage on the part of its own producers and the more investment from foreign multinationals it can attract to the region, the greater its own latitude to conduct industrial and technology policies for the benefit of local producers will be.

Problems Generated

Though the mutual convergence of the large and small firm systems of production in Baden Württemberg has resulted in the dissolution of several important problems that had plagued relations between small and large producers in the past, the interpenetration of the two systems is not without problems. I want to suggest that the current set of developments poses very important problems concerning the future governance of the interpenetrated systems that are only now beginning to be addressed in Baden Württemberg. Specifically, the problems I have in mind concern the future role of government in the region.

Traditionally, the large firm system and the small and medium-size producer's decentralized system have harbored fairly contradictory conceptions of the proper role for the state in industrial life. In the decentralized system of small and medium-size manufacturers in Baden Württemberg, government has traditionally played a very important role in the organization of production and its administration. It is an important extrafirm institution and a key source of redundancy in the system. In this system, to use a more technical language, government is a node in the complex production network in the region. The large firm system that emerged in the post-World War Two period, however, viewed the government with considerable reserve. Those elements of production that the large firm system did not seek to control directly through vertical integration, it generally preferred to leave for the market system to organize. State interference in the direct affairs of production has been consistently rejected with great ideological contempt. Large firms prefer to keep the state out of their networks.[22]

These conflicting perspectives on the proper role of the state in the organization of production were possible to reconcile in the period of mass production because the boundaries between the large firm system and the small and medium-size system were fairly clear. The state's traditional role in the affairs of the small and medium-size producer system could be viewed as "Mittelstandförderung" (promotion of small and medium-size independent producers) or "Mittelstandspolitik" (policy for small and medium size independent producers) more generally; that is as something clearly distinct from the affairs of large firms. But, as large firms intensify their subcontracting practices and decentralize their operations, the boundaries that once distinguished the affairs of small and medium-size producers from those of large producers are becoming blurred. Will this emerging mutual integration of the large into the small result in a set of conflicts around the proper role for the state in the administration of production and its administration?

There are some signs that this is the case. The governor of Baden Württemberg throughout the 1980s, Lothar Spaeth, was an extremely aggressive advocate of a strong role for government in the regional economy. In his view (which still seems to be representative of the government administration that has replaced him), the current economic environment creates the need for the government to assume the responsibility for the cultivation and extension of a regional infrastructure of information. Informatics systems, telecommunications systems, research institutes, trade associations, independent producers, and all areas of emerging technology need to be brought together and interlinked, he argued, and it is folly to believe that market processes alone will accomplish this. Moreover, the more current trends progress, the more important regional governments become vis-à-vis other, in particular national, levels of government. The needs of regional networks for stable channels of know-how transfer and for the financing of information must be met by the state, and the local state is the only government body in a position to do this. In Spaeth's view, this logic is intensified by all tendencies toward European integration (Spaeth 1988, 1991). Unsurprisingly, most of the other organizations within the system of small and medium-size firms, such as the chambers of commerce, tend to agree with Spaeth's assessment that there are new and expanding infrastructural needs in the traditional decentralized system. But, they are eager to ensure that the state's capacity to shape process in the system does not expand in a way that limits their own.[23]

Against these voices are those of the national level industrial associations representing the interests of large German business, large corporations themselves, and the national level banks that are tied to the corporations. These groups regard the aggressiveness with which local governing bodies engage in the local economy with considerable concern. They are interested in having a healthy infrastructure of dynamic specialist firms but cannot understand why the market is incapable of maintaining that infrastructure. Interference with the market only prolongs the life of inefficient producers by providing them with access to information and financing that they would otherwise never acquire and that they anyway cannot take advantage of appropriately. Moreover, the engagement of the Spaeth government in export promotion is disruptive to the existing, national level and private channels of export infrastructure that have for years served the purposes of Germany's major exporters (i.e., of large firms).

This debate has been developing in Baden Württemberg since the middle of the 1980s. It is being conducted in a systematic and continuous way and shows no sign of either resolving itself or falling into polarized crisis. Nevertheless, at the limit, there are two possible ways in which this conflict can be resolved. In one scenario, the movement of large firms into the system of decentralization will result in a transformation in their understanding of the proper role of government and other extrafirm institutions in the flow of industrial resources. Liberal rhetoric about the market will be abandoned and a new rhetoric emphasizing the need for continuous cooperation between public and private actors in the maintenance of a decentralized system will take its place. In another, alternate, scenario, the large firm's traditional interest in leaving to the market all aspects of production that they do not themselves directly control will lead them to advocate policies that would undermine the key institutions of extrafirm support that are essential to the survival, and independence, of the small and medium-size firms.

Either scenario leaves us with a very different political economy than the one we have known up to now. The former nonliberal world would have to make its peace with the continued existence of important concentrations of capital in the shape of—albeit decentralizing—corporations. The latter liberal world (currently being glorified with the collapse of central planning in Eastern Europe) would have to invent alternative mechanisms for the socialization of risk, or suffer the consequences—and wrath—of a vulnerable and betrayed industrial middle class.

Conclusions

In the end, however, all that can be said about the current, fascinating, process of organizational and industrial transformation in Baden Württemberg is that it will be political in the broadest possible sense. I believe that this characterization is generally true in industrial organization, but in this essay I make the point that it is especially true in current relations between disintegrating large firms and dynamically innovative and decentralized systems of small and medium-size firms in industrial districts such as Baden Württemberg. The arrangement of the extrafirm institutional and practical environment in which small and medium-size producers operate and over which much of the political struggle will take place is at least as important in understanding success in the current environment as is the internal organization of individual firms. The more that larger firms strive to disintegrate and socialize their risks and their acquisition of know-how, the more attention to such extrafirm institutions and practices will become important in the study of industrial organization.

Current trends in the world industrial environment indicate that the division of labor is becoming increasingly inter- and extrafirm in its organization. Questions concerning the character of development in the new division of labor and the way in which it changes, consequently become increasingly political. The present analysis suggests that to understand the character of current changes, one has to see that producers seek not only individual profit, but an orderly environment in which they can do so.

Notes

I would like to thank Bruce Kogut for valuable suggestions in the completion of this paper.

1. Good accounts of Baden Württemberg are given by Philip Cooke and Kevin Morgan (1990), Ms. Hans Maier (1987), and Charles Sabel et al. (1989). For general discussions of the various mechanisms involved in such systems, see Charles Sabel (1989), and Jeffrey L. Bradach and Robert G. Eccles (1989).

2. For firms with more than five employees (Goelz 1990).

3. Closer case studies of the competitive strategies of producers in Baden Württemberg can be found in Herrigel (1989).

4. This and all subsequent information on the workings of the VDMA come from inter-

views conducted with the association in Frankfurt and Stuttgart in 1984–85 and 1986. There is also a dissertation on the VDMA by Hajo Weber (1984).

5. On the development of this system, see chapter five of my MIT dissertation (Herrigel 1990). See also the discussion by Weber (1984).

6. See especially the discussion of Japanese practices in Friedman (1988, chap. 4, 5). Fruin and Nishiguchi's article in this book (Chap. 12) points to homologous kinds of construction in the large Japanese enterprise.

7. Marc Granovetter (1985). treats this phenomenon extensively.

8. The following historical argument about Baden Württemberg has been drawn from my MIT dissertation (Herrigel 1990, chap. 2, 5).

9. This process is outlined in chapter five of my dissertation (Herrigel 1990).

10. On the liberalism of postwar German large corporations, see the work of V. R. Berghahn (1985). See also the critical discussion of Berghahn's views in my dissertation (Herrigel 1990, chap. 5, 6).

11. On the logic of this kind of dualist subcontracting, see Michael Piore (1980). For Baden Württemberg specifically, see Jürgen W. Hutzel (1981a, 1981b).

12. Few dispute these characteristics of the present environment. For arguments about their genesis and consequences, see Michael Piore and Charles Sabel (1984), Alain Lipietz (1985), and David J. Teece (1987) for a sampling of perspectives.

13. For a case study of this phenomenon, see Charles Sabel, Horst Kern and Gary Herrigel (1990).

14. For more detailed description of this process see Sabel, Kern and Herrigel (1990).

15. The term has been used by Charles Sabel to describe this process, see Sabel (1989).

16. For a discussion of the way in which this system worked at Daimler Benz during the 1950s and 1960s, see my dissertation (Herrigel 1990, chap. 5).

17. The strategy of this company has also been described in Sabel et al. (1989).

18. See, for example, the rather skeptical assessment of nonlocal sourcing by Baden Württemberg large firms in the paper by Cooke and Morgan (1990).

19. Interviews at IBM, summer 1990 and winter 1989, and at Hewlett Packard, fall 1987. The single best study of developments in the German electronics industry is that being conducted by Volker Wittke and Ulli Voskamp at the SOFI Institute in Göttingen. See Ulli Voskamp, Klaus Peter Wittemann, and Volker Wittke (1989) and Wittke (1989a, 1989b). Cooke and Morgan (1990) discuss similar changes at Daimler Benz. Their otherwise excellent paper is bizarrely contradictory on the matter of the disintegration of large firms. On the one hand they point out that it is happening, and, moreover, on a European-wide basis, in the automobile, engineering, and electronics firms they look at in their case studies. Yet on the other hand, they somehow think that it must not be happening if disintegrating large firms do not use exclusively local suppliers.

20. A classic treatment of this phenomenon is the earlier work of David Harvey. See his radical classic, *The Limits to Capital* (1982). Further elaborations on the theme appear in his *The Urban Experience* (1989), which also contains an extremely interesting discussion on the transformation of that old model.

21. This is a point frequently overlooked, often because analysts tend to conceive of the activities of the corporation along the lines of the old model rather than that of the new one that appears to be emerging. A paradigmatic case of work that mixes old principles and new environmental conditions in the analysis of globalization and the corporation is found in Ash Amin and Kevin Robins (1990).

22. See the discussion in Berghahn (1985) and, of course, the classic portrait of German business government relations given by Andrew Schonfield in his *Modern Capitalism* (1964).

23. Interview with Chamber of Commerce, Grossraum Neckar, July 1990.

References

Amin, Ash, and Kevin Robins. 1990. "Industrial Districts and Regional Development: Limits and Possibilities," in Frank Pyke, G. Beccattini, and W. Sengenberger, eds., *Industrial Districts and Inter-Firm Cooperation in Italy,* pp. 185–219. Geneva: International Institute for Labor Studies.

Berghahn, V. R. 1985. *Unternehmer und Politik in der Bundersrepublik.* Frankfurt: Suhrkamp.

Bradach, Jeffrey L., and Robert G. Eccles. 1989. "Price Authority and Trust: From Ideal Types to Plural Forms," *Annual Review of Sociology* **15:**97–118.

Cooke, Phillip, and Morgan Kevin. 1990. "Industry, Training and Technology Transfer: The Baden Württemberg System in Perspective." Research report, University of Cardiff.

Friedman, David B. 1988. *The Misunderstood Miracle.* Ithaca, N.Y.: Cornell University Press.

Goelz, Uwe. 1990. Unternehmen und deren Beschaeftigte in Baden Württemberg am 25. Mai 1987. *Baden Württemberg in Wort und Zahl* **38:**167.

Granovetter, Marc. 1985. "Economic Action and Social Structure: The Problem of Embeddedness," *America Journal of Sociology* **91:**481–510.

Harvey, David. 1982. *The Limits to Capital.* Chicago: University of Chicago Press.

Harvey, David. 1989. *The Urban Experience.* Baltimore: John Hopkins University Press.

Herrigel, Gary. 1989. "Industrial Order and the Politics of Industrial Change: The Case of Mechanical Engineering," in Peter Katzenstein, ed., *Industry and Politics in West Germany,* pp. 185–220. Ithaca, N.Y.: Cornell University Press.

Herrigel, Gary. 1990. *Industrial Organization and the Politics of Industry: Centralized and Decentralized Production in Germany.* Ph.D. diss., MIT Department of Political Science.

Hutzel Juergen W. 1981a. *Grosse und Kleine Zulieferer. Eine Untersuchung zur Nachfragermacht industrieller Abnehmer.* Tübingen: Institut für Angewandte Wirtschaftsforschung Tübingen.

Hutzel Juergen W. 1981b. *Interdependenzen zwischen Klein- und Grossfirmen. Eine empirische Untersuchung am Beispiel der Metallindustrie Baden Württembergs.* Tübingen: Institut für Angewandte Wirtschaftsforschung Tübingen.

Lipietz, Alain. 1985. *Mirages and Miracles.* London: Verso.

Maier, Hans. 1987. "Das Modell Baden Württemberg—Eine Skizze," *Discussion Paper, IIm/LMP 87-10a,* Wissenschaftzentrum Berlin.

Muenzenmaier, Werner. 1984. "Zur Verflectung des Automobilsektors mit anderen Wirtschaftszweigen," *Baden Württemberg in Wort und Zahl* **32**(7):211–15.

Piore, Michael. 1980. "The Technological Foundations of Dualism and Discontinuity," in Suzanne Berger and Michael Piore, eds., *Dualism and Discontinuity in Industrial Societies,* pp. 55–81. New York: Cambridge University Press.

Piore, Michael, and Charles Sabel. 1984. *The Second Industrial Divide.* New York: Basic Books.

Sabel, Charles. 1989. "Flexible Specialization and the Reemergence of Regional Economies," in Paul Q. Hirst and Jonathan Zeitlin, eds., *Reversing Industrial Decline?* pp. 17–70. London: Berg.

Sabel, Charles, Horst Kern, and Gary Herrigel. 1990. "Collaborative Manufacturing: New Supplier Relations in the Automobile Industry and the Redefinition of the Industrial Corporation," in H. G. Mendius and U. Wendling-Schroeder, eds., *Zulieferer im Netz: Zwischen Abhaengigkeit und Partnerschaft.* Koeln, Germany: Bund Verlag.

Sabel, Charles, Gary Herrigel, Richard Deeg, and Richard Kazis. 1989. "Regional Prosperities Compared: Baden Württemberg and Massachusetts in the 1980's," *Economy and Society* **18**:4.

Schnonfield, Andrew. 1964. *Modern Capitalism.* New York: Oxford University Press.

Spaeth, Lothar. 1988. "Regionalisierung des europaeischen Raums—Die Zukunft der Bundeslaender im Spannungsfeld zwischen EG, Bund und Kommunen," *Cappenberger Gespräche der Freiherr-com-Stein-Gesellschaft* **23**:1–7.

Spaeth, Lothar. 1991. *Der Traum von Europa.* Stuttgart: Deutsche Verlags-Anstalt.

Teece, David, J., ed. 1987. *The Competitive Challenge: Strategies for Industrial Innovation and Renewal.* Cambridge, Mass.: Ballinger.

Voskamp, Ulli, Klaus Peter Wittemann, and Volker Wittke. 1989. "Elektroindustrie im Umbruch. Zur Veränderungsdynamik von Produktionsstrukturen, Rationalizierungskonzepten und Arbeit. Zwischenbericht." Göttingen: SOFI.

Weber, Hajo. 1984. "Intermediaere Organization: Zur Organization von Wirtschaftsinteressen zwischen Markt, Staat und Gewerkschaften," Ph.D. diss., Universitaet Bielefeld.

Wittke, Volker. 1989a. "Elektronisierung und Rationalisierung. Zur Veränderungsdynamik von Produktionsarbeit in der Elekroindustrie," in L. Preis, R. Schmidt, R. Trinczek, eds., *Trends betrieblicher Produktionsmodernisierung,* pp. 130–136. Opladen, Germany: West Deutscher Verlag.

Wittke, Volker. 1989b. "Systemischer Rationalizierung. Zur Analyse aktueller Umbruchsprozesse in der industriellen Produktion" *SOFI Mitteilungen, Nr. 17,* December, pp. 53–68.

2

Country Patterns in R&D Organization: The United States and Japan

ELEANOR WESTNEY

Empirical studies of country patterns in R&D have been dominated by the system-level analysis of aggregate national variables. One common approach has been the comparative analysis of national data on such variables as research expenditures, patent applications, and the numbers and distribution of researchers (e.g., Okimoto and Saxonhouse 1987; Slaughter and Utterback 1990). Another approach has been to study the state's role in the R&D system (Brooks 1986; Ergas 1987; Derian 1990). However, the growing interest in the effect of institutionalized patterns in manufacturing organization on technological change and country competitiveness[1] raises the question of whether country patterns in R&D organization—patterns that cut across industries and individual firms—also influence national trajectories in the pace and direction of technological change.

The question is difficult to answer, given the paucity of data on country patterns in the organization of industrial R&D. Nevertheless, the growing interest in the similarities and differences between U.S. and Japanese firm-level R&D organization has produced at least some comparative studies to complement and, in some cases, contradict the widely shared "common knowledge" about the dominant patterns in the two countries. This chapter examines current comparative analyses of Japanese and U.S. industrial R&D and looks at their implications for theories of the relationships between country differences in technology and those in organizational patterns.

Differences in the Technological Behavior of U.S. and Japanese Firms

In the second half of the 1980s, Japanese competitive strengths in technology development have attracted increasing attention in the popular and academic business literature. A widespread consensus has emerged on some of the key characteristics of the technological behavior of Japanese firms, compared to those of the United States:

1. Shorter development times (Mansfield 1988a; 1988b; Stalk and Hout 1990; Imai, Nonaka, and Takeuchi 1985)
2. More effective identification and acquisition of external technology, on a global scale (Rosenberg and Steinmueller 1988; Mansfield 1988b)
3. More effective design for manufacturability (Aoki 1988; Rosenberg and Steinmueller 1988)
4. More incremental product and process improvement (Dore 1987, 125–144; Rosenberg and Steinmueller 1988; Aoki 1988, 237–247)
5. Innovation dominated by large rather than small firms (Scherer 1980; Abegglen and Stalk 1985; Dore 1987; Okimoto and Saxonhouse 1987)
6. Stronger propensity to competitive matching of products and processes (Abegglen and Stalk 1985)
7. Greater propensity for interfirm collaboration in developing technology (Imai, Nonaka, and Takeuchi 1985; Yamamura 1986; Westney 1987)
8. Higher propensity to patent (Hull and Azumi 1989)
9. Weakness in science-based industries, for example, pharmaceuticals, chemicals, biotechnology (Saxonhouse 1986; Sun 1989)

While these traits have been observed across several industries, not all have been subjected to rigorous measurement of the extent of the differences between Japan and the United States. And even those who are convinced of the essential validity of the characterizations do not always agree on the key factors underlying each trait. The three primary arenas of explanation have been (1) technology policy and the role of the state; (2) corporate strategy; and (3) the institutionalized organizational patterns of the firm.

Shorter Product Development Times

There have been several recent efforts to test the accuracy of the widespread popular perception of the Japanese advantage in the time taken to develop a new product. The analysis of development times for Japanese, European, and U.S. firms in the auto industry (Clark, Chew, and Fujimoto 1987) confirmed the fact that, despite considerable dispersion around the mean within each country, the Japanese firms had a clear advantage over both their European and U.S. counterparts. Edwin Mansfield's multi-industry study, using managers' assessments of the average development times and costs for Japanese and U.S. firms in their industry, showed the same pattern over the average for the six industries he studied. However, the difference was not statistically significant for two of the four industries: chemical and metals (1988b, 1158). And such data face challenges from those who believe that U.S.–Japan comparisons of new product development cycles may face unrecognized problems of definition of the "project." Westney and Sakakibara (1985) found in their comparative study of R&D in the computer industry that Japanese firms tended to engage in considerable "pre-project" research before formally defining research activity as a budgeted "project."

The auto study by Clark and colleagues, and Mansfield's research, however, have been taken to provide empirical confirmation for what many people strongly believe: that Japanese firms have been faster to develop new products than their U.S. counterparts. Both popular discussions and more academic analyses (Imai, Nonaka, and Takeuchi 1985; Westney and Sakakibara 1985; Nonaka 1990) have identified the organizational structures of product development in Japanese firms as the key factor explaining their shorter design cycles. Included in this general category are multifunctional development teams—which include technical people from manufacturing and marketing in new product development teams (Imai, Nonaka, and Takeuchi 1985; Takeuchi and Nonaka 1986)—and the mode of technology transfer from R&D to manufacturing, whereby a key project team member moves with the project to the manufacturing division and sees it through the complete product introduction cycle (Westney and Sakakibara 1985).

Mansfield suggested a third organizational factor, linked to competitive strategies rather than to internal organization, although the two are not mutually exclusive: what he has called the "elasticity of innovation cost with respect to time." His study found that the Japanese figure was twice the American, that is, "Japanese firms seem willing to devote a much greater amount of resources than American firms to reduce the time taken to develop and introduce an innovation" (1988b, 1162). Mansfield also stressed an additional explanation: greater effectiveness in identifying and utilizing technologies developed outside the firm (and often outside Japan).

More Effective Use of External Technology

Mansfield compared the time and cost for innovations based on internal and external technology between 1975 and 1985 in thirty matched pairs of firms in Japan and the United States and found that the United States suffered from an "apparent inability to match Japan as a quick and effective user of external technology" (1988b, 1167). Indeed, Mansfield asserts that the innovation time and cost advantage of the Japanese firms resides solely in their greater efficiency in using external technology, although he does not present the data to support his contention that "the average cost and time for innovations based on internal technology does not differ significantly between the two countries" (1988b, 1160, n. 9).

There is relatively little systematic analysis, empirical or conceptual, of the basis for this capacity to exploit externally generated technology. It is often ascribed to cultural factors: in particular, an absence of the NIH (Not Invented Here) Syndrome, which leads technical people to eschew technical solutions developed outside the firm. This greater willingness of Japanese researchers to explore existing solutions to problems and to search for externally available technology has been explained in turn by (1) the educational system, which emphasizes the absorption of existing (often foreign) knowledge over the capacity for originality, and (2) the socialization processes of the large corporation, which trains technical employees to value speedy and effective solutions, whatever their source (Westney and Sakakibara 1985; Rosenberg and Steinmuller 1988). Technology policy has also played a role, through government support for the creation of an on-line patent system and a range of scientific and technical data bases (Herbert 1989). But here again, the organization of the firm remains significant, and not only in providing access to and encouragement for the use of such data bases. Several of the interns from the MIT-Japan Program, returning to the United States after a year in a Japanese corporate laboratory, have reported on the institutionalized firm-level supports for external information gathering they have observed within their own research groups, including standardized procedures for attending and reporting on technical conferences; regular study groups within the lab that focus on analyzing competitors' patents or on the Western technical literature in a particular area; and extremely well-maintained and easy-to-use technical libraries and information systems.

Design for Manufacturability

That Japanese firms have been more successful than their American counterparts in incorporating manufacturing criteria into their design processes has become virtually a truism in discussions of Japanese technology behavior (Rosenberg and Steinmuller 1988). This widespread perception is based largely on concrete data from the auto industry (Clark, Chew, and Fujimoto 1987; Womack, Jones, and Roos 1990) and on less publicly available competitive product evaluations made by U. S. firms (see Westney and Sakakibara 1985). The technological aspects of this behavior include the incorporation of existing components into new designs (which can often make for more conservative design); simultaneous engineering of new components with new products; and design for efficiency and ease of production.

Design for manufacturability is seen as one of the factors in the quality advantage enjoyed by many Japanese firms, and in the shorter product life cycles observed in several industries. Not surprisingly, some of the same organizational features invoked to explain shorter product cycles are used to account for the capacity to design for manufacturability: in particular, the incorporation of technical employees from manufacturing (and in some cases from components suppliers) into development teams. The Westney and Sakakibara study (1985) of the computer industry provided some evidence for another factor: the greater prestige of the manufacturing organization within the large Japanese firm. This prestige was reflected in the much greater importance that engineers at the central R&D labs of Japanese firms assigned to manufacturing people as a reference group, compared to their U.S. counterparts. This perception of importance, in turn, may well be linked to the career path of R&D engineers: as previously pointed out, in many engineering-based industries, researchers from the central lab move at a certain point in their careers into the divisional labs attached to the manufacturing plants and eventually into line management.

Incremental Product and Process Improvement

Mansfield's multi-industry study of thirty matched pairs of firms in Japan and the United States (1988b) has provided some concrete data to support what has become a widespread perception (e.g., Okimoto 1986): that Japanese firms in general allocate more resources than their U.S. counterparts to process improvement and less

to entirely new products and processes. One explanation for this behavior is organizational: as the mobility patterns previously described suggest, Japanese firms
tend to have a greater concentration of technical personnel in production, both in
the divisional labs and on the factory floor, and therefore a greater capacity for
incremental innovation at the plant level. Another explanation is strategic: firms
compete in the marketplace (particularly the domestic marketplace) by the proliferation of products and their continuous improvement (Stalk and Hout 1990).
Whether the strategy drives the organizational capabilities or the capabilities drive
the strategy is probably an unanswerable question.

Innovation Dominated by Large Firms

The very small number of innovative start-up firms in Japan that establish a market
presence by a breakthrough technology or an innovative product has been widely
noted, as has the continuous stream of new products and new businesses developed
by Japan's very large firms.[2] Concrete data on the extent of the difference between
the U.S. and Japanese systems has been somewhat sketchy, but studies of significant
innovations in several countries in the 1970s found that, of the relatively small
number of innovations ascribed to Japan, a disproportionately large number were
attributable to large established firms (Scherer 1980). Okimoto and Saxonhouse
(1987) pointed out that, although Japanese R&D expenditures were more evenly
distributed across large firms on the one hand and medium and small-scale firms
on the other, large firms dominated in patent production and in the development
of new product niches.

Both government policy and firm-level organizational capabilities have been
invoked to explain this pattern. Large established firms have long had preferential
access to government-sponsored technology development projects, to bank funding, and to technical labor. And many scholars would argue that they have used
those resources to build systems that are conducive to continuous innovation
through their organization of R&D and their "information creation" capacity
(Imai, Nonaka, and Takeuchi 1985; Nonaka 1990).

The observations made regarding the technological dominance of large firms in
Japan should be tempered by the recognition that Japanese large firms are not as
big as their Western counterparts. In 1985, for example, Matsushita Electric (the
parent company of the Matsushita group) had 39,403 employees, of whom 2,000
were in the central research laboratory and 7,160 of whom (18 percent) were
defined as being in research and technology development; Canon had 15,800
employees, of whom 4,300 (27 percent) were in R&D; and Kao had 5,833, of whom
1,520 (26 percent) were in R&D (data supplied to the Japan Management Association, published in Nihon Noritsu Kyokai 1987). The structure of the Japanese corporation, where vertical disaggregation is spurred by the strong pressures to homog-
enize salaries and rewards within the boundaries of the firm (discussed in detail in
the following section), means that the "large" company contains technology development and final assembly for its core businesses, as well as the standard corporate
staff functions such planning and finance; it spins off component production, much

of sales and distribution, and less strategic businesses into subsidiaries. In consequence, the "large" Japanese firm avoids some of the inertia believed to come from large size (especially constraints on information flows), and by centering the company on technology development and manufacturing it raises the salience of those functions in decision making and strategy formation.

Propensity for Competitive Matching

The tendency for Japanese firms to pursue strategies that are driven primarily by a determination to match the products and performance of key competitors has been observed with admiration by some (e.g., Abegglen and Stalk 1985) and with exasperation by others. The oligopolistic structure of most Japanese industries can explain some of this behavior: as economists have pointed out, in such an industry "oligopolistic matching," in which oligopolists follow closely any move by competitors, can be the lowest risk strategy for all players.

Propensity for Interfirm Collaboration in Technology Development

The propensity of Japanese firms to cooperate on technology development has been the object of sustained, though hardly systematic, interest. Western observers have focused primarily on the large-scale horizontal cooperative projects involving direct competitors, such as the project to produce more powerful semiconductors, that are sponsored by the government and are clearly a result of governmental technology policy. But more numerous and probably more important are the various vertical technology development collaborations with suppliers and with customers.

Most large Japanese firms carry out considerable numbers of these collaborations each year (see the data provided in Westney 1989). These vary from arrangements that are virtually contract research (in which one firm carries out the project after its parameters have been decided), to genuinely joint research involving the exchange of researchers and sustained interfirm communications. This large number of collaborative research arrangements means that Japanese firms have evolved an array of organizational patterns to support such projects, especially for keeping in touch with and reabsorbing researchers sent out to other companies and for monitoring and evaluating collaborative projects (Westney 1987).

Such cooperative arrangements have not only an output agenda but also a developmental one. They have become an important way for Japanese firms to enhance their technological capabilities. A recent Ministry of International Trade and Industry (MITI) survey of Japanese manufacturing firms found that nearly three-quarters of the responding companies viewed technical cooperation with a Japanese firm as their most commonly used mode of strengthening their own R&D capabilities; over half also identified technical cooperation with companies in other industries and cooperation with foreign firms as useful avenues (Table 2.1).

Explanations of this behavior have been less numerous than descriptions of it, but they have tended to center on government antitrust policy (or more accurately its absence; see, for example, Yamamura 1986).

TABLE 2.1 Current Modes to Strengthen R&D in Japanese Firms

Technical cooperation with a leading Japanese company	73.4%
Technical cooperation with Japanese universities	72.3
Building a new R&D center within the company	60.1
Technical cooperation with companies in other industries	58.8
Hiring mid-career researchers	57.1
Cooperation with foreign companies	51.5
Utilizing subsidiaries	34.1
Technical cooperation with foreign universities	17.0
Acquisition of another company	10.9
Setting up research facilities overseas	6.2

Source: These data are from a MITI survey of manufacturing companies listed on the Tokyo Stock exchange. The questionnaire was sent to the 1,090 manufacturing companies, of whom 466 responded (42.8%) (compiled from data in Tsusho Sangyo Sho 1990, p. 74).

Higher Propensity to Patent

The higher Japanese propensity to patent has been inferred from the aggregate data on patent applications: between 1982 and 1987, the ratio of domestic patents received per 100 researchers was 99.6 in Japan and 28.2 in the United States (Hull and Azumi, 1989). The aggressive patenting by Japanese firms in the United States is a further indicator: since the mid-1980s, more Japanese firms than American have ranked in the top ten firms in number of patents received in the United States.

One explanation of this drive for patents is that under the Japanese system patents are awarded on the basis of techniques rather than basic concepts, making the requirements for a patent less rigorous than those in the United States. Nevertheless, the scale of Japanese patenting efforts has some problematic aspects. One is that the Japanese patent system is widely viewed as providing a lower level of protection for intellectual property than its Western counterparts, in part because of inadequate legal structures to enforce patents and in part because of the long-standing orientation of Japanese technology policy to dissemination rather than protection (Doi 1986). Another puzzling aspect is that the success rate of patent applications in Japan is unusually low. In the five years from 1983 to 1987 (inclusive), there were 2,521,965 patent applications; only 423,101 were granted during that time (16.8 percent). Over the same time frame, the ratio of approvals to applications was 59.4 percent in the United States, 58.6 percent in what was then West Germany, and 87.2 percent in the United Kingdom. Both these factors would, on the face of it, seem to discourage rather than encourage patenting in Japan. Yet since 1969, the increase in the number of patent applications in Japan has been 400 percent; the increase in patent approvals, 255 percent.[3]

Two kinds of explanations of this behavior—which are not mutually exclusive—have been put forward. One portrays patenting as a salient element of the competitive strategies of Japanese firms. In this interpretation, Japanese firms have three strategic motivations for intense patenting activities. One is to surround key emerging technology breakthroughs so as to force other firms to engage in cross-licensing if they are to utilize their own patented technologies. In addition, a firm can conceal its own technology trajectories from competing firms by creating a flood of patent information. Finally, Japanese firms want to avoid paying in future the large and ongoing one-way stream of royalties that many Japanese firms are even today providing to foreign firms (such as RCA) for technologies licensed decades earlier.[4]

Another set of explanations focuses on internal organizational factors: in particular, the reward structures for Japanese researchers. As they expanded their R&D expenditures in the wake of the first oil crisis, many Japanese firms looked to patents as a measure of productivity and performance in their R&D organizations. Today many leading Japanese firms not only provide incentives to their technical employees both for patent applications and for patents received (Doi 1986, 162), they also assign patent quotas to each section of their R&D laboratories.[5] Companies, which regularly publish the number of patent applications as a measure of their technological competitiveness, try to make it relatively easy for their employees to apply for patents by providing patent templates and technical support to reduce the amount of time required to write patent applications.

Weakness in Science-based Industries

Japan's science-based industries—pharmaceuticals, chemicals, biotechnology—have long been considerably weaker than their counterparts in the United States and Western Europe. Japan does not at present boast of global competitors in these industries, and the most common explanation given is the relative weakness of its scientific—as opposed to its engineering—education. U.S. universities have provided a much more favorable environment for scientific research and have produced far more advanced degree-holders in the sciences than Japan. Japanese universities, in contrast, have long given priority to the "applied" fields of engineering and medicine (Bartholemew, 1989). In engineering in 1986, for example, Japan produced 73,316 bachelor's graduates in engineering, compared to the United States' 77,061; however, it produced only 588 doctoral graduates of university courses, compared to the 3,376 in the United States (National Science Foundation, 1988).

Clearly education and technology policy is a major factor explaining this pattern. Government policy plays an additional role that influences the research base in the pharmaceutical industry, as Reich (1990) has pointed out: R&D in the Japanese pharmaceutical industry has faced major constraints imposed by the price regulations exacted by the health-care delivery system.

Interpretation and Summary

There is a logical coherence in the overall pattern of these nine traits, given Japan's position as a technology follower. The influence of followership is most obvious in the use of external technology: as Rosenberg and Steinmuller (1988) have pointed out, U.S. firms and researchers have become accustomed to their country's technological preeminence, and are only now adjusting to a world where the leading centers of science and technology are not necessarily found within their own borders. Japanese firms, in contrast, have spent decades developing organizational systems to identify and acquire foreign technology (Herbert, 1989).

Given their reliance on a global pool of technology under conditions where no single firm could hope to gain exclusive access, competition among Japanese industrial firms focuses on the speed and quality with which that technology could be embodied in products, on incremental improvements in the acquired technology, and on rapid competitive matching of products and processes. The continuous incremental improvements were far from trivial: many U.S. firms in the 1980s found themselves licensing back from Japanese firms products based on technology that they had themselves licensed to the Japanese in the 1950s or 1960s. Technology followership also give an advantage to large firms over small: the larger firms have greater resources to devote to global technology scanning and acquisition and to invest in rapid incremental improvement of that technology.

Clearly there were systemic factors conducive to these developments. Postwar Japanese government technology policy fostered technology dissemination: a disclosure-oriented patent system, an insistence in the 1950s and 1960s on multiple licensees for major technology imports, and state sponsorship of interfirm cooperation R&D. Japanese industrial policy consistently eschewed fostering a single "national champion" in any industry, perhaps because government bureaucrats felt that maintaining a small population of oligopolistically competing firms was more likely to maintain their own position of authority than the creation of a single, perhaps countervailing, behemoth. These policies in turn reinforced companies' focus on seeking competitive advantage in the application of technology and rapid incremental innovation. The universities contributed through their emphasis on foreign language training (focused on reading capability) and on keeping abreast of the Western technical literature.

While government policy and institutional influences on competitive strategy are clearly essential in explaining the technology behavior of Japanese firms, both these forces tend to operate through their influence on the organization of the large industrial firm. In eight of the nine factors described, institutionalized patterns of R&D at the firm level—in terms both of the internal organization of the technology development function and of the R&D networks among firms—play a major role. Following is a discussion of the processes that have produced significant commonalities in R&D across firms and across industries.

Institutionalized Differences in R&D Organization

The organizational patterns in industrial R&D that are institutionalized across firms and across industries can be divided into three major categories. One type is isomorphic with patterns institutionalized in other functions of the industrial firm; these are often integrally connected with and reinforced by external labor markets. A second category is isomorphic with patterns institutionalized in the professional research community as a whole; these are frequently a consequence of and reinforced by the organizational patterns that prevail in the leading research institutions, which in many countries are the major universities. A third type consists of the distinctive patterns that are a consequence of what Scott (1987) has called "imprinting" and that Cole (1978) calls "period effects": patterns that are a consequence of the time and the sequence in which the function evolved within firms.

Isomorphism with General Patterns in Industrial Organizations

Patterns institutionalized across industries in large industrial firms have received far more attention in studies of Japan than of the United States. Western researchers have been more inclined to view the Japanese firm and "Japanese management" holistically and to be struck by the commonalities across industries; witness the number of books with titles such as *The Japanese Factory* (Abegglen 1958); *The Japanese Company* (Clark 1979); *The Economic Analysis of the Japanese Firm* (Aoki 1984); and *Kaisha: The Japanese Corporation* (Abegglen and Stalk 1985). But in all countries—the United States as well as Japan—certain patterns are common across industrial firms, and these have exerted strong isomorphic pulls on the organization of industrial R&D. In the case of Japan, as described in the following, the pulls have been toward standardization across functions within the industrial firm; in the United States, they have favored differentiation. In consequence, in the United States the second type of isomorphic pulls—towards patterns institutionalized in the professional research community—have been stronger than in Japan. The pulls on the Japanese R&D function from patterns institutionalized in manufacturing can most clearly be observed in the career patterns and reward structures of R&D employees.

By now it is virtually a truism that recruitment and career structures in large Japanese firms are directed toward the development of generalists, both in management and in blue-collar positions, whereas in the United States they are directed toward bringing in and developing specialists (Aoki 1988, 49–52). These patterns in Japan can be seen in prewar industrial firms, but were strongly institutionalized in the postwar period (for an explanation of the evolution of the phenomenon, see Dore 1973). It is hardly surprising that the same patterns characterize the R&D organization of large firms.

One of the clearest indicators of the difference between Japanese and U. S. patterns is the strong resistance of Japanese companies to hiring university-trained Ph.D.'s into their research organizations. Whereas the R&D groups of large U. S. firms have formed a major market for the more than 12,000 Ph.D.'s produced in science and engineering each year, the reluctance of Japan's industrial firms to hire researchers directly from the Ph.D. programs of the universities is the major factor explaining the small scale of these programs in Japan.

A number of industrial researchers in Japanese companies do indeed boast of Ph.D.'s, but they are obtained in a program (adapted from the German model) whereby researchers employed in companies can submit papers to their alma mater and receive a Ph.D. in recognition of their contributions to the field. These degrees are granted without any of the specialized coursework and university-based socialization of the American Ph.D., and tend therefore to reinforce rather than counteract company-based socialization. In 1986, 57 percent of the doctorates granted in Japan in natural science and engineering were of this type (Kagaku Gijutsu Cho 1987).

The generalist structure of Japanese technical careers means that relatively few of those who are recruited into the R&D function spend their careers there. The "standard" career in most industries leads from R&D into divisional technical roles and then into line or staff positions in the operating divisions (Westney and Sakakibara 1985; Nihon Noritsu Kyokai 1987).

Underpinning this career structure is a marked difference from the technical career structure that prevails in most U.S. firms. In the R&D organization of large Japanese firms, as in other functions, the primary locus of responsibility for planning the employee's career rests with the company, rather than with the individual as is the case in most U.S. firms. This difference was reflected in many of the indicators in the comparative study of computer engineers by Westney and Sakakibara (1985). In assignment to projects, the most important factor for the U.S. engineers was their own expressed desire to participate; for the Japanese engineers, it was the supervisor of their last project. In training after entry into the company, Japanese engineers were far more likely than their U.S. counterparts to have been assigned to courses by their company, rather than undertaking them at their own initiative. Significantly more of the Japanese engineers agreed with the statement that "the recruitment of engineers is based on long-range personnel planning rather than immediate needs" (Westney and Sakakibara 1985). This belief is bolstered by the policy that when Japanese engineers join a company upon graduation, not only do they not know what project they will join; they do not know to what part of the company they will be assigned after the entry-level training program. And over half the Japanese engineers agreed that their performance was evaluated over a period of five to ten years, compared to just 10 percent of their U.S. counterparts.

Another aspect of R&D organization that is strongly shaped by the general patterns of the industrial corporation is the reward structure. In Japanese firms, criteria for base pay and annual increments for blue-collar workers and the nonsupervisory levels of management are set in annual spring negotiations with the company union (to which management and technical personnel belong until they reach the level of section head—usually in their mid-thirties). In consequence, wages, salaries, and bonuses are standardized across functions, and there are strong barriers impeding the use of monetary incentives to reward outstanding researchers or to differentiate across functions (Westney and Sakakibara 1985). In interviews in sixteen technology-intensive firms in Japan, Sully Taylor found that:

> Resistance to using salary as a motivator may be quite strong. One R&D manager stated that if a high performing researcher were being headhunted by another firm, his company would rather let him go than entice him to stay through a salary increase. This manager felt that increasing his salary would severely undermine the lifetime employment system by destroying the cherished sense of internal equity that the system provides. . . . This sentiment was echoed in various ways by the R&D managers at other firms, as well as the researchers themselves. . . . In short, the heavy emphasis on seniority in allocating rewards is felt to be the cornerstone of the present employment relationship between the firms and employees. . . . Changes in this part of the HRM [human resource management] system were felt

to have potentially severe repercussions throughout the company and could not be instituted as easily as other changes. Several R&D managers also mentioned the question of union resistance to changes in any part of their firm's salary structure. (Taylor, 1989, 139)

In large U.S. firms, in contrast, while there may be equally strong constraints on major differences in salary levels within a given function, reward structures are highly differentiated across functions and between blue-collar and managerial employees, but strongly isomorphic across firms in terms of function and level. In Japan, the pulls toward homogenization within the firm are extremely strong, and, indeed, provide an important constraint on the size and vertical integration of the firm.

The strong isomorphism across the functions and levels within the industrial firms in Japan has been a critically important element of their strengths in reducing development times, designing for manufacturability, and incremental product and process innovation, all of which are undergirded by the transfer of engineers across functions and by the ability of the firm to assign them to tasks (such as incremental product improvement) that may lack intrinsic interest but that have high value to the firm.

The stronger propensity of Japanese firms to patent also has its roots in intra-firm isomorphic processes: it is an outcome of the efforts of firms to develop concrete measures of productivity within their R&D function analogous to those that have been so useful in benchmarking their manufacturing processes. And at least some of the high propensity of Japanese firms to cooperate in technology development can be attributed to isomorphism with patterns institutionalized elsewhere within the industrial firm. As several scholars have pointed out (Aoki 1988; Fruin 1992), Japanese firms have a marked tendency to cooperate with other firms in several contexts. But the particular patterns institutionalized in R&D to support extensive technology collaboration, while perhaps attributable to the same underlying firm-level and environmental factors, are distinctively suited to the more intense (and potentially more intrusive) interactions required by the joint development of technology.

Isomorphism with Professional Patterns

Given the fact that isomorphism with companywide organizational patterns is so strong in Japan, U.S. analysts have tended to assume that the pulls of professionalism and professional identity are extremely weak (see, for example, Saxonhouse 1986, 127–29, and Okimoto and Saxonhouse 1987, 413). The context in which this difference has attracted most attention has been in the area of patterns of technical communication. U.S. researchers, even those in industry, are portrayed as being oriented primarily to their professional identity, and therefore as willing to publish research results and communicate freely with researchers outside their company. Japanese researchers, on the other hand, are seen as being loyal "company men," and therefore as being reluctant to share information with "outsiders."

However, this perception of the Japanese researcher is based primarily on an economically rational model of professionalization rather than on empirical research: it assumed that researchers communicate within their profession primarily to enhance their individual market value (Saxonhouse 1986, 128). In the absence of high levels of cross-company mobility, as in Japan, one would expect incentives for professional communication to be low. There is some empirical evidence that this perception is wrong: in the comparative study of R&D in the computer industry (Westney and Sakakibara 1985), Japanese company engineers were found to be significantly more likely than their U.S. counterparts to participate in professional societies, to attend professional meetings, and to believe that their company encourages them to publish the results of their work. They are also, surprisingly enough, more likely to value the approval and respect of their professional colleagues outside their own company than are the U.S. engineers. The longstanding Western assumption that "loyalty to the company" and "professional identity" are at opposite poles of a single continuum needs reassessment: the two dimensions may well be orthogonal. Companies can create an environment that fosters the "organizational professional" for whom enhancing personal reputation in the profession is also a way of enhancing the prestige of the company.

In the United States, the role of the professional researcher is epitomized and reinforced by the faculty of the major research universities. The norm of autonomy, the commitment to public disclosure and dissemination, the strong concern with external reputation, the high value on original and creative research, a higher value on the scope of opportunity to pursue self-defined research agendas than on institutional loyalty (which has made for such a high level of mobility of faculty across universities) all epitomize the professional model. The influence of the model is reinforced by the key role of research universities in the national technology system and the consequent interaction between industrial and academic researchers—and perhaps by the fact that industry often competes with universities to hire promising Ph.D. graduates. The model's effects are also perpetuated by the strong socialization of those industrial researchers who have pursued Ph.D.'s at a research university.

In Japan, the universities play a far less significant role in providing a strong model of the professional researcher than in the United States, partly because of the less salient role of the university in the national research system (National Research Council 1989). In part this circumstance is attributable to the far lower proportion of university-trained Ph.D.'s in industry, but it also results from the Japanese university not providing a strongly institutionalized alternative role model. University faculty members in Japan are not subject to the strong pressures to generate new knowledge embodied in the "publish or perish" tenure tournament of the North American research universities. The major Japanese universities recruit their faculty members overwhelmingly from the ranks of their own graduate students. Most faculty members obtain Chairs in the same university in which they did their postgraduate and even their undergraduate work, and they enjoy the equivalent of tenure from the time of their initial appointment. Their most important role in the national research system is to function not as creators of new knowledge but as sources of information: information about new technologies (domestic and foreign), about the directions of government policy (in which they play an important advisory role), and about the students who provide the future cohorts of industrial researchers. This role, insofar as it affects the definition of the role of the research professional in industry, reinforces the importance of external information gathering and dissemination.

Universities in Japan make at least one more important contribution to that model in the course of the education of scientists and engineers. In contrast to the research universities of North America, with their emphasis on fostering the ability to define and solve problems, the technical education at Japanese universities has historically emphasized the mastery of a body of knowledge, much of it from abroad (Westney and Sakakibara 1985). Technical graduates enter the industrial research setting with a strong orientation to keeping abreast of external technology developments that is often missing from North American technical education at the elite institutions, where originality is more highly valued than a "mindless" mastery of the technical literature.

There is perhaps another way in which the universities in Japan have contributed to the role of the "organizational professional" whose company identity and professional identity are not at odds, although it is difficult to measure: the long-standing bias of Japanese universities to the development of "useful" knowledge. This trait has been discussed in some detail in James Bartholemew's history of the early decades of the development of Japan's research system (Bartholemew 1989), where he documents the early dominance of engineering and medicine in the evolution of the national universities. He leaves open the question of whether this trait is grounded in Japan's status as a follower nation or whether its roots are older, in the traditional neo-Confucian emphasis on the obligation of the scholar to serve society. But among the highly advanced industrial nations, Japan remains the only country in which there are more engineering doctorates granted as a proportion of the population than natural science doctorates (National Science Foundation 1988, 51).

In summary, the model of the academic researcher in Japan is less strongly institutionalized than in the United States. Moreover, such features that are institutionalized are more compatible with at least some of the goals of industrial research, particularly the orientation to effective use of externally generated technology and to product-oriented research rather than to basic or advanced research. The greater strength of the model of the "organizational professional" in Japan, as opposed to the "academic professional," means that isomorphism with other functions in the firm is stronger, and what DiMaggio and Powell (1983) have called "normative isomorphism"—which differentiates the "professional" from other members of the organization—is much weaker.

Isomorphism Across Firms Within Industrial Research

This type of country-based patterns in R&D organization, which refers to patterns attributable to isomorphic pulls across industrial firms within the R&D function, has been the least systematically explored. There are two arenas where somewhat unsystematic observation suggests important country-level effects: one concerns the formal structure of R&D, the other the propensity for interfirm cooperation in technology development.

Historical descriptions of the evolution of R&D facilities in Japan suggests that there are strongly marked development phases that stretch across industries (Nihon Noritsu Kyokai 1987). Relatively few Japanese firms established R&D facilities before World War II; most relied for technology development on technology departments attached to major factories, whose role was primarily the identification, acquisition, and adaptation of foreign technology. The early 1950s saw an "R&D center" boom, in which many of the larger firms set up *kenkyujo* (research centers). The early and mid-1960s produced a *Chuo Kenkyujo Bu-mu* (Central R&D Laboratory boom), in which companies either consolidated their existing research centers into a single central lab or added a central lab to do advanced product development. The 1970s was a decade in which divisional laboratories proliferated; one firm has identified it as a period when the dominant thrust was toward fostering the ties between the growing technology development organization and the *jigyobu* (business divisions). Finally, the mid-1980s witnessed the establishment of basic research labs in Japan's leading companies, a development promptly dubbed the *kiso kenkyu bu-mu* (basic research boom) by the business press.

Given this apparently widely shared development trajectory, institutionalization theory would lead one to expect strong isomorphic pulls across the R&D organizations. One reason is what Scott calls "imprinting," structural features shared across organizations by virtue of the environmental conditions at the time of their establishment (Scott 1987). Another is that one would expect what DiMaggio and Powell (1983) call "mimetic isomorphism" strong mutual awareness and emulation of patterns defined as "state of the art." However, at this point the research on the development of R&D in Japan has only begun. The isomorphic pulls within industrial R&D over the five decades of its development in Japan remain a fertile ground for future institutional research.

Conclusions

As Japanese and Western researchers alike become increasingly interested in the similarities and differences between their respective countries' R&D organizations, the amount of information on which we can ground our assessments of country effect on organizational structure and the behavior of organizations will inevitably grow. But increasingly our observations and analyses of the technology systems of the two societies will be complicated by growing isomorphic pulls across societies. Currently Japanese firms are looking to the United States for organizational models on which to develop their basic research institutes. U.S. firms have developed growing interest in "learning" from how the Japanese link R&D to other functions within the firm and to customers and suppliers across the boundaries of the firm. And the growing internationalization of R&D will inevitably exert some unanticipated pressures on current patterns of R&D organization in the United States, Europe, and Japan alike. The careful documentation and analysis of evolving R&D organization is one of the most promising avenues for understanding the nature and extent of country effects on organizations, and on the forces that work to change and to reduce those effects.

Notes

1. See for example R. Jaikumar (1986) on the influence of production worker organization on the use of flexible manufacturing systems in Japan and the United States, and the more general approach in Michael L. Dertouzos et al. (1989).

2. For a discussion of the phenomenon and a succinct analysis of the economically grounded explanations for it, see Rebecca Henderson (1991).

3. These data on patents come from the annual publication of the Kagaku Gijutsu Cho (Science and Technology Agency), *Kagaku Gijutsu Yoran* (Indicators of Science and Technology).

4. This preceding discussion is based largely on several seminars on Japanese patenting behavior sponsored by the MIT-Japan Program.

5. Based on information from returning MIT-Japan program interns, several of whom have described the flurry of activity in their research group when the end of the "patent year" approaches without the group's having met its quota: researchers "brainstorm" to develop patent ideas to meet their quota, well aware that many of these proposed patents will never actually be granted or provide much value to the company.

References

Abegglen, James. 1958. *The Japanese Factory.* Glencoe, Ill.: The Free Press.

Abegglen, James, and George Stalk. 1985. *Kaisha: The Japanese Corporation.* New York: Basic Books.

Aoki, Masahiko, ed., 1984. *The Economic Analysis of the Japanese Firm.* Amsterdam: New Holland Press.

Aoki, Masahiko. 1988. *Information, Incentives, and Bargaining in the Japanese Economy.* New York: Cambridge University Press.

Bartholemew, James. 1989. *The Formation of Science in Japan.* New Haven, Conn.: Yale University Press.

Brooks, Harvey. 1986. "National Science Policy and Technological Innovation," in R. Landau and N. Rosenberg, eds., pp. 119–67. *The Positive Sum Strategy.* Washington, D.C.: National Academy Press.

Clark, Rodney. 1979. *The Japanese Company.* New Haven, Conn.: Yale University Press.

Clark, K., W. Bruce Chew, and T. Fujimoto. 1987. "Product Development in the World Auto Industry," *Brookings Papers on Economic Activity* 3:729–82.

Cole, Robert E. 1978. "The Late-Developer Hypothesis: An Evaluation of Its Relevance for Japanese Employment Patterns," *Journal of Japanese Studies* 4:2.

Derian, Jean-Claude. 1990. *America's Struggle for Leadership in Technology.* Cambridge, Mass.: MIT Press.

Dertouzos, Michael L., Richard K. Lester, Robert M. Solow, and The MIT Commission on Industrial Productivity. 1989. *Made in America: Regaining the Productive Edge.* Cambridge, Mass.: MIT Press.

DiMaggio, Paul J., and Walter W. Powell. 1983. "The Iron Cage Revisited: Institutional Isomorphism and Collective Rationality in Organizational Fields," *American Sociological Review* 35:147–60.

Doi, T. 1986. "The Role of Intellectual Property Law in Bilateral Licensing Transactions between Japan and the United States," in G. Saxonhouse and K. Yamamura, eds., *Law and Trade Issues of the Japanese Economy,* pp. 157–92. Seattle: University of Washington Press.

Dore, Ronald. 1973. *British Factory–Japanese Factory: The Origins of National Diversity in Industrial Relations.* Berkeley: University of California Press.

Dore, Ronald. 1987. *Taking Japan Seriously: A Confucian Perspective on Leading Economic Issues.* London: Athlone Press.

Ergas, Henry. 1987. "Does Technology Policy Matter?" in B. R. Guile and H. Brooks, eds., *Technology and Global Industry: Companies and Nations in the World Economy,* pp. 191–245. Washington, D.C.: National Academy Press.

Fruin, Mark. 1992. *The Japanese Enterprise System: Competitive Strategies and Cooperative Structures.* New York: Oxford University Press.

Henderson, Rebecca. 1991. "Successful Japanese Giants: A Major Challenge to Existing Theories of Technological Capability." MIT Working Paper.

Herbert, Evan. 1989. "Japanese R&D in the United States." *Research Technology Management* 32(6):11–20.

Hull, Frank M., and Koya Azumi. 1989. "Teamwork in Japanese and U. S. Labs," *Research Technology Management* 32:21–26.

Imai, K., I. Nonaka, and H. Takeuchi. 1985. "Managing the New Product Development Process: How Japanese Companies Learn and Unlearn," in K. Clark, R. Hayes, and C. Lorenz, eds., *The Uneasy Alliance, Managing the Productivity-Technology Dilemma.* Boston: Harvard Business School Press.

Jaikumar, R. 1986. "Postindustrial Manufacturing," *Harvard Business Review* 6(Nov.-Dec.):69–76.

Kagaku Gijutsu Cho (Gijutsu Seisaku Kyoku). 1987. *Kagaku Gijutsu Yoran (Showa 62 Nenpan).* Tokyo: Okura-sho Insatsu Kyoku.

Mansfield, Edwin. 1988a. "Industrial R&D in Japan and the United States," *American Economic Review* 78(2):223–28.

Mansfield, Edwin. 1988b. "The Speed and Cost of Industrial Innovation in Japan and the United States: External vs. Internal Technology," *Management Science* 34(10):1157–68.

National Research Council. 1989. *Learning the R&D System: University Research in Japan and the United States.* Washington, D.C: National Academy Press.

National Science Foundation. 1988. *International Science and Technology Update 1988* (rept. no. NSF 89-307.) Washington, D.C.: National Science Foundation.

Nihon Noritsu Kyokai (Japan Management Association). 1987. *Senshin Kigyo sanjusha in miru Kenkyujo Un'ei Kasseika Jitsureishu.* Tokyo: Nihon Noritsu Kyokai.

Nonaka, Ikujiro. 1990. "Redundant, Overlapping Organization: A Japanese Approach to Innovation," *California Management Review* 32(3):27–38.

Okimoto, D.I. 1986. "The Japanese Challenge in High Technology," in R. Landau and N. Rosenberg, eds., *The Positive Sum Strategy,* pp. 541–68. Washington, D.C.: National Academy Press.

Okimoto, Daniel, and Gary Saxonhouse. 1987. "Technology and the Future of the Economy," in K. Yamamura and Y. Yasuba, eds., *The Political Economy of Japan,* Vol. 1: *The Domestic Transformation,* pp. 385–419. Stanford: Stanford University Press.

Reich, Michael R. 1990. "Why the Japanese Don't Export More Pharmaceuticals: Health Policy as Industrial Policy," *California Management Review* 32(2):124–50.

Rosenberg, Nathan, and W. Edward Steinmueller. 1988. "Why Are Americans Such Poor Imitators?" *American Economic Review* 78(2):229–34.

Saxonhouse, Gary. 1986. "Industrial Policy and Factor Markets: Biotechnology in Japan and the United States" in Hugh Patrick, ed., *Japan's High Technology Industries,* pp. 91–169. Seattle: University of Washington Press.

Scherer, F. M. 1980. *Industrial Market Structure and Economic Performance.* Chicago: Rand McNally.

Scott, W. Richard. 1987. "The Adolescence of Institutional Theory," *Administrative Science Quarterly* **32**:493–511.

Slaughter, Sarah, and James Utterback. 1990. "U. S. Research and Development: An International Comparative Analysis," *Business in the Contemporary World,* Winter, pp. 27–35.

Stalk, George, Jr., and Thomas M. Hout. 1990. *Competing Against Time: How Time-Based Competition Is Reshaping Global Markets.* New York: The Free Press.

Sun, Marjorie. 1989. "Japan Faces Big Task in Improving Basic Science," *Science* **243**(March 10):1205–07.

Takeuchi, H., and I. Nonaka. 1986. "The New Product Development Game," *Harvard Business Review* **1**(Jan.-Feb.):137–46.

Taylor, Mary Sullivan. 1989. "A Transactions Cost Analysis of Japanese Employment Relationships." Ph.D. diss., University of Washington.

Tsusho Sangyo Sho Sangyo Seisaku Kigyo Kodoka. 1990. *Sogo Keieiryoku Shihyo: Seizogyo hen.* Tokyo: Okurasho Insatsu Kyoku.

Westney, D. Eleanor, and Kiyonori Sakakibara. 1985. "The Organization and Careers of Engineers in the Computer Industry in Japan and the United States." MIT-Japan Program Working Paper.

Westney, D. E. 1987. "Domestic and Foreign Learning Curves in Managing International Cooperative Strategies," in F. Contractor and P. Lorange, eds., *Cooperative Strategies in International Management.* Lexington, Mass.: Lexington Books.

Westney D. E. 1989. "Internal and External Linkages in the MNC: The Case of R&D Subsidiaries in Japan," in C. Bartlett, Y. Doz, and G. Hedlund, eds., *Managing the Multinational.* London:Croom Helm.

Womack, James P., Daniel T. Jones, and Daniel Roos. 1990. *The Machine That Changed the World.* New York:Rawson Associates.

Yamamura, Kozo. 1986. "Joint Research and Antitrust: Japanese vs. American Strategies," In Hugh Patrick, ed., *Japan's High Technology Industries: Lessons and Limitations of Industrial Policy,* pp. 171–209. Seattle: University of Washington Press.

3

Work Organization in Japan and the United States

JAMES R. LINCOLN

This chapter focuses primarily on work and company organization in the United States and Japan and, secondarily, on the impact of organization on the work attitudes and behaviors of Japanese and American manufacturing employees. It draws heavily on the empirical results of a large survey study of plants in both countries that I conducted with several colleagues in the early 1980s (Lincoln and Kalleberg 1990).

The topic is by no means a new one. The extent to which the keys to the competitive power of Japanese manufacturing companies lie in the discipline and commitment of Japanese labor and whether that discipline can be, in turn, traced to the management and structuring of the Japanese firm have been *the* comparative management questions of the 1980s. Always in the background of recent discussions of Japanese and Western management styles is the question of whether Japanese work organization is usefully cast as a new organizational form, one which (for a variety of reasons) the Japanese hit upon first and have therefore seized comparative advantage from, but is nonetheless the model toward which progressive and competitive North American and European firms are also inexorably drifting. As the successes of Japanese manufacturing at home and abroad have accumulated, this speculation has fascinated many writers, but the most sophisticated and provocative treatment of the topic remains Ronald Dore's (1973) thesis of "welfare corporatist" organization as a holistic organizational control system likely to materialize in late-developing economies.

At the time Dore first put forth his ideas about the economic and administrative rationality of Japanese-style work organization, most thinking on the distinctive institutional features of the Japanese economy was in a strongly culturalist vein. The departures from mainstream Western, particularly American, practice evident in Japan could only be construed as the quaint residues of particularistic values and customs, carried over from Japanese feudalism and signalling that the Japanese economy had yet to make the transition to full modernity. However, as we enter the 1990s, the Japanese model is becoming the new orthodoxy of rational economic organization (see, e.g., Aoki 1988; Fruin 1992). Explicit or not, the influence of Japanese practice is clearly evident in much current, revisionist economic and organizational theory concerned with the internal management and external transactions of modern capitalist firms.

Yet even as the Japanese model of organizing has acquired mainstream legitimacy in the theories of scholars and the practices of managers, there is renewed talk—especially in Japan—of its demise or, at least, metamorphosis. To what extent are the most striking contrasts fading and convergence taking place as adjustments are made on both sides in the interest of implementing new techniques and enhancing efficiency? From the perspective of classic modernization-convergence theory, institutional variations in management style and economic organization are always transitory, because the pressures of competitive efficiency and the rapid diffusion of physical and organizational technology break them down. The prediction that Japan would soon shed its distinctive and exotic management and employment practices has been in circulation since Western observers first encountered them (see, e.g., Abegglen 1958). As Dore and his colleagues documented in a recent assessment of Japanese labor trends, the rate of actual change has consistently lagged behind the predictions (Dore, Bounine-Cabale, and Tapiola 1989). In the current period of reduced economic growth, high wages, and an aging workforce, shifts are taking place in Japan (some of which are discussed in the following sections). But their overall extent and impact seem generally small as yet, or confined to certain limited sectors of the Japanese economy.

Contrary to the expectations of an earlier generation of convergence theorists, the amount of recent change, particularly in factory organization, may well have been greater in the United States than in Japan. In large part fueled by the pressure of competition from Japan, American industry during the 1980s abandoned many time-honored management methods and embraced new ones that are open attempts to mimic Japanese practice. Quality circles, work team organization, strong cultures, participatory decision making, job rotation, broad and permeable job boundaries, just-in-time production systems, and long-term, high-trust "relational" contracts with suppliers are among the Japanese-originated methods that have swept through United States manufacturing, encouraged, perhaps too often, by the extravagant claims of consultants and journalists of the power of Japanese management to reverse American industrial decline.

The cultural, historical, and political–economic processes through which these practices arose and grew to be dominant forms within the Japanese economy are complex and much debated (Lincoln, 1990). My general view, following, in particular, the arguments of Cole (1979), Dore (1973), and Gordon (1985), is that those processes represent the residues of state and corporate strategies over the course of Japan's industrialization to organize and discipline the workforce. These strategies were, in turn, selected and shaped by struggles with Japanese labor. They have become institutionalized for two reasons: (1) their thoroughgoing legitimation— even sanctification—over time in Japanese cultural ideology (the firm as a family, etc.); and (2) their apparent effectiveness in the postwar era in fostering flexible, innovative firms and dedicated, loyal employees. A discussion of the first reason is beyond the scope of this paper. The second reason, apparent efficacy, is the motive for the current rapid diffusion of "Japanese" practices through the economies of Japan's Western competitors, so many of my comments here address it.

What, then, are the primary areas in which contrasts in the work organization of U. S. and Japanese factories are evident? I suggest the following:

1. Organization design—the differentiation of labor into jobs, departments, and divisions, and the shape and functioning of status and authority hierarchies.
2. The structure of decision making—the differentiation and allocation of decision-making roles among individuals and positions.
3. The structuring of internal labor markets—the recruitment, training, and allocation of labor within the firm; compensation and promotion systems and their incentive and motivational effects.
4. The organization of unions and industrial relations.

Admittedly, these are complex topics deserving of lengthy treatment, and few of the observations made here will be wholly unfamiliar to readers having even a passing acquaintance with Japanese management practice. In light of the wide availability of more detailed treatments of these topics (Lincoln and Kalleberg 1990; Aoki 1988; Dore 1987), my presentation is based on breadth rather than depth.

Organization Design

I begin with the problem of organizational design, the vertical and horizontal division of labor within the organization. Many observers have commented on the distinctiveness of Japanese organizational structures, and a fair amount of relevant evidence has become available.

A pervasive difference in work organization between U.S. and Japanese firms concerns the degree to which job responsibilities and functional specialties are differentiated, formalized, assigned to individuals, and made the basis for advancement and reward. Rigid, formal division of labor in this sense has historically been much more characteristic of U.S. than Japanese organization. The differences appear in many areas, such as job classification and design, functional specialization, and hierarchy.

Job Classification and Design

Job classifications are kept simple and broad in Japanese firms, with most factory production workers, for example, falling within a single classification. Job descriptions, if they exist at all, are typically short and couched in vague terms. These patterns contrast sharply with the traditional job design practices of large U.S. firms that differentiate jobs into hundreds of discrete titles, do systematic job evaluations to ascertain the scope and depth of job responsibilities, record these in great detail in formal job descriptions, and make them the basis for compensation decisions.[1]

A number of observers have documented the reasons behind the preoccupation of U. S. firms with formal job design and classification (Jacoby 1985; Cole 1979).

One powerful historical force has been the scientific management movement, which, in Federick Taylor's teachings, saw the minute analysis and delineation of job duties and the elimination of worker discretion as critical elements in the rationalization of production and the transfer of control to management. Ironically, another force in the same direction was the emergence of "job control" unionism in the United States (Piore 1982). Unions took up formal job classification and descriptions as devices for curtailing management discretion in the task assignment process and giving workers rights to tightly circumscribed areas of job responsibility.

Strong cultural arguments have also been made for the low level of job or occupation consciousness in Japanese society (Cole and Tominaga 1976). It is proposed that there are deep-seated differences in the social structural attachments of Japanese and Western people. Westerners (perhaps Americans in particular) identify heavily with their occupational positions and roles, and only secondarily with the organizations and groups in which those positions and roles are embedded; hence, the pervasive pattern in the U.S. economy of people pursuing careers within occupations that take them across a series of employing organizations (see Chapters 2 and 7). The Japanese, so this argument goes, link themselves first to groups and only secondarily to functional positions within them. Indeed, the usual presumption is that the two orientations are incompatible in some degree. A strong affiliation with a group implies a willingness to take on any of the responsibilities arising from group membership.[2]

In keeping with the culturalist perspective is evidence that a low degree of specialization and a high degree of responsibility for a range of organizational functions are characteristic, not only of Japanese companies, but of other Japanese organizational settings as well (Rohlen 1983). Much like the Japanese factory worker who is held accountable for the cleanliness and condition of his work station and equipment (see Chapter 7), Japanese school children routinely do janitorial cleanup and minor maintenance in the classroom and around the school.

Japanese factories avoid narrow delineation of job boundaries, job proliferation, and a rigid one-to-one matching of workers and jobs. They screen for talented generalists fresh out of school and invest heavily in training them for a wide array of responsibilities. In so doing, they ensure that workers develop broad skills and can be flexibly adapted to variations in production scheduling and demand. The wide variety of production processes and product lines (including short production runs and small lot sizes) within the Japanese plant places a particular premium on this capacity. The traditional American production system of large economies of scale achieved through long production runs of highly standardized products and low unit cost is more tolerant of the rigid occupational division of labor characteristic of U.S. factories (see Chapter 12). Clearly, another critical factor in the importance Japanese firms attach to a flexible workforce that can quickly be redeployed is *shushin koyo seido,* the lifetime employment system. In sharp contrast with U.S. (though less so with European) norms, this system sets severe limits on the company's leeway to terminate employees whose particular job skills and specialties are no longer in demand.

It is important, however, not to be misled by the observation that extreme division of labor and narrow job design are in general more endemic to American than Japanese industry. Japanese organization is not synonymous with fluid, amorphous, organic management where formal structure is absent and coordination is achieved through strong shared values and a cohesive enterprise community. It is in some respects extraordinarily rigid and bureaucratic, a point to which any American academic who has spent time in a Japanese university can readily attest.

Moreover, in Japanese manufacturing a high degree of task specialization and industrial engineering refinement is often in evidence. Although Japanese forms of worker participation and work team production are sometimes grouped by job redesign enthusiasts together with such European innovations in work reform as the well-known Saab and Volvo experiments, there are marked differences (see Chapter 6). In the Swedish case, job design and task assignment are to a striking degree the prerogatives of the production team. Workers enjoy real autonomy in choosing the operations to be performed and who does what. In the New United Motors Manufacturing, Inc., plant in Fremont, California (the Toyota–GM joint venture), production teams and job rotation are central features of the factory organization, but workers experience little freedom in determining how production tasks are to be performed. "Standardized work" is NUMMI's motto. A refined set of work specifications is provided by Toyota's industrial engineers. Workers do have input into job design—the plant provides training and incentives for worker participation in task design—but the criteria against which all refinements are made are rigorous industrial engineering standards. Workers learn time-and-motion study and other techniques for reducing cycle times and increasing task efficiency. In the view of NUMMI's critics, the NUMMI workforce has been co-opted into practicing Taylorism on their own jobs (Parker and Slaughter 1988). The plant reaps the benefits of industrial engineering efficiency as well as the motivational rewards that shopfloor participation brings. Though some scholars argue that the organization of the Japanese factory trades off economies of specialization for those of flexibility (Aoki 1988; Fruin 1992), the NUMMI plant, it appears, succeeds in having it both ways.

Although Japanese pay systems formally allocate a portion of the Japanese worker's compensation on the basis of job area (*shokukin*), differences in job boundaries and responsibilities typically play a small part in wage determination (Kalleberg and Lincoln 1988). In response to claims that such American-style management methods were a modern and rational approach to compensation, job-based pay systems diffused rapidly in Japanese industry (Daito 1984). But, as a number of researchers have documented, the job or occupational wage system in Japanese firms more often than not is a front for a system of distributing wages chiefly on the basis of experience, age, and personal or family characteristics (Aoki 1988; Marsh and Mannari 1977).

Functional Specialization

The Japanese propensity to reject Western habits of organizing around functional specialties is not confined to job design. Narrow specializations are likewise typical neither of organizational subunits nor management careers. Japanese companies rarely have the array of specialist staff departments—finance, planning, law, and so on—found in U.S. firms. Functions such as personnel and human resources, on the other hand, are of much broader scope and authority. Recruitment, screening, and training responsibilities, which U.S. personnel departments share with line managers, in Japan are normally the province of only the personnel department. On the other hand, personnel management is quite often combined with various general administrative and housekeeping functions in a large and powerful "general affairs" department. In sharp contrast with U.S. business culture where human resource management tends to be a low-prestige, low-pay professional responsibility, Japanese personnel managers are central figures in the hierarchies of Japanese companies and are well-positioned for career moves into top executive jobs.

The relative absence of functional specialization within the Japanese firm can be traced to several factors. One direct consideration is the greater industrial specialization and lower vertical and horizontal integration of the Japanese company (Clark 1979; Abegglen and Stalk 1985). Japanese firms subcontract to formally independent suppliers for many parts and services that U.S. companies transfer from another corporate division (see Chapter 12). This policy of subcontracting leads to less differentiation within the organization in the business specialties, functional cultures, and career paths of managers and professionals.

As in the case of production jobs, a factor in the low specialization of management occupations is the premium the Japanese firm places on a flexible, multi-skilled workforce that can be redeployed as circumstances change. The traditional assumption that managers will spend their careers within the firm and that higher positions are filled through internal promotion and reassignment plays a major role in this regard (see Chapter 7 for evidence that Japanese firms do not always conform to this model). Management-track employees in manufacturing industries typically begin their careers with a stint on the production line, or, at least, as in Toyota's case, by undergoing the same training that production workers receive. The U.S. pattern of terminating surplus workers in a declining specialty and recruiting to a growing one experienced people from the outside has simply not been an option for Japanese companies.

Also in part attributable to the long-term career attachments of Japanese employees to their firms is a conviction that effective top management demands long experience across a range of specialties and divisions within a single organization. An American-style competitive labor market for executive manpower, grounded in the belief that a talented professional manager can be effective across a range of corporate cultures and business settings, is quite foreign to the Japanese.

Analogously, the boards of directors of Japanese companies are largely composed of senior managers; outside directors are scarce and the ones that exist are typically placed there by affiliated companies or regulatory agencies (*hakken yakuin*). Virtually unheard of are American-style "free-lance" directors sitting on the boards of multiple corporations yet holding no management position in any (Gerlach 1991). Overall, the generalist thrust of Japanese education and the relative absence of formal business school training for Japanese managers—which in the U.S. produces large numbers of functional specialists committed to a professional career in marketing, finance, or accounting—has been a factor in the low specialization of the Japanese company (see Chapter 2).

Our research on 106 manufacturing plants and 8,302 of their employees in the central Indiana and Atsugi areas speaks to these observations regarding functional specialization in several ways (Lincoln and Kalleberg 1990).[3] We measured the functional specialization of the plant using a standardized interview scale based on that devised by the British "Aston" group of organizational researchers (Pugh et al. 1968). The Aston scale consists of a set of twenty specialist responsibilities common in manufacturing organizations. The question we posed to each plant was whether each such specialty was the sole responsibility of at least one employee. In our version of the scale, the overall scale score was simply the proportion of the scale items to which specialists were assigned sole responsibility.

Our study found a substantial difference between the U. S. and Japanese samples in the number of functional responsibilities performed by specialists: the mean was .75 in the U. S. (standard deviation = .260) and .328 (standard deviation = .287) in Japan. Other studies using similar structural measures have generally produced similar results, though (owing in part to our large sample) not always so clear-cut (Azumi and McMillan 1981; Hsu, Marsh, and Mannari 1983). Moreover, we found no statistically significant difference between the Japanese and U. S. samples in the effects of various antecedent conditions. As other studies found, functional specialization proved greater in large plants, in independent companies (vs. branch plants and subsidiaries where the relevant specialist department or individual was often located elsewhere in the corporation), and where the workflow production process was more rigid and integrated. None of these variables, however, had anything approaching the statistical impact on the specialization index of a dummy variable for an American versus Japanese plant.

Hierarchy

The structure of the Japanese firm's authority and status hierarchy is also distinctive in a number of important respects. Moreover, along with low degrees of job fragmentation and functional specialism, it is widely regarded as a factor contributing to the cohesion and loyalty for which the Japanese firm is renowned (Aoki 1988; Dore 1973).

For one thing, Japanese organizations decouple status ranking and job responsibility to a striking extent. Whereas shifts in status within U. S. companies typically involve changes in job responsibility as well (e.g., the movement of engineers into management positions), Japanese status systems are more closely analogous to civil service, military, and even academic ranking systems in the United States. That is, an upward move is a reward for merit, experience, and seniority, but does not necessarily entail a change in responsibility nor an increase in management authority. Also similar to military and academic titles in the United States, Japanese ranking systems are quite uniform across different companies, so much so that Clark (1979) refers to the "standard ranks." These range from *shacho* (president), *fukushacho* (vice-president), and *senmu torishimariyaku* (director) to *bucho* (department head), *kacho* (section head), and *hancho* (team head). The first three positions typically involve seats on the company's board of directors. The interval from *bucho* to *kacho* (including intermediate deputy positions) encompasses managers who are not directors but who are also ineligible for membership in the enterprise union.

Kakaricho and *hancho* positions (subsection head and team head) comprise supervisors who typically are enterprise union members.

These titles have considerable honorific significance, outside as well as inside the workplace. Much as the titles "professor" or "colonel" would be used in the United States, managers are addressed as *"kacho"* or *"bucho."* Though the titles imply leadership of an organizational unit (*"bu"* - department; *"ka"* - section), some managers may hold the title without the supervisory responsibility over a work unit (as a brigadier general may lack a brigade). What the title does index clearly is the employee's location within the company's status hierarchy and thus conveys important information to outsiders. In business negotiations between Japanese companies considerable care is taken to match the status positions of the representatives of the respective firms. Avoiding mismatches in the rank or responsibility of negotiating company officials is a concern of Western managers as well, of course, but American business titles often convey quite ambiguous information as to the level of the person holding them. At my own university, the proliferation of "vice-president" positions among semiprofessional administrative staff has robbed the title of most meaning.

Just as there is in principle no limit to the number of faculty who can attain full professor rank—the odds of promotion being wholly determined by the "supply-side" criteria of individual merit and seniority—the traditional ranking system of the Japanese company also moved people more or less regardless of whether higher positions had been vacated (Yoshino 1968). Seniority and age are the triggering mechanisms in this process but they are most important at the early stages of an employee's career. Later on, they become *necessary* conditions for inclusion in the pool of promotion candidates for which the sufficient conditions are talent and ability. The Japanese internal labor market is thus a far cry from the demand-driven vacancy chain systems that White (1970) has studied.

Yet as Japan's economic growth has slowed and aging of the workforce has progressed, companies have moved to limit the proliferation of managerial ranks and dampen expectations for promotion prospects. A recent corporate decision at Toyota represents a strong move in this direction, one with heavy symbolic significance for Japanese corporate culture. Toyota effectively eliminated the position of *kacho* (section head). However, in the fashion discussed above, the new system permits employees who by virtue of seniority and experience warrant promotion to *kacho* to enjoy *kacho*-level rank and compensation, though not the authority and responsibility the position once bestowed. They are even permitted to include the *kacho* title on their name cards, but its use as a term of address within the company is discouraged. The action was part of a general program to limit management overhead and restrain the seniority escalator that historically moved people into lower and middle management positions with almost automatic regularity (see Chapter 2). Toyota's objective, first of all, was to foreclose the operation of the "Peter Principle" whereby valuable and (in the present tight Japanese labor market) scarce engineers and technicians are promoted into mediocre managers.

A finely layered status and authority pyramid with narrow spans of control is highly characteristic of Japanese organization (Chapter 7; Aoki 1988; Dore 1973). Our survey of 55 American plants and 51 Japanese plants found the latter, despite smaller size (means of 461 vs. 571 employees), averaging 5.5 administrative levels as opposed to 4.9 in the U.S. sample. Our approach to measuring hierarchical depth, moreover, focused on major administrative divisions and likely missed many of the secondary titles (deputies and assistants) that proliferate in Japanese firms.

The suggestion that Japanese companies have "tall" hierarchies may seem at odds with much recent commentary in the popular business press. American consultants and executives, often as a rationale for middle-management reductions at home, are fond of contrasting the "lean, flat" hierarchies of Japanese corporations with the bloated management bureaucracies of large U.S. firms. As earlier noted, Japanese companies tend to be smaller and more industrially focused than diversified U.S. firms, and therefore less likely to have decentralized, multidivisional structures (Chapter 12; Fruin 1992). Coupled with a less specialized, more flexible corps of middle managers, they enjoy certain administrative economies in the deployment of white-collar personnel. In this sense, they do tend to be more lean and streamlined than many U.S. firms. On the other hand, Japanese offices are notoriously unproductive, using far less automation (computers, word processors) and more people employed in redundant ceremonial and personal service roles, such as the "office ladies" (*oh-eru's*) whose chief responsibilities are to bow to visitors and serve tea.

The other feature of Japanese status hierarchies that has attracted broad attention is the low level of overall inequality between the highest and lowest ranks. As Abegglen and Stalk (1985, 194) put it: "Both within the kaisha, and in comparison with compensation levels in other countries, the lower ranks of the kaisha do well and the higher ranks do not do as well in total cash compensation."

Our own survey likewise produced a good deal of evidence of lower hierarchical inequality in Japan, not only in earnings (Kalleberg and Lincoln 1988), but also in employees' assessments of the complexity of their jobs and the control they could exercise over them (Lincoln and Kalleberg 1990). Moreover, the contrast between workers' and managers' assessments of the intrinsic rewards of their jobs and in the degree they allowed for teamwork and cohesive relations proved much greater in the United States. In sum, one of the most consistent findings running through our data analysis was that job rewards and experiences were segmented by rank to a greater degree in the United States than in Japan.

Decision-making Structure

Centralized Authority and Group Consensus

The structure of decision making is another aspect of the organization of the Japanese firm that has drawn considerable international interest. Both at the shopfloor and management levels, Japanese decision making is characterized as decentralized, bottom-up, and consensus-seeking. Much attention has been focused in particular on the phenomena of quality circles, *nemawashi* and *ringi-seido,* practices often portrayed as exotic Eastern rituals encapsulating the networking, participatory flavor of Japanese decision making. Japanese CEOs and other top corporate management are cast as passive, symbolic leaders, who lend their formal authority to and accept responsibility for a great many decisions in which they had little direct hand (Yoshino 1968). Yet such characterizations are regularly belied by the Moritas (Sony), Tsutsumis (Saison), Matsushitas, and other assertive, mediagenic, and entrepreneurial CEOs who dot the Japanese corporate landscape (see Clark 1979). The claim that every decision is supported by an organization-wide consensus is also at odds with numerous indications that Japanese corporate decision making, much like Japanese politics, is given to factionalism and power struggles among competing coalitions pursuing largely local agendas (Vogel 1975). Just how decisions are made in Japanese organizations understandably remains to many a matter of considerable confusion.

The highly touted flexible and participatory nature of Japanese decision making is linked directly to other distinctive features of Japanese organization. Little formal differentiation of tasks and responsibilities implies a correspondingly low degree of decision-making compartmentalization and differentiation. When the boundaries of jobs are broad, permeable, and overlapping, decision roles will be as well, such that teamwork and sharing become the only viable way of making decisions. Correspondingly, when employees are cross-trained in multifunctional skills and their career paths take them through a variety of job experiences, the information and expertise that are input to decisions naturally overlap and team interdependencies in the decision process result. The American system prizes a close match between the requirements of a specialized position and the capacities of a specialized person. The result is a neat matrix of segregated functional roles and a highly individualized system of delegated decision making.

Ironically, the U.S. pattern of differentiated and delegated decision roles implies greater formal decentralization of authority than does the Japanese system where role separation and decision delegation are low. Formal authority is concentrated in the Japanese firm or plant; a high proportion of decisions require formal approval by top management before implementation can proceed. Clark (1979) has made the interesting argument that much of the fabled networking and consensus building found in Japanese companies is a means of coping with the absence of real delegation. Without the authority to make decisions on their own, Japanese middle managers have little choice but to *nemawashi* (network and negotiate).

U.S. firms favor systems of delegation that grant autonomy to managers in charge of self-contained operations. As long as a division or department manager is achieving satisfactory results, higher management is content to stay aloof from day-to-day decisions. Such models of decentralization are widely advocated by Western organizational theorists for their presumed efficiency gains over the centralized, unitary organizational designs that require heavy top management input into routine operations and thus divert time and energy from long-range strategic planning (Chandler 1962; Williamson 1975).

Our research on 106 factories in the United States and Japan produced strong evidence of greater concentration of formal authority in the Japanese plants we surveyed (Lincoln, Hanada, and McBride 1986; Lincoln and Kalleberg 1990). We used a modified version of the Aston centralization scale, which requires management informants to score each of thirty-seven standard decisions as to the level in the management hierarchy where the decision is made (where 6 = higher corporate unit, 5 = plant manager, . . . , 2 = first-line supervisor, 1 = direct worker). Our application of this scale drew a clear distinction between the position with the *formal authority* to make the decision and the position where the decision was de facto (in practice) made. We found formal authority for the decisions in the Japanese plants averaging 5.0 on the scale; the U.S. score was 4.66. Though small in absolute terms, the difference is large relative to the total sample variation in this measure and is thus statistically significant at a high level of confidence.

On the other hand, when our management informants were asked to indicate the de facto level at which each decision was typically made, the pattern reversed: among the U.S. plants, the average centralization score was 4.36. In the Japanese sample it was 3.82. Thus, the gap between formal and informal authority in the U.S. plants was small; no more than one-third of a level. In Japan, de facto centralization averaged more than one full level below the rank possessing the formal authority and much lower than in the U.S. organizations.

The results from the de facto centralization scale are consistent with the conventional portrait of Japanese decision making as bottom-up: the impetus for decisions and the primary motive force behind them comes from middle management (Nonaka 1988). The *ringi* system illustrates this point. Every *ringi-sho,* stamped with the personal seals (*inkan*) of lower-ranking department heads, must land on a high-level executive's desk for final approval. The decision is not made until the chief affixes his seal to it (much like a U.S. governor or president signs off on bills approved by the legislature), but the role is a highly passive one. Moreover, as a number of observers point out, the circulation of the *ringi-sho* is the ritual formalization of a decision that has been worked out through extensive informal consultation. The likelihood that the top executive will refuse to sign it is therefore essentially nil.

Of course, the appearance of passivity on the part of top executives in the Japanese decision process may be quite misleading. The term, *ato-* (after) *ringi,* implies the engineering of consensus around a decision top management wishes to see made and the entrusting to loyal subordinates of the responsibility for moving it through the usual channels (Vogel 1975). This pattern underscores the importance of appearances of consensus and harmony in the Japanese organization, even while it testifies that Japanese decision making may be a good deal less "bottom-up" than it seems (see also Nonaka 1988).

Our empirical results showed a very strong statistical association between the practice of *ringi* in the plant and the de facto decentralization of decisions as measured by the Aston scale. We measured the prevalence of the *ringi* system by asking our management informants whether, for each of the thirty-seven Aston decisions, the *ringi* process was used. The plant's score was the proportion of the decisions made in this fashion. Across the fifty-one Japanese plants, the average proportion was .267 (Lincoln, Hanada, and McBride 1986). Contrary to the preceding reasoning, however, plants that used the *ringi* method extensively appeared to be no more centralized in the formal authority sense than those that did not.

Quality Circles as Shopfloor Participatory Decision-making Devices

No contemporary discussion of the Japanese workplace, nor, indeed, of modern forms of work structuring and control, can ignore the implications of quality circles for the reactions of employees to job and employer. These are programs in which groups of workers meet to discuss quality and productivity improvements in the production process, then propose and carry out changes (Thomas and Shimada 1983; Cole 1979, 1980, 1989). A Japanese innovation, they were heavily influenced by the principles of statistical quality control devised by W. E. Deming and other American experts. Already near-universal in Japanese industry and rapidly expanding in the United States, quality circle activity has come to symbolize participatory work reform, and strong claims have been made for its effectiveness in motivating commitment and cooperation on the part of managers and workers (Ouchi 1981).

Cole (1979) has estimated that one out of every eight employees in the Japanese workforce was a member of such groups in 1978. In our Japanese sample, surveyed in 1982–1983, 81 percent of the plants reported having quality circle programs, and 76 percent of their employees claimed to be members, for a 94 percent participation rate. In our American sample, 62 percent of the plants had quality circle programs. However, only 27 percent of the U.S. employees reported that they were members of quality circle-type groups, for a 44 percent participation rate.

While one might well expect quality circle programs in the U.S. to be generally weak gestures at shopfloor participation, some observers find the programs in Japan also failing to hold the interest of workers, particularly as their novelty wears off. Cole (1980) notes that workers have come to perceive circle participation as yet another chore demanded by management. A personnel manager in a showcase automobile plant informed us in a personal interview that attendance at circle meetings had fallen to roughly 50 percent, and the state of the program was a matter of serious concern to the company. Odaka (1982, 232) quotes Japanese workers' complaints that management is often lax in providing the training, time, and facilities necessary for quality circle activities. Tokunaga (1983, 323) argues that the participation of Japanese workers in quality circles and zero-defect groups is semicompulsory and is often considered in personnel evaluations. He cites a 1970 survey of union members showing that only 7 to 10 percent of the workers responding felt a "sense of active involvement in the (quality circle) work," as opposed to feeling burdened by it.

While the primary function of shopfloor small group programs is the enhancement of quality and productivity, a secondary function of equal importance is the fostering of a sense of participation in and influence over workflow decisions among workers. Indeed, quality circles are perhaps the most widely implemented expression of the movement to upgrade the quality of work life through enriched jobs and increased teamwork. Our interviews with American managers regarding their hopes and motivations for circle activity revealed that their expectations were in many cases pinned more on the potential payoffs in work force morale and motivation than on tangible improvements in product quality per se.

Indeed, much of the interest in Japanese decision-making styles is prompted by the speculation that they play a role in building the loyalty and commitment among employees for which the Japanese firm is famous. Our survey produced surprisingly strong confirmation for this hypothesis. First, we found that quality circle participation *in both countries* led employees to report higher commitment to the company and satisfaction with the job. The effect was somewhat larger in the United States, owing, we surmised, to the greater novelty value of such programs in American work settings.

Second, we also found statistical evidence, under a large number of controls, that employees of Japanese plants that practice *ringi-seido* were more committed to the organization. This effect, moreover, was calculated over *all* employees in the sample, the majority of whom were production workers. *Ringi* is a management-level decision-making device in which rank-and-file workers are unlikely to be direct participants. We speculated that the use of *ringi* is symptomatic of a generally participatory decision-making climate in the plant, to which workers as well as managers respond. (The effect of Aston formal and de facto centralization indices are partialled out from our estimate of the effect of *ringi* on commitment.)

Finally, our data showed that the "distinctively Japanese" combination of high formal centralization and low de facto centralization was statistically associated *in both countries* with higher levels of employee commitment to the organization and perceived job autonomy, intrinsic rewards, job complexity, and the like.

Internal Labor Markets

Worker Experience

I have touched on the process whereby employees of Japanese companies climb long career ladders over the course of their tenure with the firm. More broadly, the internal labor market organization of the Japanese firm includes recruitment of new graduates into entry-level positions after an intensive screening process; subjecting them to intensive on-the-job training in skills and values that are heavily firm-specific (Dore and Sako 1989); advancing them in status and compensation with rising age, seniority, and family size; and, finally, retiring them at the relatively early age of 55 to 60 with a lump-sum severance payment. In an earlier era, the Japanese employment system was castigated by Western critics and not a few Japanese as feudal, anachronistic, and an impediment to economic and administrative efficiency (Abegglen 1958; Yoshino 1968). In the wake of the Japanese economic miracle, the general persistence of these institutions has challenged Western observers to uncover the hidden rationality in the Japanese firm's approach to managing its human resources.

Much of the work by economists and sociologists on internal labor markets and specific human capital has fueled efficiency explanations of this sort (e.g., Aoki 1984, 1988; Burawoy 1979; Edwards 1979; Doeringer and Piore 1971; Lincoln 1990; Williamson 1975, 1985). Where technology is uncertain and fast changing, skills are latent, contextual, and firm-specific. They cannot be purchased on the external labor market but must be bred within the organization, in large part through learning-by-doing and the kinds of apprenticeship and mentoring relations (e.g., *sempai-kohai*) that are common in Japanese firms. Because they take the form of uncodified know-how and are realized through team interdependencies, such skills are also hard to measure and reward, particularly at the level of the individual employee. Consequently, experience may be the best overall index of human capital and thus the criterion on which promotions and compensation are meted out. This reasoning also explains the Japanese company's penchant for rendering a large share of compensation (up to 40 percent) in the form of bonuses that can be tied to company and divisional performance (but in practice tend to be a relatively fixed part of annual compensation that is subject to collective bargaining).

Change in Japanese Employment Practice

There is some irony in the apparent fact that, just as social science theory appears to be converging toward an acceptance of the rationality of Japanese forms of economic organization (e.g., Aoki 1988; Lazear, 1979), reports of change in the Japanese system are proliferating. There is little question that, in the current era of slower growth and an aging workforce, Japanese companies have growing concerns about the long-run consequences of *nenko joretsu* (seniority grading) and *shushin koyo seido* (lifetime employment). Japanese companies are acutely conscious of the age distribution of their workforce; most large firms use demographic life tables to monitor employee age composition. When the work force is young and the company is rapidly expanding, these systems impose little burden on the firm and are in fact apt to be less costly than Western-style alternatives.

But under present economic and demographic conditions, the costs of the Japanese practice are rising. Companies are responding, as Toyota has, by dampening the proliferation of traditional titles such as *kacho,* and by seeking alternatives to seniority as mechanisms of internal promotion. Many large firms are proclaiming their abandonment of the seniority principle as a means of promoting and compensating employees. Embarrassed by their use of systems that Westerners have labeled feudal and inefficient, Japanese managers have long been inclined to downplay the prevalence of such practices to outsiders or to disguise them in nominal job evaluation systems and the like. Recent analyses of Japanese labor force data still show much stronger age and experience effects on compensation and promotion patterns than in Western countries (Hashimoto and Raisian 1985; Kalleberg and Lincoln 1988), but shifts do appear to be taking place.

In comparison with U.S. practice, Japanese merit compensation schemes reward not past performance so much as accumulated ability and skill (Daito 1984). Nissan assembly workers' wages, for example, are directly tied to the number of jobs they have learned (personal interview with plant managers, January, 1990). One of the hot new trends in Japanese management development in the current reduced-growth era is an examination system designed to screen for talented middle managers deserving of top executive careers. At a company I visited, the exam involved a week of essay writing and case analysis, much in the fashion of a Ph.D.

prelim. However, as one manager in the midst of the exam process confided, selection into the pool of candidates eligible to take the exam is at least half the battle.

In appraising performance potential and value to the firm, Japanese supervisors' apply the test of loyalty and commitment, using as evidence diligence and reliability of work behavior. This system, known as *satei,* results in a rank ordering for merit pay purposes of the employees within a section (Endo forthcoming). It is a source of considerable anxiety and competitiveness among workers. Japanese employees' almost nonexistent absenteeism and their extraordinary (to Americans) penchant for failing to take advantage of all the vacation time to which they are entitled are less indicators of deep-down psychological commitment to work and organization than they are direct reflections of the organization's performance appraisal process (Okuno 1984).

Another quite visible trend, however small as yet in terms of overall impact on the labor market, is the inclination on the part of large companies to hire midcareer employees (Nagashima 1990). Japanese newspapers and magazines feature large ads aimed at luring talented experienced people away from their present positions. In the era of an aging workforce, one reason for this trend may be the company's smaller lifetime commitment to a more senior employee. But clearly another is the accelerating pace of technological and product development change in key industries, which has made it difficult for firms to supply through internal training the number of technical specialists they need. A third factor is the increased presence of foreign companies in Japan which, at a severe disadvantage in the labor market for recent graduates, have aggressively pursued midcareer people with premium compensation packages, creating a competitive market at this level and helping to legitimize job changing.

Unions and Industrial Relations

The structure of unions and collective bargaining is another domain of work organization in which there appear to be substantial differences between the United States and Japan, differences with clear implications for employee work commitment and cooperative industrial relations. With very few exceptions (e.g., the Seamen's Union), Japanese unions are enterprise unions, each representing the employees of a different firm. Approximately 90 percent of all Japanese unions are enterprise unions and 80 percent of all union members belong to them (Shirai 1983). Enterprise unions are typically organized into loose national federations, but do not bargain on an industry- or occupation-wide basis. Moreover, the enterprise union organizes both blue- and white-collar employees up through second-line supervision (typically below the *kacho* or section head level). The fact that a single union represents employees in diverse occupational groups within a common firm has been a significant force for standardizing working conditions and payment levels and systems across occupational boundaries. Indeed, the abolition of "status discrimination" between blue- and white-collar employees was a key collective bargaining objective of Japanese unions in the early postwar era (Gordon 1985; Koike 1983).

The enterprise union works closely with management in administering company welfare services and employee social-recreational programs (Rohlen 1974). Moreover, in striking contrast to U.S. norms, leadership positions in Japanese enterprise unions provide a bridge to a management career (Hanami 1979; Shirai 1983, 139). Furthermore, Japanese unions have traditionally shunned the American practice of demanding restrictive work rules and protective job classifications (Cole 1971, 232). Indeed, detailed job titles, formal job descriptions, and job-related criteria for pay and advancement have been conspicuously absent from Japanese employment practice, whereas job rotation and extensive cross-training are the rule (Aoki 1984; Hanami 1979, 39).

In general, Japanese collective bargaining contracts, like other legal instruments in this society less litigious than our own, are phrased in very flexible and general language (Hanami 1979, 52). Grievance procedures as well lack the formality and structure typical of U.S. industrial relations, and problems on the shopfloor tend to be handled in an informal and ad hoc way (Cole 1971, 230–231). Though Japanese unions, particularly in the tumultuous formative period of Japanese labor relations (the 1920s and 1930s), have certainly, at times, shown strong resistance to the exercise of arbitrary supervisory authority (Gordon 1985, 78). They have, in general, not challenged the prerogative of management to set the criteria for job design and labor allocation, so long as employment security guarantees were preserved. Indeed, the extreme flexibility with which Japanese companies rotate, retrain, and transfer workers is very much an adaptation to the constraints imposed by the permanent employment and seniority wage systems, two institutions in which postwar Japanese unions have had a considerable stake and fought hard to defend (Gordon 1985, 362). Moreover, Japanese unions have been active partners in the development and diffusion of joint consultation committees, quality circle programs, and other participatory workplace arrangements (Cole 1979; Koshiro 1983). The notion, widespread in U.S. labor circles, that participation is tantamount to complicity and thus a threat to union autonomy is generally foreign to the Japanese industrial relations scene. On the contrary, unions have at times sought to make companies live up to the Japanese managerial ideology of the firm as an enterprise family by demanding the creation of explicit structures for worker participation and enfranchisement (Gordon 1985, 346).

The enterprise union is thus considerably more dependent on the company than is the typical craft or industrial union in the United States. It has a major stake in the firm's competitive position. This connection places limits on how far the union is willing to push the company in a labor–management dispute, and it fosters an impulse on the union's part to identify with company goals. Moreover, the boundaries between union and management are less sharply drawn than in the United States, and the relationship between the two is typically closer and more cooperative. These considerations have led some observers to conclude that Japanese unions have effectively been co-opted by management and are akin to "company unions" in the historical U.S. sense; that their dependence and docility works for rather than against the discipline and commitment of the Japanese workforce (Galenson 1976; Hanami 1979, 56; Shirai 1983).

In this view, enterprise unions function as an instrument in the overall "welfare corporatist" strategy of labor control that, in Dore's (1973) view (see also Lincoln and Kalleberg 1990), is the logic that drives the Japanese employment system. Welfare corporatism, as Dore used the term, refers to the total complex of welfare services, employment practices, and organizational structures that are distinctive of large Japanese companies and that operate to build a strong, paternal bond between the worker and the firm. This reasoning, in stark contrast to the U.S. case where the abundance of evidence testifies to the contrary, suggests the hypothesis that the effect of membership in a Japanese enterprise union is to raise the Japanese worker's commitment to the company and satisfaction with the job.

Other observers of Japanese industrial relations, while acknowledging the structural dependence of enterprise unions on Japanese firms, nonetheless see Japanese unions bargaining hard on wage, benefit, and job security issues (Cole 1971; Gordon 1985; Shirai 1983). They credit unions with the rapid postwar rise of aggregate wage levels in the Japanese economy, and with many of the distinctive institutions of the Japanese employment system (permanent employment, seniority wages, etc.). Some of these practices—occasionally mislabeled "traditional" by Westerners—were the outcomes of hard-fought union-management struggles, notably in the early postwar years. The incidence of Japanese strikes, as Shirai (1983, 136–37) has demonstrated, has been within the range of Western economies. Yet the size and duration of Japanese work stoppages is generally low by North American and European standards, and most—particularly those associated with the *Shunto* Spring strike offensives—are brief, symbolic affairs. Still, careful students of Japanese industrial relations would probably agree that Hanami overstates the coincidence of interest between the Japanese firm and its enterprise union (see, e.g., Shirai 1983).

The evidence from our study showed that the job satisfaction and company commitment of U.S. workers were sharply lower in unionized than in nonunion plants (Lincoln and Boothe, forthcoming). These results were consistent with virtually all similar U.S. research (see, e.g., Freeman and Medoff 1984). In the Japanese sample, on the other hand, union membership bore no statistical relationship to job satisfaction and only a small negative relationship to company commitment. Of at least equal interest was the evidence that unionized U.S. workers held jobs that on intrinsic job quality criteria were inferior to those of nonunion American workers: quality circle membership was lower and the jobs in general displayed lower skill complexity and autonomy. On all three counts the opposite pattern held in Japan: greater complexity, autonomy, and quality-circle activity in *unionized* plants. It appears that in large measure the reason for the dissatisfaction of the U.S. union members was the rigidity and narrowness designed into their jobs, in part, at least, by union work rules and job classifications.

Conclusions

This paper has briefly reviewed a number of dimensions on which the organization of Japanese and U.S. companies seems to vary in important ways: vertical and horizontal division of labor, decision-making, internal labor market structure, and industrial relations. As global labels such as "welfare corporatism" imply, there is a wholistic logic to Japanese as well as to U.S. patterns of work organization. That logic may be better revealed through a broad-scope march through a variety of topics than through a fine-grained treatment of a few.

The distinctive features of Japanese organization include long-term employment, seniority promotion, flexible and overlapping role assignments, extensive cross-training, team production, cohesive work groups, strong vertical relationships, finely graded hierarchies combined with low inequality, broadly participatory yet formally centralized decision making, enterprise-based unions, a rich bundle of employee welfare services, and ceaseless efforts to build morale and commitment through appeals to core company values, rigorous screening and socialization of recruits, and an abundance of ritual and ceremony.

Just how much Japan's distinctive forms of company organization and industrial relations should be credited for the astounding competitive power of Japan's manufacturing economy (in particular) remains an open question, as does that of how much U.S. organization is to blame for the difficulties facing American industry. Alternative arguments abound—the role of culture as a source of work motivation, the macroeconomic management of the economy by government ministries, the abundance of cheap capital, the lower transaction costs produced by Japanese-style "relational contracting."

Yet the prima facie case is a strong one. The evidence from our comparative survey study demonstrates with considerable consistency that the structural designs and management practices associated with "Japanese" management yield dividends in employee satisfaction and commitment whether they are practiced by Japanese or U.S. firms (Lincoln 1989; Lincoln and Kalleberg 1990). The same conclusion is prompted by the generally impressive performance on productivity, quality, and industrial relations criteria of Japanese-owned U.S.-based manufacturing "transplants" such as NUMMI. The advantages of Japanese work organization seem to center on a more flexible and efficient use of human resources, and the capacity to motivate and channel extraordinary high levels of work-force discipline and commitment.

The question of change still looms large. Will Japanese firms, faced with an aging workforce, slower growth, more competition from abroad, and rising aspirations for leisure, mobility, and affluence on the part of the Japanese people ultimately jettison what the world has come to know as Japanese management? Will old-line convergence theory, humiliated in the 1980s by the specter of Western companies scrambling to imitate Japan, be vindicated in the end? It may be too soon to tell. But reports of the demise of Japanese organizational forms and management styles, like that of Mark Twain's, have been exaggerated in the past and, I suspect, remain so.

Notes

1. For evidence that factory jobs in Britain, as in the United States, display less task breadth and are more likely to form the basis for economic reward, see Chapter 7 by Whittaker (this volume).
2. Examples include *sempai/kohai* (senior/junior) relations, *oyabun/kobun* (patron/cli-

ent) relations, and *oyagaisha/kogaisha* (parent-company/child-subsidiary company) relations.

3. Plants were sampled from the following manufacturing industries: transportation equipment, nonelectrical machinery, prefabricated metals, electrical machinery, food processing, chemicals, and printing. Within each plant, interviews were conducted with top plant executives and documentary information was collected on the management, personnel practices, and production processes of the factory. We also conducted questionnaire surveys of representative samples of employees in each plant. More details of the sampling, research design, and measurement are given in Lincoln and Kalleberg (1985; 1990).

References

Abegglen, James C. 1958. *The Japanese Factory: Aspects of Its Social Organization.* Glencoe, Illinois: The Free Press.

Abegglen, James C., and George Stalk, Jr. 1985. *Kaisha: The Japanese Corporation.* New York: Basic Books.

Aoki, Masahiko. 1984. "Risk Sharing in the Corporate Group," in Masahiko Aoki, ed., *The Economic Analysis of the Japanese Firm,* pp. 259–64. Amsterdam: North-Holland.

Aoki, Masahiko. 1988. *Information, Incentives, and Bargaining in the Japanese Economy.* Cambridge, U.K.: Cambridge University Press.

Azumi, Koya, and Charles McMillan. 1981. "Management Strategy and Organization Structure: a Japanese Comparative Study," in David J. Hickson and Charles McMillan, eds., pp. 155–72. *Organization and Nation: The Aston Programme IV.* Farnborough, Hampshire, U.K.: Gower.

Burawoy, Michael. 1979. *Manufacturing Consent: Changes in the Labor Process under Monopoly Capitalism.* Chicago: University of Chicago Press.

Chandler, Alfred D., Jr. 1962. *Strategy and Structure.* Cambridge, Mass.: MIT Press.

Clark, Rodney. 1979. *The Japanese Company.* New Haven, Conn.: Yale University Press.

Cole, Robert E. 1971. *Japanese Blue Collar: The Changing Tradition.* Berkeley and Los Angeles: University of California Press.

Cole, Robert E. 1979. *Work, Mobility, and Participation.* Berkeley: University of California Press.

Cole, Robert E. 1980. "Learning from the Japanese: Prospects and Pitfalls," *Management Review,* **69**(Sept.):22–42.

Cole, Robert E. 1989. *Strategies for Learning.* Berkeley: University of California Press.

Cole, Robert E., and Ken'ichi Tominaga. 1976. "Japan's Changing Occupational Structure and Its Significance," in Hugh Patrick, ed., *Japanese Industrialization and Its Social Consequences,* pp. 53–96. Berkeley: University of California Press.

Daito, Eisuke. 1984. "Seniority Wages and Labour Management: Japanese Employers' Wage Policy," in Shigeyoshi Tokunaga and Joachim Bergmann eds., *Industrial Relations in Transition,* pp. 119–30. Tokyo: University of Tokyo Press.

Doeringer, Peter B., and Michael J. Piore. 1971. *Internal Labor Markets and Manpower Analysis.* Lexington, Mass.: D. C. Heath.

Dore, Ronald. 1973. *British Factory, Japanese Factory: The Origins of Diversity in Industrial Relations.* Berkeley: University of California Press.

Dore, Ronald. 1987. *Taking Japan Seriously.* Stanford: Stanford University Press.

Dore, Ronald, Jean Bounine-Cabale, and Kari Tapiola. 1989. *Japan at Work: Markets, Management, and Flexibility.* Washington, D.C.: OECD (Organization for Economic and Cooperation Development) Publications and Information Center.

Dore, Ronald, and M. Sako. 1989. *How the Japanese Learn to Work.* London: Routledge.

Edwards, Richard T. 1979. *Contested Terrain.* New York: Basic Books.

Endo, Koshi. Forthcoming. "Satei (personal assessment) and Inter-worker Competition in Japanese Firms." *Industrial Relations.*

Freeman, Richard B., and James L. Medoff. 1984. *What Do Unions Do?* New York: Basic Books.

Fruin, W. Mark. 1992. *The Japanese Enterprise System.* New York: Oxford University Press.

Galenson, Walter. 1976. "The Japanese Labor Market," in Hugh Patrick and Henry Rosovsky, eds., *Asia's New Giant: How the Japanese Economy Works,* pp. 587–672. Washington, D.C.: Brookings Institution.

Gerlach, Michael L. 1991. *Alliances and the Social Organization of Japanese Business.* Berkeley: University of California Press.

Gordon, Andrew. 1985. *The Evolution of Labor Relations in Japan: Heavy Industry, 1853–1955.* Cambridge, Mass.: Harvard University Press.

Hanami, Tadashi. 1979. *Labor Relations in Japan Today.* Tokyo: Kodansha International Limited.

Hashimoto, Masanori, and John Raisian. 1985. "Employment Tenure and Earnings Profiles in Japan and the United States," *American Economic Review* **75**:721–35.

Hsu, Cheng-Kuang, Robert M. Marsh, and Hiroshi Mannari. 1983. "An Examination of the Determinants of Organizational Structure," *American Journal of Sociology* **88**:975–96.

Jacoby, Sanford M. 1985. *Employing Bureaucracy: Managers, Unions, and the Transformation of Work in American Industry, 1900–1945.* New York: Columbia University Press.

Kalleberg, Arne L., and James R. Lincoln. 1988. "The Structure of Earnings Inequality in the United States and Japan," *American Journal of Sociology* **94**(Suppl.):S121–S153.

Koike, Kazuo. 1983. "Internal Labor Markets: Workers in Large Firms," in Taishiro Shirai, ed., *Contemporary Industrial Relations in Japan,* pp. 29–62. Madison: University of Wisconsin Press.

Koshiro, Kazutoshi. 1983. "The Quality of Life in Japanese Factories," in Taishiro Shirai, ed., *Contemporary Industrial Relations in Japan,* pp. 63–88. Madison: University of Wisconsin Press.

Lazear, Edward. 1979. "Why Is There Mandatory Retirement?" *Journal of Political Economy* **87**:1261–84.

Lincoln, James R. 1989. "Employee Work Attitudes and Management Practice in the U. S. and Japan," *California Management Review* **32**:89–106.

Lincoln, James R. 1990. "Japanese Organization and Organization Theory," in Barry M. Staw and L. L. Cummings, eds., *Research in Organizational Behavior,* vol. 12, pp. 255–94. Greenwich, Conn.: JAI Press.

Lincoln, James R., and Joan Boothe. Forthcoming. "Unions and Work Attitudes in the U. S. and Japan," *Industrial Relations.*

Lincoln, James R., and Arne L. Kalleberg. 1985. "Work Organization and Workforce Commitment: A Study of Plants and Employees in the U.S. and Japan," *American Sociological Review* **50**:738–60.

Lincoln, James R., and Arne L. Kalleberg. 1990. *Culture, Control, and Commitment: A Study of Work Organization and Work Attitudes in the U.S. and Japan.* Cambridge, U.K.: Cambridge University Press.

Lincoln, James R., Mitsuyo Hanada, and Kerry McBride. 1986. "Organizational Structures in Japanese and U.S. Manufacturing," *Administrative Science Quarterly* **31**:338–64.

Marsh, Robert M., and Hiroshi Mannari. 1977. *Modernization and the Japanese Factory.* Princeton, N.J.: Princeton University Press.

Nagashima, Hidesuke. 1990. "Changing Jobs Is No Longer Taboo: Labor Crunch, Corporate Restructuring Yielding Opportunities," *Japan Times,* February 28.

Nonaka, Ikujiro. 1988. "Toward Middle-Up-Down Management: Accelerating Information Creation," *Sloan Management Review* **29**:9–18.

Odaka, Kunio. 1982. "The Japanese Style of Workers' Self-Management: From the Voluntary to the Autonomous Group," in Velnko Rus, Akihiro Ishikawa, and Thomas Woodhouse, eds., *Employment and Participation,* pp. 135–48. Tokyo: Chuo University Press.

Okuno, Masahiro. 1984. "Corporate Loyalty and Bonus Payments: An Analysis of Work Incentives in Japan," in Masahiko Aoki, ed., *The Economic Analysis of the Japanese Firm,* pp. 387–412. Amsterdam: North-Holland.

Ouchi, William G. 1981. *Theory Z.* Reading, Mass.: Addison-Wesley.

Parker, Mike, and Jane Slaughter. 1988. *Choosing Sides: Unions and the Team Concept.* Boston: South End Press.

Piore, Michael J. 1982. "American Labor and the Industrial Crisis," *Challenge* **25**:5–11.

Pugh, D. S., D. J. Hickson, C. R. Hinings, and C. Turner. 1968. "Dimensions of Organization Structure," *Administrative Science Quarterly* **13**:65–91.

Rohlen, Thomas P. 1974. *For Harmony and Strength.* Berkeley: University of California Press.

Rohlen, Thomas P. 1983. *Japan's High Schools.* Berkeley: University of California Press.

Shirai, Taishiro, ed. 1983. *Contemporary Industrial Relations in Japan.* Madison: University of Wisconsin Press.

Thomas, Robert J., and Haruo Shimada. 1983. "Work Organization and Quality Control Practice in the U. S. and Japanese Auto Industries." Paper presented to the American Sociological Association (September). Detroit, Michigan.

Tokunaga, S. 1983. "Marxist Interpretation of Japanese Industrial Relations with Special Reference to Large Private Enterprises," in Taishiro Shirai, ed., *Contemporary Industrial Relations in Japan,* pp. 313–29. Madison: University of Wisconsin Press.

Vogel, Ezra F., ed. 1975. *Modern Japanese Organization and Decision-Making.* Berkeley: University of California Press.

White, Harrison. 1970. *Chains of Opportunity.* Cambridge, Mass.: Harvard University Press.

Williamson, Oliver E. 1975. *Markets and Hierarchies: Analysis and Antitrust Implications.* New York: Free Press.

Williamson, Oliver E. 1985. *The Economic Institutions of Capitalism.* New York: The Free Press.

Yoshino, Michael Y. 1968. *Japan's Managerial System: Tradition and Innovation.* Cambridge, Mass.: MIT Press.

4

The Societal Effect in the Strategies of French and German Machine-Tool Manufacturers

ARNDT SORGE
MARC MAURICE

Research and theory about comparative advantage in societies or national econo-mies have tended to neglect some of the most important factors: work organization; the skills and knowledge of the work force and the way these are developed; the relations of producers to clients, suppliers, and other organizations or institutions; and the nature of entrepreneurial dispositions or strategies. Since the 1970s, how-ever, we have seen an increasing number of international comparisons covering these factors, particularly, comparisons conducted by what Rose (1985) has called the Aix Group to denote the group of scholars located at the University at Aix-en-Provence. Following the larger Franco-German comparison by Maurice, Sellier, and Silvestre (1977, 1982), the Aix Group's primary tenet has been that similar or near-identical industrial goals in similar task environments can be achieved in ways that are substantially different concerning work organization, human resources, and industrial relations. An organizational unit's societal context explains why units adopt and maintain different patterns, which prevail without regard for dif-ferent industrial goals and contexts (e.g., the nature of products and production technology, size of units, dependence, regional location).

The comparison can be expressed in terms of the "functional equivalence" of the contrasted organizations and of their human resources, industrial relations, and social stratification modes. Child (1972) noted that different organizational struc-tures and processes may be functionally equivalent with regard to the same goal. In the Aix studies, there was no indication that units in one country, as part of the matched pairs of enterprises compared across societies, were more successful by any criterion in a particular unit size band or technical situation.

The second tenet of the Aix Group on comparative advantage qualifies this con-clusion of functional equivalence. Empirical comparisons have revealed a remarkable affinity between mass- and continuous-process production regimes and French patterns; earlier work had revealed an affinity between unit- and small-batch production regimes with German patterns. The latter tended to accommodate the medium-sized mechanical engineering firms that make investment goods; French patterns could be likened to the traits characterizing larger firms in the automobile and petrochemical industries.

Maurice, Sellier, and Silvestre (1977) had previously suggested that societal patterns are also related to the position that sectors have gained or lost within the international division of labor. Later, notably thanks to a series of Anglo-German comparisons led by Prais and others building on an Anglo-German comparison closer to the Aix Groups (Sorge and Warner 1986; Maurice, Sorge, and Warner 1980), Anglo-German differences in human resources and organizational factors were shown to be strongly related to product strategies and productivity. British patterns were associated with the production of more price-elastic standardized goods at a lower rate of overall productivity, whereas German patterns were associated with less price-elastic and more customized products made at a higher level of productivity (Steedman and Wagner 1987, 1989). Similar differences had been suggested by Sorge et al. (1983) and Campbell, Sorge, and Warner (1989).

It is tempting to suggest that the success of companies with particular generic strategic, technical, organizational, and human resources characteristics is related to the affinity between societal institutions and matching task environments. Firms will survive and grow when there is a relatively good fit between societal and sectoral or market segment characteristics. Hence, there is, for instance, a large and successful population of medium-size investment goods engineering firms in Germany. In Britain and France, large batch-producers or defense, electronics, and specialized high-tech manufacturers are more competitive.

Our major thesis, therefore, is that societal context constitutes competitive advantages and disadvantages in specific industries. Such an approach links the societal effect framework of the Aix Group and the neo-contingency framework, which maintains that organizational structures and processes are interdependent with a firm's business strategy and market segment (Miles and Snow 1978).

To investigate this thesis, we looked at the machine-tools producing industry as a case for testing neo-contingency theory in a Franco-German comparison, by examining recent changes in the industry over time. Although machine-tool producing sectors experienced difficulties in many countries after the mid 1970s, the sectoral crisis in France was much more severe than in Germany.

Machine-tool industries are generally distinguished by an absence of very large firms and an often artisanal mode of production. There is also a strong continuity from workers' to technicians' and engineers' jobs regarding training backgrounds and contents, and the skills and knowledge required. The emphasis on the proximity of shopfloor and engineering competencies, and on both vertically and laterally overlapping work tasks also characterizes industrial firms in Germany.

We therefore hypothesize that machine-tool makers had been doing better for a long time in Germany because *sectoral* patterns there corresponded more closely to *societal* patterns, allowing German producers to engage in more flexible production and to more quickly explore opportunities for "flexible specialization" (Piore and Sabel 1984) or "diversified quality production" (Sorge and Streeck 1988). Conditions favoring the latter business strategy would seem all the more important with the declining demand for machinery after the end of the long-running postwar boom phase.

But, surprisingly, the French machine-tool industry had more customized development and production, smaller production runs, much smaller average plant and enterprise sizes, more skilled craft workers, and fewer semiskilled workers and engineers. These results from the initial investigation are contrary to those obtained in previous Franco-German comparisons addressing manufacturing at large.

In this chapter we first present an analysis of long-standing differences between the French and German sectors. We then compare what happened during the recent crisis and transformation of the industry. Finally, we interpret the resulting overall picture.[1]

Characteristics of Machine-Tool Manufacturers in France and Germany

Personnel

The German machine-tool industry reached the climax of its postwar expansion in 1971, when it employed 125,000 people. It subsequently went through phases of decline and rejuvenation, stabilizing at 93,000 employees at the end of 1986 (Wobbe and Manske 1987, 30; VDW 1986). The French industry in 1974 stabilized at 27,000 employees, after having grown more quickly than the German one during the postwar expansion (Perrin and Réal 1976, 214). It then plummeted to 11,000 employees at the end of 1987 (*Le Monde Economie,* 1 March 1988, 37), a 60 percent decline compared to a 25 percent loss of previous maximum employment in Germany. It is significant that the German sector, having been outperformed by the French after World War II, reached its crisis point three years earlier. Yet it pulled out of the crisis much less affected by the reduction of employment and bankruptcies.

According to Perrin and Réal (1976), the personnel structure of the two industries mirrors these differences in market orientation and production systems, but it runs counter to everything we know about Franco-German differences in manufacturing at large. Craft workers made up 50 percent of all personnel in the industry in France; noncraft blue-collar workers, 10 percent for the period before 1980 (Podevin 1986, 37). In Germany, the figures were correspondingly about 40 percent and 25 percent at roughly the same time.[2] The German machine-tool firms' greater number of unskilled workers and smaller number of craft workers cannot be explained by reference to different methods of classification; if anything, the French classification of craft workers is more narrow and restrictive.

The same picture is revealed when we compare the shares of professional engineers. The German industry has a much larger share, because it puts more effort into product development and design. Nevertheless, German firms appear to have gone a longer way toward larger batch production than French firms, which have more unit and small-batch production; and both have the personnel structures to match—more skilled workers in France and more engineers and unskilled workers in Germany (Maurice and Sorge 1989, 10–11).

There are parallel differences with regard to plant and enterprise sizes. The French plants and enterprises were about half as large as the German ones, on average, in the second half of the 1970s. This difference, too, points to the French industry having a more artisanal, and the German industry a more industrial, profile.

One difference, however, does not quite fit this picture. By all accounts, the professional careers of workers, managers, and supervisors on the one hand, and design and development personnel, on the other, are generally more separated in France than in Germany. Similarly, the geographical distance between head office/development functions and production is sometimes greater in France. Such findings are in greater accord with previous Franco-German comparisons that had shown greater continuity of working careers in Germany, starting from basic education and training processes to production and higher technical functions.

Economic and Social Settings

There are important differences in how the two machine-tool industries are embedded in their respective economic and social settings. In Germany, the industry enjoys numerous and close relationships with technical universities especially in Aachen, Berlin, and Stuttgart (see Chapter 1). The production, engineering, and machine-tool departments and institutes enjoy high standing, draw good students, are quite generously staffed, and maintain close collaboration with firms in development projects. The academic establishment supports the industry and is in part financed by it through contract research and development.

In France, however, departments of production engineering and machine-tools have less prestige and less presence in the leading engineering schools (grandes écoles). The industry is not backed by an academic establishment as large and reputed as in Germany, and the cross-fertilization between the two is much less in evidence (see, e.g., Assemblée Nationale 1985).

It is also illuminating to look at the position of the machine-tool industries within the larger industrial sectors of mechanical engineering. Whereas the German mechanical engineering industry (excluding automobile, armaments, and naval and aerospace engineering) employed over 1,200,000 people in 1985, the French industry had 563,000 employees (Delouvrier 1987). In Germany, that industry is the largest exporting industry and, in a way, the nation's pride; in France, its inferior role is the cause of some concern (Académie des Sciences, 1980).

According to Delouvrier (1987, 52), 58.8 percent of personnel in German mechanical engineering work in plants with more than 500 employees; in France, only 32.6 percent do. At least some of the differences that apply to the machine-tool firms also characterize the broader field of mechanical engineering, although to a more limited extent. The French mechanical engineering industry seems not more industrial but rather more artisanal than the German industry. But, as in the machine-tool industry, working careers in German mechanical engineering differ from those in the parallel French industry, with more segmented careers and departmental structures in the latter (compare the small-batch plants in Maurice,

Sellier, and Silvestre 1977, 1982). Furthermore, there is no evidence that German mechanical engineering firms have more semi- and unskilled workers, as we found for the machine-tool industry (Maurice and Sorge 1989).

On a continuum from artisanal to modern industrial structures (Fig. 4.1), the machine-tool industry in most European countries falls toward the artisanal end and the industrial average toward the industrial end, with the mechanical engineering industry somewhere in the middle. The distance between industries on this continuum is not the same for France as for Germany. There seems to be a greater variance of personnel structure types, production systems, and generic product market types in France, with machine-tool manufacturing in particular more removed from the prevailing industrial norm. In Germany, the mechanical engineering and the machine-tool industry are closer to each other on the continuum.

Also, the industrial norm in Germany is more toward the artisanal end—though the more artisanal industry of machine tools is more toward the industrial end than in France. In France, the variance is larger, because its more artisanal industry is closer to the artisanal end of the spectrum than in Germany and the industrial norm is closer to the industrial end.

Domestic and International Markets

Consider the implications for the domestic conditions in which a machine-tool industry operates. In its domestic national economy, German mechanical engineering is a fairly large client for the German machine-tool industry; in the French national economy, other industrial sectors are a more important client for its machine-tool industry. French machine-tool makers' domestic clientele tends to segment its workflow hierarchically and laterally to favor single-purpose automation and, therefore, tailor-made installations. These demand characteristics favor concepts of machines that do not require the professional autonomy of machine-tool setter-operators.[3] The opposite applies in Germany; its machine-tool makers cater to clients that emphasize less organizational differentiation of workflow, require flexible but standard machine-tools, and favor the socialization and use of professionally autonomous operators.

France

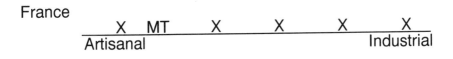

Germany

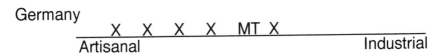

Figure 4.1 Variations in structure of work. MT = machine tool industry; X = other industries.

It is important to consider that machine-tool making firms have many characteristics that are the opposite of their clientele's. Mass production and process industries increasingly automate earlier, and they mechanize flows between different stages of the process by transfer lines, assembly lines, automatic feeding and transport, and so on, up to fully continuous operations. In such industries, forms of automation that are dedicated to a specific purpose are more appropriate. Therefore, in France, industries with large-scale production are interdependent with a machine-tool industry characterized by unit and small-scale production. Here, machine-tools are more developed or manufactured to order. It is important to note that a manufacturing industry dominated by large-batch or mass-production firms and large concerns will be congenial to manufacturers of customized machine tools, and these suppliers therefore will feature the opposite traits of their clients.

But in unit and small-batch production, automation for a specific purpose would mean less flexibility than the production system requires, as is the case in Germany. A user population strong on small and medium-size batches is interdependent with small-to-medium size batches in machine-tool firms. It is important here to note that manufacturing industry typified by small-batch production of investment goods for more differentiated markets will be congenial to more industrial machine-tool firms that make greater numbers of machines having more flexible standards.

Of course, it would be wrong to assume that investment goods industries such as machine-tools are mainly dependent on domestic national markets. More commonly, export ratios exceed 50 percent of turnover. But the orientation toward international markets comes about in different ways and to different extents. Marked by a national policy of protecting domestic producers up until the Second World War, French entrepreneurs had become accustomed to concentrating on home markets and maintaining relationships with the national government to stabilize domestic industrial structures and demand (Lévy-Leboyer 1979). Export markets were, more frequently, in former colonies or countries that had been opened through diplomatic activity, such as in post-World War II Eastern Europe. Exports were thus more dependent on political relations, concentrated on specific world regions, and less buttressed by global sales and service subsidiaries.

German machine-tool firms, by comparison, had acquired a leading position in various international markets before World War II, but they had done so very gradually (Daly and Jones 1980). Although the machine-tool industry has "traditional" traits, its prominent position in the German export economy is a more recent phenomenon of modernization. It thrived on liberalized export markets, and it was fortified by the gradual construction of a worldwide sales and after-sales service network. This network includes both sales and service companies independent of particular manufacturers and company-specific sales and service subsidiaries.

Governmental Support

French machine-tool makers, despite the liberalization of export markets for industrial goods on a worldwide scale, have continued to be more dependent on the national government. Or, rather, the dependence is particularly focused on governmental policy to structure the industry, provide financial assistance, and generate demand for products at critical moments. This pattern, established much earlier, is vividly seen in the evaluation of the government program to stabilize the industry in the crisis that began in the early 1980s (Assemblée Nationale 1985).

In Germany, the industry's dependence on government is different. It is focused not on industrial structure policies or financial or demand management, but on the embeddedness in a supporting network of education, training, and research institutions, out of which grew a policy to promote product and process innovation in production engineering. Put simply, whereas French policies tried to control and manage the industry in terms of structure, finance, and demand, German policies aimed to increase industry performance through innovativeness, disposable qualified manpower, and linkages between producers, clients, and R&D institutions (Foray 1987).

Industrial Policies

Such contrasts are not unrelated to the differences in markets, production systems, work organization, and professional careers previously described. However, neither do they amount to the same thing. French industrial policy appears to work well where demand for goods is easily predictable or can be planned, and where innovation requirements are substantively concentrated rather than dispersed over different market segments and over time. This condition explains successes in aerospace, energy generation, telecommunications, and other public utility industries (Groenewegen 1989). The German type of industrial policy, however—dispersed and differentiated demand, competitive or contestable markets, diverse and piecemeal innovation paths—seems better suited to the goods and markets that figure more prominently in the German economy and exports.

Inevitably, societies have generalized basic patterns in industrial policy, beyond conditions applying in specific industries. Similar to organization and human resources patterns, the different industrial policy regimes found in different countries also have an affinity with requirements in specific markets, products, and types of innovation. It is therefore no accident that the results of French industrial policy are epitomized by the Minitel, the nuclear power station, generations of Mirage fighters, the fast train TGV (*train à grande vitesse*), and despite its European character, the Airbus. The symbols of German industrial policy are different and usually less glamorous: the workshop programmable computer numerically controlled lathe, the abortion pill, earth-moving equipment, and the fertilizer plant that can also make nerve gas.

The Transformation of the Industries, 1975–1987

A historical comparison shows how societal context and demand characteristics influenced the abilities of the machine-tool industries in Germany and France to respond to the introduction of new technologies and the growth in international competition. The immediate period after World War II had seen a narrowing of the quantitative economic differences between the French and German machine-tool industries. Output and employment had somewhat higher rates of growth in the French industry than in the German one (Perrin and Réal 1976). Furthermore, there was no evidence at the end of this period of a technological gap between the two countries. If anything, the French industry had benefitted from its close relations with the strong domestic aerospace client industry for an earlier adoption of NC (numerical control) techniques. The aircraft industry had everywhere been the major seedbed for NC techniques, first in the United States and then in Britain and France.

The NC technique, which was new in the 1950s, required substantial development of organizational, personnel, and planning capacities for programming machines largely away from the shopfloor, and for debugging and running job and batch-specific machining programs. It was therefore a technique more fitting for manufacturers with the capacity and will to install substantial planning groups—larger enterprises and firms in "elite" industries. That requirement accounts for its slow progress until the middle of the 1970s. Until then, conventional methods of automating machine operation (cam or plugboard control, for instance) were cheaper, if firms that applied them had reasonably large batches in production. The postwar period was indeed one of frequently growing average batch sizes, particularly, in the end, in consumer-oriented large-batch and mass-production industries.

Large-batch production in machine-tool-applying industries and customized production of machine tools were suited to the individual requirements of large-batch or mass producers. French producers and users of machine tools thus were well matched: the task environment was identical with societal predispositions. Therefore, French machine-tool producers outpaced the German competition at that stage.

However, after the mid 1970s, changes in the international system of currencies and payments, in financial flows, and in oil prices brought the lasting boom phase to an end and notably brought problems in some investment goods industries. These industries are more sensitive to trade cycle fluctuations than those catering directly to the consumer. A worldwide crisis in machine-tools started to develop, because the slower growth of disposable income and of the goods market's reduced need for additions to single-purpose automation and for investment goods on the whole.

This crisis came at different times, took somewhat different forms, and received different handling in the two countries. Our summary covers the broad situation with regard to employment; production, including export/import factors; technology and its effects on relations between suppliers, manufacturers, and clients; industry structures; personnel structures of firms;[4] and government intervention.

Employment

The immediate postwar growth in machine-tool industry employment was radically reversed starting in the 1970s. In Germany, the most severe reduction happened between 1970 and 1976, with a drop from 125,000 to 96,000. Thereafter, one finds a fluctuation finishing at 93,000 employees in 1986. In France, the most intense periods of labor-shedding were after 1976 and, again, notably after 1981, thus at a time when the German industry was picking up. The overall drop is from 27,000 employees in 1974 to 11,000 in 1988. (All statistics are from Maurice and Sorge 1989.)

Production

There is no reason to suppose that the terms of trade developed differently in the two national economies. Research by Debonneuil and Delattre (1987) showed that differences in exchange rate changes and inflation rates between France and Germany cancelled each other out over the period discussed here. A macroeconomic explanation, which would have reflected on differential export/import advantages, is therefore ruled out.

Domestic demand for machine tools (domestic demand = domestic production − exports + imports) has evolved differently in the two countries. Controlling for price changes, in Germany demand increased 15.8 percent in 1977 and 19.2 percent in 1978; in France, demand decreased by 28.4 percent and 29.5 percent. In the following years, changes are in the same direction and differ less in the two countries. But after about 1977, CNC machines—which improved on the earlier NC generations and became attractive for a wider clientele beyond the original core of NC users—started to be sold more widely. This circumstance seems to have occasioned an increase of demand in Germany more quickly than in France.

Such an increase could be expected from what we know about users in the two countries. Whereas Germany puts more emphasis on the autonomy of the skilled worker at "his" machine, in France, a greater division of labor exists among operators, setters, and programmers (Maurice et al. 1986; Sorge et al. 1983). German machine-tool users may have taken to CNC machines more quickly than their French counterparts because they saw them as breaking with the previous cumbersome division of labor among planning, programming, and machine operation.

Domestic production of machine-tools evolved differently over the whole period. German production developed more or less in parallel with world production, but production in France fell in real terms from 1980 on and particularly after 1982 (DAFSA 1977). One is tempted to infer that French industry missed the opportunity of the rapidly growing CNC demand because of initially smaller demand at home and the later entry of domestic producers into that market. This situation can be related to the fact that French producers were less oriented toward users demanding flexible standard machines and were less acute in perceiving that CNC differed from NC machines.

Of course, many of the problems of European and, notably, American manufacturers of machine-tools after 1977 were related to the Japanese penetration into foreign markets on a wide front, offering inexpensive standard CNC machines without electronic control problems. The Japanese were the first to use CNC techniques to overcome a deep domestic crisis in machine tools, achieving a more systematic integration of electronic control system and machine design and offering handy and reliable machines very competitively (Nohara 1987).

The Japanese advance was much stronger in France even before the industry's crisis, climbing from a market share of 47.5 percent in 1971 to one of nearly 60 percent in 1985. In Germany, the Japanese market share increased from 21.9 percent in 1971 to 31.5 percent in 1980, then decreased, and finally began to climb again (Leborgne 1987). To some extent, the profile of machines offered by German makers is probably somewhere between that of the Japanese and that of the French manufacturers. The Japanese mainly make standard machines produced in very large batches. Germans produce machines that are more standardized than those of the French but less standardized than those of the Japanese, giving some more weight to customization and breadth of the product spectrum.

Differences are also substantial in the overall machine-tool trade balance. The German industry has guarded an export surplus (although this has tended to shrink), whereas the French industry turned an initial export surplus into a growing deficit.

Technology

Although the share of NC machinery installed with potential customers had been roughly the same in France and Germany, German firms had, by 1977, adopted CNC machinery more quickly than their French counterparts (Mense 1983, 8). The share of NC machines in domestic production was lower in France during the crucial period but then climbed after 1980 and 1984 more steeply, finishing at the same a level as in Germany. That level was achieved differently in the two countries. Manufacturers of conventional machines frequently went into receivership in France, while the changeover was carried out by a largely stable population of firms in Germany.

Did manufacturers take advantage of the opportunity to approach clients and manufacturing tasks that had up until then been unfamiliar with NC machines? The answer may depend on producer–user relationships and the "social construction" of producers as actors.

During the formative period of CNC systems, no electronics enterprise emerged in France to take over an important role in systems design in close relationships with machine-tool makers. The individual machine-tool manufacturers sometimes tried their own hand; but, lacking financial resources and experience, they largely failed (Assemblée Nationale 1985, 22–23). Manufacturers were, it will be remembered, already much smaller than in Germany, had status, and had fewer links in the wider industrial and societal context. Later—but too late to stay the massive onslaught of the competition—the enterprise NUM was set up to pool efforts, operating as a subsidiary of Télémécanique.

In Germany, firms such as Siemens and AEG had made NC systems. Siemens, which successfully entered the CNC market, was helped by the demands of machine-tool firms for a revision of earlier systems concepts and by teaming up with the market leader, FANUC of Japan. But despite the emergence of Siemens and other smaller domestic control-system makers, leading large machine-tool makers also entered the systems market themselves. They were dissatisfied with conventional concepts, keen to guard their own application knowledge and integrate it into system design, and suspicious of yielding parts of what they perceived as their own value-added to supplying electronics firms.[5]

Better linked with financial and R&D institutions, possessing higher status, and being much larger on the average than French makers, the leading German companies launched themselves into CNC and other systems. They used the opportunity to introduce concepts more oriented toward shopfloor programming and use of operator knowledge. Government programs reinforced this trend and put a premium on workshop-oriented forms of programming, developed jointly by machine-tool makers and users, electronics firms, and system houses. They contributed to establishing a cooperative network among suppliers, manufacturers, and users, including collaboration between competitors.

Thus, what happened after 1977 in the two countries fits into previously established patterns, despite substantial technical, social, and economic change. In Germany, government and corporate policies were directed at maintaining the autonomy of the skilled worker on "his" machine and put in place appropriate systems and forms of work organization. Novel systems were designed that would maintain and develop existing patterns of organization and the distribution of skills. To some extent, the articulated interests of large company users and of smaller plants with less developed production bureaucracies coincided and reinforced each other. For instance, the specifications issued by the German engineering firm MAN coincided with those of small companies, pointing out the need for a workshop programming option if machines were to be bought more widely.

Such concerns were less in evidence in France, where CNC introduction followed the established NC logic more closely. The upgrading of setters separate from operators, and of technicians and foremen, as well as the insertion of more highly technically trained manpower on the shopfloor, became the main focus of company policies. Actors exacerbated the existing qualificational and hierarchical segmentation of workshop personnel and adjacent technical and planning functions. To be sure, case studies have revealed a drive to augment skills and knowledge in the workshop and to bridge the gap vis-à-vis planning departments (Maurice et al. 1986). But these attempts to augment skills are carried out by selectively placing people with higher technical qualifications in shopfloor jobs early in their careers, rather than by elevating the level of craft worker training collectively, as happens in Germany. An example is the reform of apprenticeship training for the metal trades. The training curriculum for machining mechanics now provides for an obligatory module in CNC machine programming and operation.

Technician qualifications in France, at levels between the *brevet d'études* (vocational degree) and higher engineering education, are nowadays largely obtained through vocational education before joining the workforce. Technicians in Germany are still, for the purposes of the manufacturing areas and professions under discussion, ex-craft workers with an apprenticeship, shopfloor experience, and supplementary technical education that is not available to noncraft workers (Drexel and Méhaut 1989). The introduction of CNC machines is more linked to the proliferation of new or higher qualifications in France. In Germany, it is accompanied by the introduction of new skills and knowledge requirements into existing education and training profiles, starting from craft worker apprenticeships. Thus, increasingly the first level of training in France (corresponding to the German apprenticeship-cum-vocational school course) is considered insufficient for responsible machine-setting and programming functions. But apprenticeship in Germany goes on to be associated with preparation for responsible autonomy.

The distinctive factor explaining the differences in the transformation of the machine-tool industries is the professional continuity between worker, technician, and engineering occupations in Germany, and the professional discontinuity and distance in France regarding status, education, remuneration, and careers. Such differences are reproduced in the midst of technical change, although a number of technical and business challenges are somewhat similar. The perpetuation of professional and organizational structures, therefore, does not simply respond to the evolution of techniques or markets; it also predisposes enterprises to pursue particular variants of new techniques and explore particular markets that have an affinity with these structures.

Industry Structure

The German machine-tool industry was quicker to use the opportunity provided by the advent of CNC machines for a more original departure from previous NC concepts and to push innovation through more rapidly. Nonetheless, the greater continuity inherent in professional structures in Germany occasioned less abrupt structural changes, allowing a smoother progression despite more pervasive technical change at the start of the crisis. For France, the greater segmentation and discontinuity in professional education and career ladders is linked with more abrupt and visible structural change.

Let us examine what happened to the structures of the machine-tool industries. In the past, the average enterprise and plant size in Germany had been twice as large as in France. During the crisis, the differences became even greater. It is reasonable to suppose that this increase in the disparity in the size among German and French plants was due to the shedding of labor in France or the bankruptcy of smaller plants and companies in Germany. However, that is not what happenned. More severely hit by bankruptcies were the large French firms. The French government had started a national program to stabilize the industry in the beginning of the 1980s, which might have been likely to particularly benefit larger firms. But exactly the opposite happened. The small firms were more resistant to the crisis, although they were less concerned by the rescue program, whereas most of the larger producers (those in the market for standard machines) went bankrupt or were sold to foreign groups (Assemblée Nationale 1985).

Those that survived were primarily the small specialty producers, the more artisanal firms that are more strongly represented in France. Only one large firm came out fairly well: Renault Machine-outil, the largest firm in the industry. But it is a specialty manufacturer of dedicated machines for the automobile industry, such as transfer machining-centers and robots. The fact that it was then a fully state-owned enterprise does not explain why it came well through the crisis, for wherever the government tried to help elsewhere in the machine-tool industry, it failed (as is shown later).

By comparison, average sizes were not much reduced in Germany. The number of companies in the industry fluctuated; during the critical years, some firms also entered the industry (DAFSA 1977). Ownership patterns in Germany remained fairly stable, with companies remaining largely in the hands of families and to some extent with banks or firms outside the industry. In France, there was first a wave of mergers and concentration in the hands of larger groups, but it was precisely these firms that subsequently were taken over by foreign competitors or went into receivership. In the new structure, Renault Machine-outil is by far the dominant firm; there is a smaller tier of medium-size companies owned by industrial groups or foreign enterprises, and a now relatively more important large tier of small companies. The structure is more polarized between a dominant enterprise and the population of quite small firms, but the firms that remained in French ownership and survived are even more likely now to be characteristic specialty manufacturers of customized machines (Assemblée Nationale 1985).

In France there is a strong emphasis on metal-cutting machines (lathes, milling, drilling, boring). In Germany, metal-forming machines such as presses amounted to 29 percent of sales in 1985 and to 37 percent of its exports in machine-tools. For a long time France has had a consistently greater share of metal-cutting machines—arguably the most "elite" metal-working machine-tool category—in its production and there has been only a slight tendency for this difference to lessen. It is interesting that the comparative advantage of Germany appears to be stronger for the "cruder" machine types than for the more "refined" ones.

These observations complement those made earlier. Germany is stronger not only on standard and modularized machines, but also on the heavy and crude machines. France has for a longer time specialized more in the "noble," tailor-made machine types that symbolize the "arts and crafts" side of the industry. This difference, which has persisted throughout all the fluctuations of the period considered, does not indicate an absence of sophisticated technique in the German industry. Rather, Germany's strength seems to lie in linking the crude, heavy, and standard character of machines with technical sophistication (expressed in precision, reliability, and advanced control systems), whereas the French firms seem to have drawn a distinction between the noble and the crude, the tailor-made and the catalogue product.

Personnel Structure

A parallel phenomenon can be observed for personnel categories. In France, the percentages of engineers, technicians, and craft workers with more demanding qualifications have increased, while the percentage of unskilled workers has decreased. In Germany, however, changes were much smaller. For instance, the decrease in the share of unskilled workers was 2 percentage points in Germany but 4 in France, even though the German share was nearly twice as large in the beginning of the period covered.

In France, firms are increasingly recruiting personnel with diplomas above the CAP *(certificat d'aptitude professionnelle)* level, which roughly corresponds to the German craft worker certificate, for functions in production departments (Hillau 1985). This recruiting trend has not happened in Germany. Similarly, one does not find the distinction between technician and worker training curricula in initial vocational education in Germany, at least not in the production engineering trades discussed here. The continuity of the qualificational spectrum and working careers remains intact in Germany. The spectrum is modernized, but there is no shift of emphasis or increase in discontinuity. In France, there is an attempt to upgrade production functions and have greater career and professional continuity from the shopfloor to preparatory and planning jobs, but the effect is to make shopfloor workers more stratified according to their levels of vocational education and attached career prospects.

Government Intervention

Even the behavior of political actors and their administrative bodies during the critical period seems to have operated within limits defined by long-running characteristics of each societal system. In France, the government tried to help the sector by generating public demand for machine-tools. This artificial demand alleviated the crisis for a year or two, after which it became particularly severe. The government further stimulated the creation of larger enterprises through mergers, but the new enterprises proved much less resilient than the small producers. Financial aid lessened some problems but was unable to prevent the decline in any noticeable way. Support for education, training, and research and development activities was considered beneficial but, in the last resort, not instrumental in decisively improving the status of the industry, or its contacts with outside R&D activities in universities or *grande école* schools of technology. The French firms were insufficiently mobilized to make use of programs (Assemblée Nationale 1985, section 41).

Crudely put, either the major measures taken had no visible effect or, where an effect might have been expected, such as in the promotion of innovation, measures were less important or not taken up by those expected to benefit from them. Lack of contact between individual firms, and between them and the world of higher technological education apparently could not be overcome by short-term measures. Government intervention can be expected to work well where it has a more lasting and pervasive influence on demand for products, which is far from the case in the machine-tool industry.

Industry-specific support in Germany was different. First, there was no direct concern with the structure of the industry, and financial support or management of demand was absent. A piecemeal system of subsidies for specific individual innovation projects considered technically worthy of support was gradually developed into a scheme that put a premium on cooperative research and development. This scheme allied producers of machine-tools with similar products, users, universities, and engineering development institutes, manufacturers of control systems, and specialized software houses. The focus shifted from specific projects in individual firms to generic techniques in many firms, and to interfirm cooperation between competing producers, users, system houses, and R&D institutes. An accent was also placed on workshop-oriented systems and methods of CNC (BMFT 1986).

It is again striking that the government in Germany subsidized what the industry in question was more likely to do anyway. Government intervention thus reinforced a societally specific trend. The trend that was reinforced in France led to the demise of the industry, whereas that reinforced in Germany had a stabilizing influence. The mindframe and the institutional setting of actors in the two societies worked to activate a response more rooted in patterns specific to the society than the problem at hand. The German response seems to be more in line with helping the sales of machine-tools or other investment goods, whereas the French response seems to be conducive to helping sell fighter planes and Minitels.

Interpretation

The Germany machine-tool industry entered the critical period earlier than the French one. It made use of the emerging CNC techniques to create new markets for selling NC machine tools, beyond the originally more restricted NC users. In that way, it compensated for declining demand for conventional machine tools, with which it was confronted earlier than the French industry. The German industry integrated forward into design of CNC control systems more systematically, although domestic electronics firms were already more established in making control systems for NC machines. It tried to improve on the design made available by electronics firms, going more in the direction of workshop programming to tap previously underdeveloped markets. In doing so, it was helped by greater overlap of user concepts regarding NC system properties and work organization between, for instance, small and large companies.

German machine-tool producers were already manufacturing more universal, nondedicated machines that can be operated flexibly, and they continued this policy by more systematically entering the market for universal CNC machines with operating flexibility, made in batches. Domestic-user concepts stressing flexibility in universal machines thus went hand in hand with a more industrialized machine-tool industry that produced catalogue machines on a larger scale. The German industry could apparently better afford backward integration into CNC system design and manufacture than the French. It had much larger firm and plant sizes, which spread overhead and development costs on the basis of greater economies of scale.

To achieve economies of scale, the adoption of the novel CNC systems that stress artisanal capabilities of the users thus depended on the greater foothold achieved by the German manufacturers' industrial principles of design and manufacture. The German industry explored new markets more quickly because its own structure and user expectations better prepared it for entering the new markets for CNC machines. The innovation required from manufacturers was substantial, but it also showed remarkable affinity with types of user requirements that were familiar to the machine-tool industry.

Despite the technical innovation required, the personnel structure in Germany did not change much. The industry in Germany now shows in all respects a comparatively striking measure of structural stability, again supporting the interpretation that it was better prepared for the innovation carried out. However, that advantage consisted of greater familiarity not with NC machines but with the types of machines and users that CNC was likely to open up as a new source of demand: standard lathes, small-batch production, smaller plants with nonbureaucratic work organization, and plants outside the aircraft industry in general. An affinity with such markets was crucial at a time when users increasingly stressed flexibility of machines and ease of operation.

Another important element in the explanation of Germany's advantage over France is that, despite individually greater backward integration into CNC system design and manufacture, there was also greater cooperation between makers of machines, and between them and electronics firms, software houses, nonindustrial research and development institutes, and machine users. Intensive collaboration alleviated problems with which individually operating firms were confronted. Another factor is the higher status of production engineering within German industry and academia vis-à-vis other specialties, and of machine-tool firms vis-à-vis other reputed industrial manufacturers.

The German industry maintained its position by using a particular series of technical innovations to open up new markets for NC machines. It was better prepared than France for that step because it was already oriented to specific market segments and user interests, and because its firms, the industry, and its core professions were embedded in the wider social and industrial structure.

The opposite story emerges for French machine-tool makers. They opened up new markets through CNC much less quickly and to a lesser extent. They were already less represented in these markets but more successful in dedicated customized machines requiring less flexible operations, installed with users in high-tech industries, larger companies, or plants with longer production runs. The French industry entered the crisis later, and its slow reaction was exacerbated by its orientation toward market segments and user interests different from those that provided latent new demand for CNC machines. Furthermore, collaboration between makers to share professionally novel (electronic and software) development efforts was much more difficult. Finally, the distance between machine-tool makers' and user industries' profiles along a number of dimensions ranging from strategy to personnel structure, and the distance between machine-tool makers and R&D outside the industry itself, further increased the French industry's difficulties.

Because of these linked disadvantages, the French backward integration of machine-tool makers into CNC systems and software development was stalled from the beginnings. Hence, the industry was less capable of opening up new market segments for NC machines. It was less prepared to explore not only new export markets, but also new domestic markets that became more profitable in the drive toward differentiated quality production. Consequently, the emerging markets were better captured by foreign (notably Japanese) competitors. But it is again also true that demand for CNC machines was, in France, slower to take off and assert itself on a wider scale, as it did in Germany.

These difficulties are related to the visibly sharper discontinuities in virtually all aspects of the French machine-tool industry and personnel structures. The survival of companies in the industry depends on their ability to maintain the classic role of the small manufacturer of customized machines under the new aegis of CNC or, alternatively, on being bought by a foreign competitor. As a result, the surviving French firms are characterized by sharper changes, in the form of a shrinking work force, changes in ownership or in personnel structure, or in all these aspects.

Conclusions

Throughout our account, we find syndromes crossing several functional areas: orientation toward market segments; quantitative importance of industries and types of users in the economy; manpower socialization; careers and personnel structures; organizational structures; organized linkages with other firms and R&D institutes; firms and plant sizes; and patterns of governmental support.

Some observers and analysts would tend to single out key variables, as follows. First, a machine-tool industry more or less has the inverse properties of the industries that buy its products. This circumstance helps to explain why the differences between these French and German industries are in many ways the opposite of what has been established for manufacturing as a whole. Second, the industries that survived the competitive struggle were already geared toward the market segments that grow and offer higher profit margins—in this case, markets for universal, flexible types of CNC machines.

This argument is plausible and powerful. It conforms with the more general view of the importance of fit in a neo-contingency theory argument: in this specific industrial case, the German firms did better, because their existing markets and their less artisanal profile in internal operations better prepared them for achieving a fit with the requirements existing for the industrial development and manufacture of CNC machines to capture new markets for an innovation.

The argument in fact refines contingency treatment by allowing for different market types with their own organizational and human resources connotations within the same industry. It also allows for a "subjective fit" between the professional and entrepreneurial tendencies of actors in an industry and potential markets that have not yet been crystallized in large-scale demand behavior. Furthermore, the argument does not assume unidirectional determination between environment, context, and internal structuring of organization and human resources. Rather, it is founded on the notion of affinity among certain market segments, organization patterns, socialization and personnel structures, and other factors.

In that way, the argument responds to a great deal of the criticism of the first wave of contingency theorists (see Schreyögg 1980). It might therefore seem that the societal-effect perspective turns into a branch of the neo-contingency perspective, by considering specific organization and human resource patterns as linked with an orientation to specific market segments. But the overlap is due to a broadening of both perspectives, rather than elementary reference points of the approaches coming closer together.

Consider not only the plausibility but also the loopholes of the neo-contingency argument in accounting for what happened in the French and German machine-tool industries. First, it is not that clear that the German industry was better prepared to achieve fit with emerging markets, notably differentiated quality production on the part of industries applying machine-tools, and with new technological potential offered by CNC techniques. Manske and Wobbe (1987) found that, in the period covered here, the number of separate machine models and variants tended to increase in the larger machine-tool manufacturers, such that universal machines were more and more tailored to requirements in smaller market segments and according to customer specifications.

Thus, the German machine-tool industry was in itself drifting toward differentiated quality production, as were the industries that it was supplying. To that extent, differentiation and broadening of the product range favored a higher measure of artisanship in the manufacturers' own production systems. Thus, contextual changes moved firms in the direction of what is more characteristic of the French competitors, namely, more customized manufacturing. Hence, the French industry also enjoyed potential benefits as it entered the crisis, at least as far as its internal production systems are concerned. Furthermore, although it took off later, the market for more flexible CNC machines also developed in France, and flexible automation "signals" were also clear there. So, the production systems of French machine-tool producers favored differentiated quality production more so than those in Germany.

In fact, neither the artisanal nor the industrial strength of manufacturing systems tipped the balance, but it was, rather, the way that opposed contingencies and arrangements systematically linked and intertwined that provided an advantage. The German machine-tool industry resembled user industries in intertwining craft and higher engineering functions, bringing artisanal and R&D work closer together; putting manufacturers into more intimate collaboration with reputed and technologically advanced institutions outside the industry; and more comfortably bridging the gap between mechanical and electronic and software engineering. The French machine-tool makers and the whole industry, by comparison, were more weakly integrated with their environment.

At this stage, a fit between internal arrangements and external contingencies is less important than a fit between institutionalized patterns in the specific industry and the wider society and economy. The German machine-tool industry was favored by the fact that institutionalized social structures and relations are conducive to bridging gaps between artisanal and industrial systems of production, between practices in small and in large firms, between craft and technological professions, between noble and less noble branches of engineering. The French industry had the disadvantage of larger gaps and discontinuities in the structure of its firms, between firms, and between institutions in the society at large. The institutional isolation of this machine-tool industry and the discrepancy between its own and prevalent societal patterns are of overriding importance for explaining its demise.

In all this, the professional habitus and behavioral predisposition of actors influence the interpretation of market signals and the assessment of costs and benefits attached to innovation projects. We therefore discard any kind of determinism, notably the view that product market differences have more or less set the ball rolling. We prefer the interactive view inherent to the societal effect approach: the reciprocal conditioning of multiple factors in differentiated societal and functional spheres explains why differences between societies originate and persist.

In that respect, the societal effect approach offers an explanation that goes beyond the neo-contingency framework. Notably, it considers success to result from the ability of actors to harmonize requirements arising from distinct and opposed contingencies. To that extent, the societal effect approach is universalistic and goes against the grain of contingency thinking. It sees the competitive effectiveness of collective actors as built on the capacity to transcend and recombine distinct contingency-specific requirements and solutions. Therefore it has a dialectical view in which success in achieving specific tasks depends on the actors being embedded in relations and structures that are not task-specific. This setting enables actors to do well in a broader environmental niche or to seek out niches that are not well circumscribed in terms of specific contingencies.

We are aware that the ball may be bounced back from the neo-contingency side. The organizational, career, and human resources discontinuities that characterize the French machine-tool industry and French manufacturing in general are more conductive to performance in other industries. The effectiveness of this kind of arrangement thus varies according to the task or industrial context in which it is found. But, again, the existence of such an arrangement is due not only to proven performance but also to institutionalized patterns.

Institutions predispose actors to seek out specific tasks, strategies, or goals, and they may lead them more toward particular industries or market segments than toward others. Here, too, the ball is bounced back from the neo-contingency side, since a specific affinity between institutions and industries or markets is assumed. To elaborate linkages between the evolution of sectoral structures in an economy and structures of organization and human resources, the societal effect approach must consider relationships put forward by neo-contingency theorizing and research.

But it uses such theory and findings differently. Actual organization and human resource patterns are not merely an approximation of ideal-type or average patterns linked with particular strategies or contingencies, but are subject to the working of elementary societal mechanisms. These are essentially ambiguous with regard to strategies or contingencies. Society characteristically contrives to bring about stable combinations of opposed or conflicting elements, such that their opposition becomes a source of long-run continuity and of change, much like a theme that persists in a music piece despite, and because of, variations.

Although it is interesting to explore the intertwining of neo-contingency and societal effect arguments, the foundations of the two approaches are different. Intertwining the approaches provides a comprehensive account of events and prevents tunnel vision, but this integrative effort combines contradictory elements. The comparison presented here shows the importance of the societal effect perspective, and it helps to underline the value of this perspective for the study of other industries. The neo-contingency perspective is now more compatible with an interactionist perspective, but the societal effect approach makes a multi-paradigmatic perspective (Morgan 1986) more systematically a part of its program.

Notes

1. The discussion that follows is based on Maurice and Sorge (1989).
2. These figures were made available by the German Association of the Mechanical Engineering Industry (VDMA), based on statistics of the Federal Office of Labor.
3. See Chapter 7 for a description of the setter, operator, and programmer tasks.
4. For more detailed treatment, see Maurice and Sorge (1989, 15–40).

5. This was a substantial revision of previous policy with regard to NC systems; on the basis of interviews with company representatives, Perrin and Réal (1976) had reported that the German competition was unlikely to venture into CNC systems design.

References

Académie des Sciences. 1980. *Les sciences mécaniques et l'avenir industriel de la France.* Rapport de l'Académie des Sciences à Monsieur le Président de la France. Paris: La Documentation Française.

Assemblée Nationale. 1985. *Rapport d'information déposé par la Commission de la production et des échanges sur l'industrie de la machine-outil, par Bruno Vennin.* Document nr. 2621. Paris: Assemblée Nationale.

BMFT (Bundesministerium fuer Forschung und Technologie). 1986. *Fertigungstechnik. Stand des Programms der Bundesregierung.* Bonn: BMFT.

Campbell, Adrian, Arndt Sorge, and Malcolm Warner. 1989. *Microelectronic Product Applications in Great Britain and West Germany. Strategies, Competence and Training.* Aldershot, U.K.: Gower.

Child, John. 1972. "Organizational structure, environment and performance: The role of strategic choice," *Sociology* 6:1–22.

DAFSA. 1977. *L'industrie européenne de la machine-outil à métaux.* Paris: Collection Analyse du Secteur.

Daley, Anne, and Daniel T. Jones. 1980. "The machine-tool industry in Britain, Germany and the United States," *National Institute Economic Review* 92:53–63.

Debonneuil, Michèle, and Michel Delattre. 1987. "La 'compétitivité-prix' n'explique pas les pertes tendancielles de parts de marché," *Economie et Statistique* 203:5–22.

Delouvrier, Paul. 1987. *Les industries de biens d'équipements.* Etude présentée par la section des activités productives, de la recherche et de la technologie du Conseil Economique et Social. Paris: Journal officiel de la République Française.

Drexel, Ingrid, and Philippe Méhaut. 1989. "Der Weg zum Techniker: Aufstieg oder Seiteneinstieg?" in K. Düll and B. Lutz, eds., *Technikentwicklung und Arbeitsteilung im internationalen Vergleich.* Frankfurt: Campus.

Foray, Dominique. 1987. "PME et politique technologique en Allemagne Fédérale," *Annales des Mines,* November, pp. 20–25.

Groenewegen, John. 1989. *Planning in een markteconomie. Indicatieve planning, industriebeleid en de rol van de publieke onderneming in Frankrijk in de periode 1981–1986.* Delft: Eburon.

Hillau, Bernard. 1985. "La remise en cause des filières professionnelles dans la machine-outil," *Formation-Emploi* 12:50–53.

Leborgne, Danièle. 1987. "Equipements flexibles et organisation productive: Les relations industrielles au coeur de la modernisation. Eléments de comparaison internationale," in *Aspects de la crise,* vol. 1, chap. 5. Paris: CEPREMAP.

Lévy-Leboyer, Maurice. 1979. "Le patronat français, 1912–1973," in M. Lévy-Leboyer, ed., *Le patronat de la seconde industrialisation,* pp. 137–88. Paris: Les éditions ouvrières.

Manske, Fred, and Werner Wobbe. 1987. *Computergestuetzte Fertigungssteuerung im Maschinenbau. Gestalt ungshin weise für Technik, Organisation und Arbeit.* Duesseldorf: VDI-Verlag.

Maurice, Marc, and Arndt Sorge. 1989. *Dynamique industrielle et capacité d'innovation de l'industrie de la machine-outil en France et en RFA.* Document 89-1. Aix-en-Provence: Laboratoire d'économie et de sociologie du travail.

Maurice, Marc, François Sellier, and Jean-Jcques Silvestre. 1977. *La production de la hiérarchie dans l'entreprise. Recherche d'un effet sociétal.* Research report. Aix-en-Provence: Laboratoire d'économie et de sociologie du travail.

Maurice, Marc, François Sellier, and Jean-Jacques Silvestre. 1982. *Politique d'éducation et organisation industrielle en France et en Allemagne. Essai d'analyse sociétale.* Paris: Presses Universitaires de France.

Maurice, Marc, Arndt Sorge, and Malcolm Warner. 1980. "Societal differences in organizing manufacturing units. A comparison of France, West Germany and Great Britain," *Organization Studies* **1**:59–86.

Maurice, Marc, François Eyraud, Alain d'Iribarne, and Frédérique Rychener. 1986. *Des entreprises en mutation dans la crise. Apprentissage des technologies flexibles et émergence de nouveaux acteurs.* Research report. Aix-en-Provence: Laboratoire d'économie et de sociologie du travail.

Mense, Harald. 1983. *Datensammlung zum Bericht "Informationstechnik."* Karlsruhe: Kernforschungszentrum.

Miles, Raymond E., and Charles C. Snow. 1978. *Organizational Structure, Strategy and Process.* New York: McGraw-Hill.

Morgan, Gareth. 1986. *Images of Organization.* Beverly Hills: Sage.

Nohara, Hiroatsu. 1987. *Les acteurs de la dynamique industrielle au Japon. Étude exploratoire dans l'électronique et la machine-outil.* Research report. Aix-en-Provence: LEST-CNRS.

Perrin, Jacques, and Bernard Réal. 1976. *L'industrie des biens d'équipements mécanique et l'engineering en France et en Allemagne de l'Ouest,* vol. 2. Research report. Grenoble: Institut de recherche économique et de planification.

Piore, Michael, and Charles Sabel. 1984. *The New Industrial Divide.* New York: Basic Books.

Podevin, Gérard. 1986. "Renaissance d'un secteur: Les mutations structurelles et relationnelles dans la machine-outil à métaux," *Formation-Emploi* **15**:33–43.

Rose, Michael. 1985. "Universalism, culturalism and the Aix Group," *European Sociological Review* **1**:65–83.

Schreyögg, Georg. 1980. "Contingency and choice in organization theory," *Organization Studies* **1**:305–26.

Sorge, Arndt, and Wolfgang Streeck. 1988. "Industrial Relations and Technical Change: The Case for an Extended Perspective," in R. Hyman and W. Streeck, eds., *New Technology and Industrial Relations,* pp. 19–47. Oxford: Blackwell.

Sorge, Arndt, and Malcolm Warner. 1986. *Comparative Factory Organisation. An Anglo-German Comparison of Management and Manpower in Manufacturing.* Aldershot, U.K.: Gower.

Sorge, Arndt, Gert Hartmann, Malcolm Warner, and Ian Nicholas. 1983. *Microelectronics and Manpower in Manufacturing. Applications of Computer Numerical Control in Great Britain and West Germany.* Aldershot, U.K.: Gower.

Steedman, Hilary, and Karin Wagner. 1987. "A second look at productivity, machinery and skills in Britain and Germany," *National Institute Economic Review* **87**(4):84–95.

Steedman, Hilary, and Karin Wagner. 1989. "Productivity, machinery and skills: Clothing manufacture in Britain and West Germany," *National Institute Economic Review* **89**(2):41–57.

VDW (Vereinigung Deutscher Werkzeugmaschinenhersteller). 1986. *Key Figures of the West German Machine Tool Industry 1986.* Frankfurt: VDW.

Wobbe, Werner, and Fred Manske. 1987. *Computerunterstützte Fertigungssteuerung im Maschinenbau. Gestaltungshinweise für Technik, Organisation und Arbeit.* Düsseldorf: VDI-Verlag.

II

NEW TECHNOLOGIES
AND NEW PATTERNS
OF ORGANIZING

5

Rationalization and Work
in German Industry

HORST KERN
MICHAEL SCHUMANN

In *Industriearbeit und Arbeiterbewusstsein* (Industrial Work and Workers' Consciousness), published in 1970, we argued that Taylorism was still in force in several German industries in the 1950s and 1960s. Work restructuring had caused a double polarization of the work force: between many unskilled workers and a few skilled ones within "direct" departments, on the one hand, and between a majority of direct workers and a minority of skilled indirect workers, on the other hand. But in a follow-up study, *Das Ende der Arbeitsteilung?* (The End of the Division of Labor?) published in 1984, we found many cases in which management could increase efficiency only by relaxing the division of labor and by utilizing the work force within a more complex and more highly integrated work organization. We concluded that the old Taylorist parallelism between increased efficiency on the one hand and downgrading and dequalification on the other had become outdated (Kern and Schumann 1989).

More generally, we interpreted the situation of German industry as one of radical transformation, when new approaches toward automation were being invented and implemented. We viewed this process as a fundamental change of the structures of industrial work, as a redistribution of living conditions in society, and as a challenge for politics. We believed that new "concepts of production" lay just around the corner.

To determine whether our hypothesis has been confirmed in the ensuing years, this chapter examines recent empirical studies on rationalization of three key sectors of the German economy: the automobile industry, the chemical industry, and the machine-tool industry. We also look in more detail at the situation in the electrical-electronics industry, a relatively new area of interest for German scholars (see Kern and Schumann 1992; Voskamp, Wittemann, and Wittke 1989).

New Concepts of Production: Flexible Automation and Skilled Work Integration

In the new research, we found no evidence of any steps to make production more efficient by increasing the division of labor. In fact, the opposite is the case. No matter how ambivalent industrial change may be, utilization of the work force is no longer hindered by the Taylorist dogma. The efforts to achieve more efficiency no longer depend upon increased subdivision of operations and a rigid fragmentation of tasks: more and more frequently they rely upon the use of task integration and the expansion of the scope of responsibility. The controversies within management concerning the pros and cons of labor division, controversies that were still vivid in 1984, have been more or less settled. The champions of the old paradigm are losing the fight; within management, no influential faction seriously presents a conceptual alternative to the strategy of integrated work organization.

One indication of the integration of work is the importance of highly skilled blue-collar workers, who have further "qualified" themselves by additional education and training. Qualified workers currently represent 12 percent of the blue-collar workers in the automobile industry, 39 percent of those in the chemical industry, and 87.5 percent of those in the machine and tool construction industry. (For the electrical/electronics industry, no statistics are available). In many cases, these workers take on an entirely new role in industrial work—that of "systems controller" (Schumann et al. 1989). If, in addition, one takes into account the "indirect" functions (maintenance, quality control, preparatory functions) as well as the "tertiary" sectors (white-collar workers), even such a classic mass-production industry as the automobile industry, can be classified as an "everyman's industry." The critical mass of qualified workers necessary for a move of skills toward high qualifications and professionalization seems to be available now.

These findings suggest that our initial belief in the evolution of new work forms has been confirmed. Yet this affirmation has to be qualified. Industrial work faces fundamental change only in those sectors in which the enterprises have combined two strategies: massive utilization of flexible automation, and an integration of the work organization. It is only at this point that traditional Taylorist production work gives way to a system of controlling and regulating tasks through a revision of the demarcations between production, maintenance, and quality control. *Both* the strategies of flexible automation and integration of functions are necessary for the development and spread of qualified production work. Organizational change without radical technological change creates *less* momentum for structural change of work. When the technological side of the production process exhibits little change in the direction of flexible automation—that is, where the workers remain the direct producers of the product—it is obviously difficult to do away with Taylor's legacy.

We can recognize the significance of the technological factor for the initial push toward change in all of the surveyed branches. In the automobile industry, for example, high-tech sectors more frequently have a fairly homogeneous work force at the level of highly skilled production workers, whereas the low-tech sectors still mainly exhibit a traditional structure. In the electrical-electronics industry, too, the technological differentiations are very prominent. The move beyond Taylorism is obvious in the manufacturing of electronic components, particularly in processes that are extensively automated by machine systems and complex assembly robots. Under such technological conditions, simple work disappears to such an extent that the Taylorist division of labor between unskilled "everyman's work" and highly skilled specialist tasks loses its significance.

We do not mean to imply that everything is static in low-technology areas. The new modes of organizing industrial work do influence these areas, particularly as the trend toward market differentiation increases the need for flexibility in production. Complex products and variant high-quality models are almost impossible to manufacture in a rigidly subdivided work organization. However, if the new demands from the market are not met with drastic changes in production techniques, the transition gets stuck halfway. For example, the operations of manual workers, which were traditionally separated, are now also bundled in these sectors; but this simply is an organizational change that results only in semiskilled jobs that may be more complex than those they replace, but nevertheless remain at a level below that of the skilled workers. All these changes lead to a paradox: on the one hand, concepts including new modes of personnel policy have, indeed, prevailed. On the other hand, the impacts of this change for the structure of industrial work is softened, slowed by the lack of technological dynamics.

We do not want to argue, however, that the prevailing differentiation between high-tech, low-tech, and mixed sectors is caused purely by technology itself. The failure of final assembly to become automated is not due to a lack of technological capacity; this move could be made technically, as examples in Japan have already demonstrated. Rather, the transition has stalled for economic reasons. The necessary capital is so large that the break-even point could only be realized many years after the investment. In addition, the works councils, an important factor in Germany, have not supported higher automation for fear of losing jobs. The technological prerequisites for comprehensive automation are in place, but they are blocked by socioeconomic factors.

Just as it is not necessary for the high-tech areas to have an integrated work organization, neither is it impossible in the low-tech areas to move in this direction. Without a doubt, low-tech workers could be brought up to the level of the skilled workers by redesigning jobs, as some successful examples of integrated assembly work in auto production prove. However, companies do not do so normally because they believe that a more traditional organization still suffices in the low-tech areas. Under these circumstances and in their perspective, the incremental costs that the restructuring would necessitate do not make much sense.

In our earlier work (1984) we underestimated these inhibiting factors. First, the diffusion of flexible automation is taking longer than we presumed. The automation in assembly, as we had expected, did prove to be *the* engineers' task for the 1980s; but the users of new technology failed to take advantage of all the possibilities. As a result, the gap between high-tech and low-tech areas is now deep and relatively stable. Second, the personnel policy of relying more on qualified workers (which is new to the concepts of production) in the low-tech areas has had quite limited effects. The nonautomated assembly sectors in mass production continue to rely on semiskilled workers. Hence, the segmentation of the work force has been more drastic and longer lived than we had assumed.

This finding leads us to formulate one aspect of our argument more drastically than we did in 1984. As a consequence of the rapid and radical application of the new production and personnel policy concepts in the growing (but still not dominant) high-tech areas, and of the persistence of Taylorist concepts in the shrinking (but still, by no means, abolished) low-tech areas, the working conditions for the corresponding employee categories are drifting far apart—further, perhaps, than we had predicted. More than ever, there is a need for policies that aim to counteract this trend.

Dialectics in the Division of Labor

We now see several reasons for widening our analytical approach to eliminate restrictions that we had observed in 1984. To arrive at the right research design means choosing an enlarged field for analysis.

Our most important analytic category, the "new production and personnel policy concepts," exemplified one restriction. We had focused on the changes in production and correlated changes in human resource management. These changes doubtless play a key role in industrial restructuring, but focusing only on this dimension risks missing the point. The structural change taking place in industry is *comprehensive* change, and none of the manifold activities of firms—product design technical planning, production, logistics, purchasing, and marketing—is excluded from this process. Not only are all of these activities included, but they are becoming more and more systematically interrelated in the process of change and are increasingly confronted with the imperative of strict coordination ("systemic rationalization"; see Altmann et al. 1986, 191; Baethge and Oberbeck 1986, 22). The sociological analysis of industrial rationalization has to take these new interrelations into consideration, and it can only do so by expanding its perspectives.

What has to be treated more seriously will become clear if we outline more precisely the new quality that the rationalization has won since our initial research. Today firms have at their disposal better and broader technologies and organization techniques, which are exploited in increasingly complex rationalization projects. If in the past rationalization was more or less limited to a more efficient shaping of the dimensions of direct production (such as automating a series of operations or reorganizing the division of labor), rationalization now includes the coordination and integration of formerly isolated departments. The improvements in communication and transport technologies even allow the orientation of restructuring to targets beyond the location of one plant. Instead of the physiognomy of individual plants being treated as constants, the interfaces between plants are becoming increasingly more dynamic. Operations are moved to those localities that appear to offer the greatest comparative advantages for carrying them out (lowest labor cost, best work force, most favorable industrial relations, strongest synergistic effects, optimal transport system, etc.). As a result of the abolishment of national barriers (the integration of the European Economic Community, opening of the borders toward the East), the relocalization of industry also increasingly gains an international dimension. Rationalization today signifies enormous spatial shifts. New plants and subsidiaries are established in other regions or nations. Mergers and takeovers amass. New partners come together for joint ventures.

While it is not possible yet to recognize any basic blueprint of change, some developments appear to be more likely than others. First, potent manufacturers of final products turn to *outsourcing* some parts and drawing them from suppliers to whom they can stipulate their own price, delivery, and quality conditions. This approach is used primarily in the case of standard parts; the production of technically valuable or net value-added intensive components is usually kept within one's own enterprise. This dividing line cannot be strictly established, however, with respect to components or component systems (modules) that are constructed out of new materials or are based on new technologies (e.g., parts made of synthetic materials, ceramic parts, electronic modules). The adjective "new" indicates that these components are located outside the realm of the traditional know-how of the manufacturers of final products. In such instances, the manufacturers of final products look for a competent supplier whose expertise can save them research and development costs, and can minimize innovation time. The inherent danger in this structure is the fact that the manufacturer of final products could become dependent on the supplier. In order to minimize this danger, however, the manufacturers of final products build up their own development competence, without eliminating the supplier completely. It is indeed plausible that the manufacturer of final products could even divest a traditional product line in order to finance a commitment in technologically and economically promising areas.

Second, suppliers are afraid of becoming dependent on a few large clients. The position of an interchangeable reproducer of standard parts is generally not considered to be a comfortable one. Greater independence can be achieved by emphasizing technologically more demanding and complex products that necessitate *special know-how;* one possibility is for the supplier to outsource standard parts or to move the production of standard parts to peripheral branch plants. The *diversification* of products is also a means of mitigating the dependency; having more than one large customer cuts down the risk. In instances in which one's own competence or capital are too limited to carry out such maneuvers, firms combine their resources by means of takeovers, joint-ventures, and mergers.

Third, a company's success in these adaptations depends more and more on the competence and capacity of its *R&D* department. This dependence results in enlarged staffs deployed in these areas, particularly as engineers. Furthermore, the efficiency and creativity of R&D are becoming key criteria in industrial restructuring. Some firms operate, thereby, along the lines of organizational independence and spatial concentration of research and design shops. As a rule, the location of the main branch is turned into a headquarters in which R&D jobs are concentrated, in addition to staff work. The production operations, on the other hand, moves successively to branches and affiliations outside the traditional geographic areas of industrial concentration (or even to a foreign country). Obviously the companies expect to improve their chances of overcoming bottlenecks in the supply of manpower, as well as taking better advantage of the differences in labor conditions. They also hope for greater potentials for further rationalization; "purified" sectors ("pure" R&D locations versus "pure" manufacturing locations) are often regarded as especially likely targets for rationalization without any compromise.

But this assumption may prove false in the long run. We suspect that such divisions will miss synergistic effects (mutual inspiration between production and design, joint utilization of the infrastructure, etc.). Hence there are also adverse examples: the establishment of "mixed" locations where certain products/operations are designed and produced. Companies that follow the division model today might later find themselves forced to allocate R&D to production facilities that have since been decentralized. If the main locations have in fact been robbed of their most efficient production lines (and if it should be too expensive to reinstall them), these main shops could wind up becoming purely administrative sites.

Conclusions

All of these important changes—whose exact contours have yet to be determined—force us to expand the analytical horizon of future sociological research in this field. The "new production and personnel policy concepts" topic must be studied and interpreted in its relation to these trends. Revision of the interfaces between the departments within the firms; dissolving of the demarcations between the firms (relations between manufacturers of final products, suppliers, machine and tool producers); intensified interrelations and linkages between firms and their social environment (political organizations, government, local authorities, private associations, etc.); relocation of production (new regional concentrations); globalization of production and a revision of the international division of labor—each of these changes influences and is influenced by the course that the technological and organizational change in production areas will take. Together, they constitute the comprehensive process of systemic rationalization, and industrial sociology should keep this totality in mind when carrying out further research.

Expanding the perspectives in this way makes possible new insights, among them the recognition that the reduction in the division of labor within production (our argument in our 1984 book) not only demands specialization on higher levels, but also fortifies it. The differentiation of the environment as a precondition for internal integration—the division of labor between the manufacturers of the final products and the suppliers, between private enterprises and the infrastructure, between the individual industrial nations, as well as between these and the NICs—could be the hypothesis to explain future developments.

References

Altmann, N., M. Dies, V. Döhl, and D. Sauer. 1986. "Ein neuer Rationalisierungstyp! Neue Anforderungen an die Industriesoziologie," *Soziale Welt* **37**:191–207.

Baethge, M., and H. Oberbeck. 1986. *Zukunft der Angestellten* (Future of White-Collar Workers). Frankfurt-M./New York: Campus-Verlag

Kern, H., and M. Schumann. 1970. *Industriearbeit und Arbeiterbewusstsein* (Industrial Work and Workers' Consciousness). Frankfurt-M.: Europäische Verlagsanstalt.

Kern, H., and M. Schumann. 1984. *Das Ende der Arbeitsteilung?* (The End of the Division of Labor?). Munich: C. H. Beck.

Kern, H., and M. Schumann. 1989: "New Concepts of Production in West German Plants," in P. Katzenstein, ed., *Industry and Politics in West Germany. Toward the Third Republic,* pp. 87–110. Ithaca, New York: Cornell University Press.

Kern, H., and M. Schumann. 1992. "New Concepts of Production and the Emergence of the Systems Controller," in P. S. Adler, ed., *Technology and the Future of Work,* pp. 111–48. New York: Oxford University Press.

Schumann, M., V. Baethge, U. Neumann, and R. Springer. 1989. "Breite Diffusion der neuen Produktionskonzepte—zögerlicher Wandel der Arbeitsstrukturen" (The Broad Spread of the New Model of Production—A Halting Transformation of the Structures of Work), *Soziale Welt* **4**:47.

6

National and Company Differences in Organizing Production Work in the Car Industry

ULRICH JÜRGENS

We are experiencing a far-reaching change in the automobile industry that is comparable in its historical consequences to the diffusion of the Taylorist–Fordist regulation model decades ago. Criticism of Taylorism–Fordism has grown since the beginning of the 1980s, especially, and the demand for greater emphasis on human resources and the self-regulation of work by the workers themsevles has been experiencing an enormous upswing in the public discussion in Western countries. One hears of the "new plant revolution" (Lawler 1978). A mixture of ideas on questions of work motivation, the design of work (in both social and technical terms), and industrial democracy that have been developing over decades have now come to fruition and been translated into textbooks for personnel policy (e.g., Milkovich and Glueck 1985), as well as for industrial engineering and production engineering (e.g., Barnes 1980). Titles such as *Improving Productivity and the Quality of Work-life* (Cummings and Molloy 1977), *Productivity Gains Through Worklife Improvements* (Glaser 1976), and *High-Involvement Management* (Lawler 1986) signal a new way of thinking among managers.

The signs of dissolution of the Taylorist–Fordist model for labor regulation are obvious. But what will come after it? A clear answer to this question is not possible at present. In view of the many facets of the current radical changes in the automobile industry, we are faced with considerable difficulties in interpreting the direction and pace of the change and getting to its essence. It is difficult to track down the actual changes, despite the loudly proclaimed objectives of the companies. One of the problems lies in properly assessing the inertia of the established structures, institutions, and attitudes.

In the following I would like to address several questions:

- What are the directions of change that can be established in the most important dimensions of how labor is deployed in the factory?
- What influence do company affiliation and national affiliation have in regard to the differences observed?
- Are there converging or diverging developments in the company- and nation-specific forms of regulation?
- Are there models for future forms of labor regulation and what are the prospects for their stabilizing and spreading?

My observations are based on research carried out in 1983 through 1986 in assembly plants of three automobile companies (designated as Company A, B, and C), two of them with their headquarters in the United States and one headquartered in Germany.[1] Two of the firms were multinationals, allowing for country comparison. In order not to succumb to the danger of investigating the rare orchids of development we selected our sample of plants on the basis of their comparability in terms of the product (front-wheel drive subcompact cars) and the production volume (mass production). In this manner we attempted to control for the influences of the product type and production technology as much as possible to isolate the differences that arose from work organization and labor relations. This approach corresponds to the principles of "most similar design" (compare Przeworsk and Teune 1970) and of the comparison of "matched" pairs, and with it we were able to detect differences in the directions of change among companies, among countries, and between factories of one company in the same country.

Directions of Change

Strategies for Job Integration

"Integration" is a key concept used to describe the restructuring of car production in the 1980s. Common to all intervention measures is the understanding that the forms of specialization enforced by Taylorism–Fordism have turned out to be dysfunctional, obsolete, or exaggerated. The costs of coordination required by separating functions and competences have become too high. Flexible production and high technology require a more integrative approach.

Integration refers both to the horizontal and vertical separation of tasks and functions. And it refers both to management and supervisory jobs as well as to rank-and-file production or administrative jobs. In fact, many of the new concepts for management organization, technical systems, and work organization (such as project teams, computer-integrated manufacturing, group work) aim at a higher function integration, too. For now, I am only refering to the job design aspect, that is, the task structure of the individual employee.

According to our findings, the main focus of the measures undertaken by the companies at the time of our study was on the horizontal aspect of work structuring, and, in particular, the integration of direct and indirect production tasks. This classic differentiation has increasingly become a hindrance to a more effective and efficient work organization. Tasks that had become the basis for separate departments and lines of hierarchy—such as quality control, equipment maintenance, and material handling—are being partially merged again with direct production tasks. Shopfloor politics of "job control," which were based on the formalized structures of the division of labor, are increasingly losing ground against such measures toward "job enrichment."

In our research, the aspect of vertical integration was often touched upon when it came to measures of dismantling hierarchies and decentralizing competences. But, in practice, we observed only timid and mostly symbolic steps toward "enriching" the jobs of line managers or operators with planning, budgeting, and control functions.

Employee Participation

Measures to increase employee participation were widely discussed in all of our research sites. The existence of all kinds of small group activities such as quality circles, problem-solving groups, and voluntary study circles was regarded by most of the people we talked to in the companies as an essential difference between the Japanese and the Western companies, and as a major factor explaining the success of the Japanese firms.

The actual activities in the factories exhibited considerable differences in this field, however. We found two directions of thrust in the management strategy:

> *The first* aimed at individual work behavior and motivation and at the quality of labor relations. In the process, management strives to reduce individual and collective resistance (absenteeism, strikes), and to create or improve the identification of the workforce with the company's goals.

> *The second* direction of thrust aimed at exploiting more fully the capabilities and experience of individual workers and the informal personal networks among them. This potential is to be mobilized for work-related solutions to problems and for improvements in the operative work process.

We found the first direction of thrust to be prevalent in those cases where the problem scenario was seen very much in an industrial relations context; the second direction of thrust was found to be prevalent in those cases where the problem scenario was defined in terms of new tasks and new qualification requirements due to the introduction of new technology and higher automation levels.

Shopfloor Self-regulation Through Group Work

Group work principles also played an important role in the strategies of all companies. Theoretically, group work could be a means to achieve many objectives at the same time: a greater job flexibility among individuals (by practicing job rotation), enhanced responsibility of shopfloor workers for cost and quality (by delegating quality control, machine maintenance, and process control responsibilities to the group), and improved social relations in production (by less direct control and more mutual help and support between workers and supervisors).

Group work meant task integration in the horizontal and vertical dimensions, and it meant a certain degree of self-regulation by shopfloor workers regarding their work. The range of tasks to be delegated to the group and the extent of self-regulation varied widely in the discussions about group work in the different companies, but at the time of our research only a few cases could be observed where group work had actually been introduced.

Substitution of Human Labor with Automation

In the beginning of the 1980s, the development of technologies seemed to many company strategists to offer the possibility of dramatically increasing automation levels. This condition was true especially in the area of assembly work where labor relations were poor and where the process layout had remained virtually unchanged since the introduction of the assembly line. Robots, sensors, and computers seemed to offer the potential to strive for the "unmanned" factory. Obviously, no company could afford to remain outside of this technological trend by failing to acquire know-how for high-tech production.

According to our findings not all of the companies regarded high technology as the key to future competitiveness. Only some of them invested heavily in advanced high-tech process technology.

Reduction of Line-paced Jobs

Tying work rhythm and performance to the pace of the assembly line has been a central characteristic of Taylorist–Fordist production organization. In the 1980s, some companies began to abolish the assembly line as the backbone of its work organization even in mass production assembly plants. Whole modules of assembly operations were taken off the main line in order to be done on stationary work places. Such organization can deal more efficiently with an increased variety of car models and options produced in the same plant.

Thus, the number of workplaces that are uncoupled from the flow of the assembly line is increasing in many plants. The gradual abolition of the assembly line in favor of stationary workplaces and the establishment of work areas outside the main line flow allows job design to be more oriented to meaningful division of tasks, and less dominated by the priorities of the moving conveyor belt. This reorganization is reducing the share of extremely short-cycle, repetitive operations. Nevertheless, the classic assembly line still governs the majority of jobs in assembly operations; the new modules (preassembly areas) only comprise one-third of the jobs, even in the factories having such areas.

But not all companies shared the view that the reign of the assembly line is coming to an end. This is definitely not the message that could be taken from the Japanese car plants we visited, although they were not part of this study. Since Japanese ideas of production organization were increasingly becoming a model for "best practice" in the 1980s, advocates of the assembly line still had a strong position. There were cases where the assembly line was even brought back into areas where process planners had originally set up stationary workplaces.

Skilled Workers for Direct Work

It has often been stated that work in the modernized factories of the car industry will increasingly become the domain of skilled labor. With increasing levels of automation, direct work is being done by machines, and the tasks of controlling and maintaining these machines and preventing breakdowns would become dominant, requiring technically skilled workers. In these circumstances, skilled workers would normally be synonymous with journeyman, workers who had gone through apprenticeships as mechanics, electricians, and the like.

According to our findings, it is too early to speak of auto production as the domain of skilled labor because, for one reason, we found a polarization of qualification requirements in the areas of high-tech production.

On the one hand, new jobs of system-monitoring and systems-management with more demanding qualification requirements are emerging; on the other hand, there is the emergence of less qualified jobs, such as feeding parts ("residual work"). But this "left-over work" is losing its importance as the mechanization gaps will probably shrink in the future. From the point of view of management, wage costs would be better minimized by segmentation of the few highly qualified jobs from the many lower qualified jobs. But the increased importance of avoiding machine down times would demand, on the other hand, that all of the workers assigned to installation could detect process irregularities as early as possible, intervene preventively, and support the experts in the event of a disruption. That is why plant management, indeed, should have an interest in deploying skilled workers at the "residual work places" even if they would be overpaid for what they would be doing most of the time.

This arrangement would require a new type of skilled worker who runs the equipment that performs "residual jobs," as well as performs maintenance and system-control tasks. The questions are whether enough skilled workers are available and whether they or the union accept these conditions. In this respect we found a special situation in the German plants. Only here, availability and acceptance could be expected and only here we found examples of auto work becoming skilled trades work. Due to the oversupply of skilled workers, many low-tech assembly jobs were given to skilled tradesman who were thus being deployed "below status" on unskilled jobs. The fact that most skilled tradesman accepted this measure (although grudgingly at times) can also be explained by the labor market situation.

Summary

In summarizing these changes we see a general trend of breaking away from the traditional forms of control over production work. In the traditional automobile factory organized along Taylorist–Fordist lines, everything is geared to prescribing the course of work to the last detail by staff above the "shopfloor" level. Machine-pacing of work through the assembly line, standardization of work performance by the industrial engineering experts, and direct monitoring by the line supervisors is a control structure of Taylorism–Fordism that does not tolerate self-regulation by the workers. This constellation, which stifles initiative and a sense of responsibility among the workers, is now beginning to loosen up in the course of developments that soften the deterministic character of the traditional control structure as shown by

- An increasing number of workplaces being freed from the strict machine-pacing through alternative work design and mechanization.
- The task of setting production standards being increasingly shifted into the production planning phase, thus avoiding the direct confrontation of the experts with the "shopfloor", as was the case in the traditional work study.
- Increased demands of technical expertise requiring a different type of supervisor, who has to be able to deal with problems of process control, material flow, and the technical equipment of his or her area, rather than simply being the commander of "subordinates".
- Routine matters of labor allocation, work organization, and personnel mobility, in part, being given back to the shopfloor for self-regulation.

With these developments, room is opened up for a self-regulation of the operative tasks in the production process. The question of how much autonomy will be given in which functional areas was being debated in all the companies of our sample.

It should be emphasized that more self-regulation on the shopfloor does not mean less control by management. The control possibilities from company headquarters have been increasing, through computer-assisted information and control systems and through comparison and competition among factories, which are increasingly being used as instruments for performance regulation. These elements make it possible for the corporate headquarters to observe the performance profile of their individual organizational units and to measure them against the most efficient and successful examples in their own global company ("best practice"). The competition between factories contributes to externalizing the pressure to adapt, and to strengthening the consciousness of common (survival) interests in the factory. Parallel production of the same product at different sites, growing overcapacities in the industry, modularization of production, and increased pressure to decide on the question of "make or buy" intensify this external pressure on the factories and work forces to adjust. An increase in the self-regulation of tasks to be carried out thus does not necessarily mean the reduction of control, but rather a change in the form of control.

These general findings convey a clear message. The work reforms of the 1980s can neither be interpreted as a purely symbolic policy or even cheap propaganda of management in order to ensure the "acceptance" of the workers and the general public for personnel reduction, the introduction of new technologies, and the restructuring of the industry. Nor can a sweeping renunciation of the traditional Taylorist–Fordist production model be observed. Rather we can observe an unfinished process of development in which differing configurations of the Taylorist–Fordist regulation mode and its negation are visible. Challenges and opportunities for the employees are concentrated in a specific manner at each of these points in the process of development. At no point is there an established model. The picture of a linear improvement of work in the automobile industry through the displacement of Taylorist–Fordist forms of regulation would, in any case, be too simple. Our empirical results also make clearly visible the limitations of the negation forms of the Taylorist–Fordist work organization: separate workplaces do not necessarily mean increased time sovereignty; internal self-regulation of partially autonomous groups is not to be equated with the weakening of external controls; job integration does not mean the abolition of the division of labor, status differentiation, and the segmentation of labor markets within the factory.

Nevertheless, a growing decoupling of the systemic elements of the Taylorist–Fordist model for labor regulation can be observed. In contrast, a close connection of these elements existed well into the 1970s. Standard product, mass production and economies of scale, rigid single-purpose mechanization, strict hierarchical control over labor deployment, fragmented and low-qualified work contents, stressful working conditions, and conflicting labor relations formed a seemingly indissoluble package. According to our observations, this structural connection began to break up in the 1980s. Against the background of the diversification of demand and the development of flexible technologies, combinations are developing that are increasingly becoming more complex: product standardization and diversification go hand-in-hand; flexible and inflexible technology are combined on a microelectronic basis; jobs that require more demanding qualifications and that have been decoupled from the assembly line are nevertheless being carried out according to strictly prescribed times and methods.

The Influence of Company Strategies

We found huge differences among the seventeen plants we investigated with respect to work rules, labor deployment patterns, and direction of change. However, two of our three multinational companies had branch plants in all three research countries (the United States, United Kingdom, and Germany), so most of our plants had "sister plants" in the other countries, often producing the same or a similar product. What influence did the company affiliation, then, have in explaining the differences in reorganizing production and work organization and in the extent to which new forms of work were introduced, and which factors were stressed most in this respect?

Clearly, the companies cannot be seen as merely adapting and reacting to the trends previously described. In strategically choosing a specific direction of work reform and giving priority to certain measures, they actively influenced the trend itself. But none of the companies opted to stay outside the trend and preserve the well-established Taylorist–Fordist ways of work.

The clearest and most important difference between the companies could be found in the question of whether they oriented their strategy toward human or technical factors as the supposedly "decisive" productivity resource. This was indeed a strategic decision, although it is true that the companies were in very different positions with regard to their financial strength and thus their ability to purchase new technology at the beginning of the 1980s. But it would be overly simplified to explain the companies' decision of whether they would give priority to "technology" or to "people" as merely a matter of the power of the purse. More important was the different degree to which the companies were rudely awakened at the beginning of the 1980s. The companies that perceived their very survival to be at stake were presented with the option of making a more fundamental break with past practices or perishing.

Company A clearly emphasized the "people potential" in its reorganization measures. The focus of the measures in its factories was on decentralizing management responsibility and on integrating direct and indirect production tasks, accompanied by the institutionalization of a program for employee participation and of involving employees in problem-solving activities on the shopfloor. The concepts were based on a human relations approach; group work principles did not play a central role. A further characteristic of this strategy is the remarkable emphasis that Company A placed on increasing efficiency and rationalizing labor deployment. The use of new technologies was secondary in this strategic concept. Finally, Company A did not venture into new production concepts that do away with the assembly line.

Table 6.1 shows the differences in the directions of change taken by our three companies. Of course there are differences in the emphasis put on each of these measures by the companies and in the extent to which all of the company-specific measures could be found in all of its plants even in the same country. The table shows the company profile characteristic in the country where the companies had their headquarters because it seems plausible that here company strategies would find their most authentic expression.

In contrast to Company A, Company C clearly emphasized automation in its measures. As a complementary measure, C considerably expanded its programs for initial and further vocational training and adapted them to the new technological requirements. Less importance was attached to questions of the task integration, employee involvement, and group work principles at the time of our investigation. It was a clear policy to reduce the number of directly line-paced jobs by various measures. The most important of these was, however, assembly automation. Finally, there was a clear strategy to let skilled workers run production in their highly automated areas.

Company B's strategy could be characterized as maximizing its options. Different paths were being tested in pilot plants in the company. The long-run goal was to achieve a synthesis of the technology and the human factor strategies. To this

TABLE 6.1 Emphasis of Change Measures by Companies

	Company		
Directions of Change	*A*	*B*	*C*
1. Task integration	+		
2. Employee participation	+	+	
3. Shopfloor self-regulation via group work		+	
4. Automation as much as possible		+	+
5. Reduction of line-paced jobs			+
6. Skilled workers for direct work			+

end, the company introduced programs of employee participation, but also programs of high-tech automation aiming at the "unmanned" factory, as well as sociotechnical programs to restructure work on the basis of group work principles. But this multifaceted strategy was only valid at the company level. On the level of individual plants, we found insecurity as to which direction the development should go.

Just as important as the differences in the main emphasis of the strategies of the three companies were differences in the way they were being implemented. Profiles typical for the different companies as a whole could also be observed. For Company A, the human-factor-oriented strategy was pursued in its plants—companywide—with remarkable consistency and speed. This approach was true for the goal of job integration as well as for employee participation. A campaign, also carried out publicly in the company, attempted to secure the acceptance or toleration of the work forces and the local managements for the program. The speed and the breadth of this process of reorganization can be summed up in a paradoxial formula: the strengthening of management and employee participation on the shopfloor was pushed through by means of a tightly centralized company organization. This paradox of a new combination of highly centralized company management and the strengthening of decentralized self-regulation at the lower levels is the key to understanding the organizational change in Company A. The highly centralized form of control was faced, admittedly, with the limits of the national industrial relations. The measures could be rapidly introduced and enjoyed initial success in the company's American and German factories, whereas they were defeated for the time being by union objections in the British factories. National-specific factors came into play here.

Company B, with its strategy of maximizing its options—that is, simultaneously testing several alternatives—increased the variety in forms of factory labor regulation within its global organization. In contrast to the far-reaching innovations in production technology or work and social organization in some pilot plants, the bulk of the assembly plants remained limited to an observer role at the time of our empirical investigations. At the level of local management, a greater insecurity over the goals of future development existed than that which we had observed for Company A's local management. The diffusion process of new organizational concepts into Company B's factories proceeded in a less centralized fashion and was more strongly oriented toward individual local initiatives. In view of this pattern of diffusion, it is no wonder that the influence of the national affiliation of the factories showed through a greater extent than at Company A.

At Company C, there seemed to be no ambiguity and hesitation about how the factory of the future was to be envisioned. The future was automation and the personnel considerations concentrated on the necessary training requirements. At the time of our final investigations, however, the shortcomings of this strategy were already recognized.

Differences in emphasis and priorities as to the directions of change described—whether companies focus on human factors or technology factors—does not say anything about the quality of these measures in terms of work goals. Company A's strategy was designed to take advantage of a potential for rationalization that could obviously be attained in the shorter run. Holding back with automation meant at the same time that the layout of production technology remained largely unchanged, so that possibilities for improving working conditions through technology and process design could not be realized. Company A thus still retained the traditional forms of assembly line organization in the factories we studied. On the other hand, Company B's and C's factories had already transferred a considerable share of their assembly tasks to production areas without an assembly line. These new work structures, generally introduced in connection with new production technologies, provided significantly improved working conditions, at least from an ergonomic point of view.

The Influence of the Factories' National Affiliation

The national affiliation of the factory site turned out to be a significant intervening factor that often comes through more strongly than the influence of company affiliation. Table 6.2 shows considerable differences in the directions of change found in the various plants of the same company located in different countries. There were also differences between plants of the same company of the same country but the influence of location was clearly weaker than the influence of company or country affiliation.

As can be seen in the table, Company A's American plants emphasized task integration and employee participation; its British plants' task integration was the only major direction of change; at the German plants we found task integration, employee participation, and the deployment of skilled workers on direct production jobs as characteristic directions of change.

In the American plants of Company B, employee participation and the introduction of group work were dominant features. The company's other plants ventured into automation as much as possible and partially abolished the assembly line. Thus, the intracountry differences between Company A and B were, in fact, bigger than expressed here. In any case, Company B's British plants were characterized by new assembly concepts, as were the German plants. The direction of people-oriented measures, that is, task integration or group work or deployment of skilled workers in direct production jobs, was quite unclear in these European plants at the time of our study.

Company C focused clearly on automation and the work organization concepts. These concepts had been devised for automation areas centered around

TABLE 6.2 Emphasis of Change Measures
by Companies and Countries

Company	USA	UK	FRG
A	1, 2	1	1, 2, 6
B	2, 3	5	5
C	—	—	4, 5, 6

Note: Refer to the numbered items in Table 6.1.

skilled workers deployed in production. A three-pronged range of measures aimed at diminishing the role of the assembly line for determining speed and rhythm of the individual workers: firstly, the introduction of automated transfer-lines in assembly areas had the effect of decoupling human labor from the direct production process; secondly, areas with stationary workplaces linked by automated guided vehicles were created, though to a smaller extent than at Company B in the European plants; thirdly, due to union demands line work was organized in such a way that individual work cycles became three to four times lower than at the assembly plants in most other companies we investigated.

Among the national factors that most conspicuously influenced the direction of change in the various countries were the politics and institutions of industrial relations and of vocational training.

In the United States, the companies made the transformation of industrial relations a central element in their strategy for work reform. Since the beginning of the 1980s, the purposeful change of industrial relations has been formulated and supported jointly by the top representatives of the companies and the unions. At the local level this policy was also jointly supported in the majority of cases because it was made perfectly clear by the company headquarters that the decisions over future investments and thus over the survival of the production sites were strongly influenced by the demonstration of their willingness and ability to change. Under these conditions the change strategy focused mainly on human factors. Employee participation programs played a central role in securing the compliance with job integration or the introduction of group work.

The strategy of transformation from above had already taken root at the factory level in the American automobile industry at the time of our investigation. The traditional structure for regulating labor deployment (seniority and demarcation rules) were still partially in force. However, they had already lost their unconditional validity.

Where advanced automation projects were implemented in the United States, the importance of vocational training politics and institutions became clear although in a negative sense: not only were there too few tradesman with adequate (especially electronic-related) skills, production workers were also incapable of coping with the new technologies. Due to the status consciousness of skilled workers and union policy, the deployment of skilled workers as direct production workers (as in the German plants) was out of the question in the American plants at the time of our study.

The decisive importance of union cooperation for such a strategy of institutional change can be seen in the case of the British companies. Here it was not possible to obtain a consensus between the companies and unions at the top level and to jointly support programs for change, as in the United States. Because of the differences in the union structures, a strategy "from the top down" would hardly have had a chance of success anyway. The influence of the unions on the process of change in work has always been strong in the United Kingdom, but it was limited to establishing and consolidating veto power. This weakness of the unions led to a special selectivity furthering traditional strategies for rationalization through industrial engineering and mechanization that, because of shifts in power relations, could be pushed through almost unimpeded by management. Programs to develop employee participation or group work, on the other hand, were blocked by the unions because they required a formal agreement in the arena of industrial relations. In its inability to develop its own concepts, British management apparently perceived its scope of action to be especially limited by the dependency relations in the European networks of their companies. We observed a growing consciousness of heteronomy at the British sites. Production organization and technological equipment were seen as "German concepts" imposed upon the British factories by the European company headquarters.

But the prerequisites for greater British autonomy in developing their own solutions would have been better performance and a process of institutional change that was jointly supported by unions and management. These prerequisites did not yet exist at the time of our study, despite remarkable examples of change in behavior within individual plants. Independent innovations in work and social organization for regulating labor could not emerge under these conditions. Concepts like employee participation, group work, or production concepts without the assembly line were regarded as foreign imports from either the United States or the continent. The British constellation was apparently not particularly fertile soil for developing independent non-Taylorist forms for regulating labor in the 1980s.

Characteristic for developments in the German context is that the change in labor was being carried out in and through existing institutions. The companies' restructuring process in the German automobile industry did not include a specific strategy for transforming the institutions. The system of industrial relations remained, so to speak, outside the brackets of the restructuring. The dual system of interest representation by the union and codetermination by works councils elected by all workers as the central institution of industrial relations showed a relatively high affinity to recent trends toward de-Taylorization. Along with this affinity came a specific promotion of mechanization and forms of labor deployment centering on skilled workers.

The statutory rights of the German works council to information and participation had supported a pattern of cooperative problem-solving at the factory level. At the same time, the works council's members and union representatives have been able to develop their own concepts and alternatives for organizing work, not the least because of the institutions of codetermination. (We did not find a comparable pattern of union involvement in job design in either of the other countries studied). It has been possible, on this basis, to negotiate future oriented arrangements between labor and management. As a result, the institutions for labor policy and vocational training have been a resource for the restructuring process of the 1980s, and for highly increasing productivity in society.

The institutional peculiarities in the German context seemed to foster specific solutions in regard to work organization and patterns of labor deployment. Three indicators supporting the thesis of a special German development could be observed.

1. The exceptional vocational training and labor market situation provides the factories with a skilled worker potential that is also deployable for direct production tasks, and can thus also be used for new forms of work organization and new job descriptions in direct production. The growing use of skilled workers in direct production increases the necessity and the possibility of creating "intelligent" work structures. Corresponding to this situation, a close connection has emerged between the surplus of skilled workers and the degree of innovation in the work organization in the German assembly plants.

2. Because of legal and contractual regulations, absentee rates due to illness and the percentage of disabled workers in German plants are much higher (about three times) than in the British and American plants. To overcome the restrictions for labor deployment this situation created, management is more dependent on job design and the use of technology. Management has to improve working conditions and job design to make work more attractive. In the American and British plants, restrictions lie more in the area of informal work practices and are tackled by management in the arena of industrial relations.

3. The particular profile of demands by the unions and works councils in the Federal Republic of Germany is clearly aimed at reducing line-paced work or at least loosening the link between the individual's work rhythm and machine or assembly-line cycle times. This decoupling has led to alternative solutions in process design and work organization being considered. In contrast, a one minute cycle time was still considered by the production planners in the United States to be the ultimate in work layout for the 1980s. The average work cycles in German plants, which are much longer than in American plants, are in line with qualification requirements, even for simple line work, that are considerably higher than those in the American plants. The gap between assembly line work and the work requirements at stationary workplaces with more comprehensive tasks is clearly smaller. The smaller gap in skills among workers in Germany explains why a changeover to forms of labor without an assembly line with a given work force faces fewer difficulties there than in the American context.

In summary, the national systems of industrial relations and labor policy institutions in each of the three countries were related to systematic cross-national differences in the objectives and priorities of restructuring. Our study revealed three different nationally specific types of rationalization. In the United States the dominant pattern was participation-oriented rationalization (QWL-rationalization [quality of work life]); in Great Britain, Taylorist rationalization was still dominant; and in the Federal Republic of Germany, a type of rationalization oriented toward skilled workers could be observed. These broad national patterns of selection overlapped with the company-specific patterns.

Models for Future Development

With the dissolution of the Taylorist–Fordist control system there are, above all, two lines of development that could fulfill the function of a model for future developments: the "German model" of labor regulation revolving around the use of skilled workers, and the "Japanese model" of group-oriented labor regulation. (The "Swedish model" is not discussed here. It is in many ways similar to the German model but they differ considerably in terms of training systems and measures to upgrade skills on the shopfloor; see Berggren 1991). Both the German and Japanese developmental models are characterized by a degree of self-regulation of shopfloor work, and both employ a type of worker who, through his or her competence and willingness to accept responsibility, is clearly different from the unskilled mass laborer. Despite these common features, there are important differences between the two models (see Table 6.3).

At the center of the German model is the skilled worker and a specific under-standing of skilled work as a "profession." This understanding includes several features: interest in the work, a willingness to accept comprehensive responsibility (also crossing over the borders of one's own task area), and a large degree of self-regulation in carrying out the work. This model presupposes a "qualification offen-sive," above and beyond the direct company needs for skilled workers, which, in turn, is dependent on institutions and politics of vocational training. By this model we are referring to the societal prerequisites for a specific form of labor regulation as they exist in the educational system in the Federal Republic of Germany. It is clear that the model of skilled worker-centered work regulation is especially impor-tant for modern technology management. The typical ideal goal of the German approach is qualified labor, uncoupled from the production cycle and the rhythm of the machines. Uncoupling work from the flow of production is the prerequisite for a type of labor with increased possibilities for self-regulation and with increased responsibility.

The Japanese approach also gives a central role to skilled labor, though not in the sense of uncoupled skilled labor. Rather, the typical ideal for the Japanese model is self-regulation under the pressure of the assembly line and the production pace. Characteristic is the allocation of personnel that aims at the best possible per-formance and its permanent improvement, that is, the continual intensification of labor. This goal stands in contrast to the industrial engineering practices in Western companies that aim for "normal" performance ("fair day's work principle") and are restricted in their possibilities for a continuous review of the established time standards. In the Japanese automobile industry, the work group is the starting point for an integrated job understanding, for making flexible and expanding labor deployment, and for the qualification of the workers. Self-regulation is thus not based on skilled worker competence and a professional ethic.

TABLE 6.3 Paradigms for the Production Organization of the Future

Germany	Japan
Infiltration of skilled workers into direct production	OJT trained workers with high general-base qualification
Decoupling from the production cycle	Determined by the production cycle
Large/wholistic job content	Short, task-determined job cycle
Mixed teams (skilled/unsilled)	Homogenous teams (OJT trained workers)
High degree of team autonomy by process-design	Low degree of team autonomy by process-design

The question of the transferability of group- or skilled-worker oriented organizational alternatives is also posed for the British and American companies in view of increasing technological requirements of the future. The considerable increase in vocational training in British factories hints at the German model. Although such a development is not yet achieveable in British labor policy, there could be an expansion of the skilled worker potential beyond the needs of the skilled labor departments in British factories, with similar consequences as can be seen in the German automobile industry. Such a development is being furthered by the centralization and creation of European company branches and the corresponding standardization of production and rationalization concepts.

In contrast to the U.K. experience, the considerations of the American companies are obviously more influenced by Japanese concepts. The formation of production groups in the unskilled area and flexibility and expansion of the workers' areas of deployment is being sought. Training measures with the goal of forming groups and the teaching of group problem-solving techniques also play a much more important role in policies for worker qualification than does the training of skilled workers. In the German context, on the other hand, a potential for dealing with technology by using skilled workers can be observed, which arose through a "softening up" of the skilled worker status from above. In the long run, on the other hand, the strategy of group related retraining for unskilled workers could allow the necessary qualification potential to emerge in the American plants, too.

Transfering either the German or the Japanese management concepts poses problems. Social and cultural prerequisites play an important role in explaining the Japanese concepts. In fact it is quite disputed among "Japanologists" whether these concepts can be transferred to the West at all and whether it makes sense to isolate certain elements and use them like "recipes." Nevertheless, most Western companies are more inclined toward transferring Japanese concepts than German concepts. The strong anchoring of the German way in the structures of codetermination and the corporatist system of vocational education would set greater institutional and legal limits on the company headquarters' scope for action and decision making. Such infringements on management's prerogatives seem to be more threatening to most Western companies than the risks associated with borrowing from Japan.

In the area of the use of skilled workers and skilled-worker supported solutions, one cannot only consider the circumstances that promote them in the German automobile industry, but also the circumstances hampering them in the United States and Great Britain. The distinct skilled worker status in the Federal Republic has significantly changed in the 1980s. While the march of the skilled worker into production is already quite far advanced in the German factories, the classic separation between production tasks as unskilled labor on the one hand, and technical support functions as skilled labor on the other still dominated in the British and American assembly plants. This "German path" of labor regulation centered on skilled workers has shown itself to be advantageous for coping with the requirements of new technologies. The German factories have, in fact, been able to meet the new technological requirements resulting from the wave of modernization at the beginning of the 1980s with less friction thanks to their skilled worker potential.

Conclusions

What are the prospects for the different paths and models? What do national specific pecularities mean for the future chances of the national production sites? According to our findings, there were enormous cross-national differences in staffing levels between factories, even when these were largely similar as regards product, production technology, and degree of vertical integration (see Jürgens, Malsch, and Dohse 1989, 311ff; Krafcik 1988, 46ff). There are apparently considerable hindrances to increasing the work efficiency and correspondingly reorganizing the work organization.

In view of the efficiency of Japanese production, the cost question was of paramount importance, especially for the American companies in their adaptation strategies at their North American sites. In Europe, on the other hand, the competitive pressure of the Japanese had not been as intense up to the time of our investigation. Because of this condition, management could consider the costs with greater composure, which was all the more possible because their increasingly expensive car variants were selling well, likewise the middle and lower size categories. Also, the increased production costs of these vehicles could be passed on to the customers, in light of their reduced price sensitivity. This trend toward higher valued model and equipment variants was especially useful for Volkswagen. In the strategy of increasing the product value, an ideal line of compromise with the worker representations was found as lay-off effects due to automation and mechanization could be largely offset by the tendency toward higher valued model and equipment variants.

During the 1980s, the strategy of moving to higher valued product was the key to the success of the German automobile industry when compared to the other traditional Western manufacturing countries. This strategy also has its risks, though. The Japanese competitors have increasingly turned to higher valued cars and equipment. Because they still have considerable cost advantages over the German manufacturers, even in the segments, growing pressure on price and cost structures can be expected in the future. With a relatively uniform state of development of product technology, the traditional quality and image advantages of the German automobile industry will lose their importance as a parameter of competition.

Fundamental for the question of the future chances for the "German way" is thus the appraisal of the potential savings of future technological development. If one assumes that the competition on the world market will be decisively fought out in the arena of technology, then the goal of short-range cost savings through traditional measures for increasing efficiency would only have secondary importance. According to our findings, this assumption has more supporters in German companies than in American companies. We are not speaking of reducing wage costs in direct production through the use of technology. Rather, we are referring to computer integrated manufacturing (CIM) as a means of achieving integration and flexibility of the production processes, of cutting costs through new logistics systems, and of speeding up product and process innovation. At present, none of the automobile companies has achieved a decisive breakthrough in the field of computer integration. The strategy of a determined leap into the age of high technology, as it was attempted at General Motors, thus remains risky. A concentration on the technological solutions to future problems could lead to similar experiences as we have already seen in the 1980s. The possibilities of the new technologies were overestimated, while the chances of innovations in work and social organization were underestimated.

In the near future, with intensified competition on the world market, those companies and production sites that will be able to assert themselves are those able to effectively combine computer integration and the development of human capital, new forms of group work, and Taylorist work efficiency. It is possible that we will even see a synthesis of the Japanese and the German models: group formation, job integration, and extreme work efficiency in manual mass production according to the Japanese example; skilled-worker oriented team formation and professionalization in the high technology areas and in the service functions according to the German example. Given the present state of the industry, such a scenario is not without possibility for the 1990s. Whether it will be realized in some form or another, or whether another model will determine the future of labor in the automobile industry, can hardly be predicted in view of the continued high dynamics of development in the world's automobile industry. Today only one thing is certain: change.

Notes

1. This project, "Challenges and Opportunities of the Current Restructuring in the World Automobile Industry for its Employees," was carried out in the context of the Massachusetts Institute of Technology's research program on "The Future of the Automobile" by K. Dohse, T. Malsch, and myself. This chapter draws on the final report by U. Jürgens, T. Malsch, and K. Dohse (1989). The English version *(Modern Times in the Automobile Industry, Strategies of Production Modernization in a Country and Company Comparison)* is forthcoming from Cambridge University Press.

References

Barnes, R. M. 1980. *Motion and Time Study Design and Measurement of Work,* 7th ed. New York: Wiley.

Berggren, C. 1991. *Von Ford zu Volvo: Automobilherstellung in Schweden.* Berlin: Springer-Verlag.

Cummings, T. G., and E. S. Molloy. 1977. *Improving Productivity and the Quality of Worklife.* New York/London: Praeger.

Glaser, E. M. 1976. *Productivity Gains Through Worklife Improvements.* New York/London: Harcourt Brace Jovanovich.

Jürgens, U., T. Malsch, and K. Dohse. 1989. *Moderne Zeiten in der Automobilfabrik. Strategien der Produktionsmodernisierung und Arbeitsregulation im Länder- und Konzernvergleich.* Berlin: Springer-Verlag.

Krafcik, J. F. 1988. "Triumph of the Lean Production System," *Sloan Management Review* **30**(1):41–52.

Lawler, E. E., III. 1978. "The New Plant Revolution," *Organizational Dynamics* **6**(3):3–12.

Lawler, E. E., III. 1986. *High-Involvement Management.* London/San Francisco: Jossey-Bass Publishers.

Milkovich, G. T., and W. F. Glueck. 1985. *Personnel, Human Resource Management: A Diagnostic Approach,* 4th ed. Plano, Tex.: Business Publications.

Przeworski, A., and H. Teune. 1970. *The Logic of Comparative Social Inquiry.* New York: Wiley.

7

New Technology and the Organization of Work: British and Japanese Factories

D. HUGH WHITTAKER

A machine-tool cuts, bores, grinds, shapes, and otherwise processes metal with various tools, the movements of which are conventionally controlled by levers and handles manipulated by an operator. With numerical control (NC), the movements are controlled instead by a predetermined code or program. The program is fed into the machine's controller, and it directs the movements of the machine. As the name suggests, computer numerical control (CNC) involves the use of a reprogramable computerized controller.

NC/CNC has aroused a good deal of controversy because it allegedly enables managers to replace willful skilled craftsmen with machine minders and button pushers on the one hand, and programmers on the other, who are more amenable to management control. Managers thereby achieve through technology an end which has constantly eluded them through organizational and disciplinary means. Braverman (1974) contended that this possibility is inevitably seized upon by capitalists, while other writers (e.g., Senker 1986) have suggested that "deskilling" may represent one management strategy, but having the operator do the programming and enriching the job—"reskilling"—is equally feasible. Both views are challenged by a study of CNC use in German and British factories that found that the main determinants of CNC use were factory size and batch size (Sorge et al. 1983). The larger the factory, the more likely it is to have separate planning and programming departments, and the larger the batch, the more likely it is that tasks will be broken up. These determinants cut across country, although national differences in training and production organization were noted.

Is there a country factor in the use of CNC? The findings of Sorge and colleagues would suggest a minor one. However, if management strategies—or the institutionally embedded employment and industrial relations—do influence the way CNC is used, they should be highlighted through an Anglo-Japanese comparison, given the respective reputations in industrial relations, employment styles, and production organization.

Nine factories in both Britain and Japan, matched by size, batch size, and product are examined in this chapter. Some are technology and industry leaders, but not all; small and large factories are included. While not statistically representative, they constitute a cross section of the respective mechanical engineering industries. Machining was a central operation in each, and all except the smallest Japanese factory had at least three CNC machines. Some details of the factories are given in Table 7.1.

This chapter focuses on the organization of work around computer numerical control (CNC) machine-tools in the eighteen factories; in particular, how the various tasks are divided up, who does them, and why. It describes qualitatively different approaches to CNC use—and innovation in general—in the two countries. The approach predominant in the British factories may be termed a "craft" approach, in which a skilled (craft) operator is responsible for the machine, programmers are selected from these operators and there is relatively little unmanned and parallel operation. The "technical" approach of many of the Japanese factories, however, is characterized by a preference for adaptability (hence youth) over experience for operators and programmers, and by greater emphasis on unmanned and parallel operation. These differing approaches cut across product, factory size, and even batch size, and have implications for competitive performance.

The discussion starts with levels of automation, followed by work organization. These topics alone are insufficient to grasp the respective approaches, however. The

TABLE 7.1 The Eighteen Factories (1987)

Factory	No. of Employees	Average Batch	Product Market	No. of CNC	% of CNC	First NC/CNC
J1	7	4–5	Subcon	2	18	1982
J2*	19	2000	Subcon	6	13	1975
J4	42	4–5	Press	7	45	1979
J9	86	3–4	Diecast	28	41	1978
J45	453	2–3	Mach.W	15	17	1973
J50	504	1–3	Ind.machX	3	3	1971
J66	657	10–30	Ind.machX	10	13	1973
J140*	1400	250	Ya	181	12	1976
J180	1800	3–5	Yb	100	25	1970
B4	35	6	Subcon	3	6	1980
B8	81	6–10	Ind.machX	4	23	1984
B11	110	10–15	Ind.machX	3	13	1982
B12*	115	500+	Subcon	17	45	1975
B39	390	6–7	Mach.W	6	10	1970
B71	709	15–30	Ind.machX	18	15	1972
B145	1450	6–7	Ind.machX	39	11	1958
B80*	800	350	Ya	16	5	1967
B120	1200	4–10	Yb	30	15	1961

Notes: J = Japanese factory, B = British factory. The number following is the number of employees divided by ten and rounded. For example, J45 indicates a Japanese factory with at least 450 employees.

% of CNC means proportion of NC/CNC to total machine tools in the machine shop area(s) excluding machine tools "never used."

*Large-batch factories. Products are coded to preserve anonymity.

backgrounds of operators and programmers are important, and practices such as unmanned and parallel operation must be considered. These, in turn, are linked to broader differences in orientations to change. After considering these, implications for competitiveness are discussed.

Level of Automation

Of the group examined, the first purchaser of NC machines was one of the large British factories, in 1958. Another British factory followed three years later, and another six years after that (Table 7.1). The first of the Japanese factories made its initial purchase in 1970, a full twelve years after the first British factory. All the other Japanese factories except the smallest, however, acquired at least one NC/CNC machine during the 1970s, whereas three of the smaller British factories did not make their first purchase until the early 1980s. In other words, the Japanese were later onto the scene, but the diffusion into smaller factories was more rapid.

The smaller factories in both countries were using the machines on a stand-alone basis. No robots were involved, nor transfer machines. Some machines, however, were fitted with pallet tables to enable multiple parts to be machined automatically. These included the large-batch factories, but also individual machines in some small-batch factories, notably Japanese.

In most of the larger factories, too, the machines were used on a stand-alone basis, with at least one or two machines fitted with pallet tables. One of the Japanese factories had a mini flexible manufacturing system (FMS), with two machining centers fed and unloaded by a programmed cart on rails, as well as three flexible manufacturing cells (FMC), with CNC machines fed by robots. Another Japanese factory was on the point of installing two FMS lines. Its British counterpart had also partially installed a mini FMS, but the plan had been shelved while new owners considered rationalization steps.

Limited CAD/CAM—computerized automation from design through to manufacturing—was in operation at one of the British factories, as well as limited DNC (direct numerically controlled) in which a program is downloaded from a host computer into CNC machine controllers. At the large-batch Japanese factory forty of the CNC machines were connected by transfer machines, while at its British counterpart there were fewer transfer machines, but two machining centers fed by robots.

In sum, while the later-starting Japanese factories were purchasing CNC machines more rapidly than many of the British factories, there was not a quantum difference in the ratio of CNC to total machines, nor in the linkage of the CNC machines to more advanced forms of automation. Again, though, the Japanese factories were moving more quickly in this direction (particularly with brisk investment in the late 1980s). More striking differences lay elsewhere.

Basic Organization of Work

Fruin and Nishiguchi describe in Chapter 12 the gradual and partial uptake of just-in-time (JIT) systems, even within Japan. Of the nine Japanese factories in my survey, only the largest two had embarked upon JIT in any systematic fashion, and predictably only the large-batch one was actually organized with transfer machines linking CNC machines in process order, kanban pulling production, and on lights, and so on. Their British counterparts were in the process of introducing module production, with the large-batch factory being more thoroughgoing. This module production system was strongly influenced by traditional JIT concepts, but it also attempted to build in module costing and accounting procedures to eliminate waste and raise efficiency. Despite management interest in JIT, however, the machine shops elsewhere in both countries were laid out by and large according to machine type, sometimes with a separate CNC section, sometimes without. Again, the most striking national differences were not in physical work organization, but on the human side of the human–machine interface.

The human involvement encompasses operators' task ranges. These can be broadly divided into operating, setting, programming and related tasks. Operating means at the very least "button pushing" and machine minding. Often operators are involved in loading and unloading the work pieces from their machines, although there may be separate "slingers" to do this. Setting involves attaching the work piece to a jig or fixture so that it can be cut along the desired planes, and selecting and fixing the tools to do the cutting. Depending on the machine and work piece, setting may necessitate advanced knowledge of materials, tools, and machining processes. Thus setting ability is considered the hallmark of a skilled operator. Where batches are large there are commonly separate "skilled" setters and "semiskilled" operators, so that the setters' skills are not wasted on long periods of machine minding. Operating and setting may constitute progressive rungs on a career ladder, however. Programming involves writing a program or filling in variations on a "skeleton" program, and testing it on the machine and correcting it if necessary (proving and editing). Proving and editing may be done either by specialist programmers, setters (or foremen) or operators, in varying combinations. Then there are related tasks, such as inspection, preventive and routine maintenance, finishing and filing off rough edges (deburring) and so on, which may be done by operators or other workers.

Table 7.2 shows the ranges of tasks performed by operators in the various factories in my survey. All operators, naturally, were involved in the basic operating tasks. Almost all, with the exception of those in one large British factory and (at times) one Japanese factory were also involved in loading and unloading their machines. The demarcation in the British factory had been eliminated several years earlier in other large British factories.

The above-cited tasks took up most of the operator's time in the large-batch factories. With one exception (J2), where setting was a relatively simple operation, there were specialist setters, even in the other large-batch Japanese factory where operators did a limited range of tasks but on several machines. Where batch sizes were small, however, operators did both setting and operating. And in the large-batch factories, where setting was already separated from operating, if anyone on the shopfloor was involved in programming, it was the setters or foremen rather than operators (again with the same exception). The observations of Sorge and his colleagues (1983) about the importance of batch size are thus supported.

There were differences in the small-batch factories, however. It did appear that

TABLE 7.2 CNC Operator Tasks

	Related Tasks			Operating Setting					Programming	
	c	b	a	A	B	C	D	E	F	G
J1		——————————————————————————————							- - - - - - - - -	
J2*	- -	—————————————————————————————							- - - -	
J4		- ———————————————————————————								
J9	- - - - - - - - - - - - -	———————————————————————							-	
J45	- - - - - - - -	—————————————————————————————								
J50	- - - - - -	—————————————————————————————							- -	
J66	- - - - - - -	———————————————————————————								
J140*	—————————————————			-			- -			
J180	- - - - - -	———————————————————————————								
B4	- - - -	———————————————————————						- - - - -		
B8	- - - -	———————————————————————						- - - - -		
B11	- - - -	———————————————————————						- - - -		
B12*	- - - -	———————————————————				- - - - - - - - - -			
B39	- - -	———————————————————————						- - -		
B71		—————————————————————						- - -		
B145	- - -	———————————————————————————————								
B80*	- -	—————————————————————								
120	- - -	———————————————————————						- -		

Notes: A dashed line indicates either task done on some occasions or by some operators.
A = loading and unloading; B = button pushing, mach. minding; C = tool setting; D = machine setting; E = program proving/editing; F = simple part programming; G = all part programming.
a = deburring; b = inspection; c = parallel operating.

more operators were involved in programming in the Japanese factories than in the British, although in the majority of the Japanese factories there were also specialist programmers, and there was quite a lot of de facto programming by British operators even where programming was supposedly done off the shopfloor. The personal views of the production managers and production engineering managers influenced these arrangements. In one factory, small batches were cited as a reason why operators should be involved in programming, in others as a reason why they should not. Those who supported operator programming thought that the operator who was nearest the work process and could make the best judgements. Those who supported specialist programming cited noise and distractions on the shopfloor as well as downtime. Where there were specialist programmers, programming in large factories was carried out in the production engineering office, and in small factories, in the foreman's office.

There were also differences between the countries in terms of related tasks. These were more likely to be seen as part and parcel of the Japanese operator's job, although there were full-time inspectors, as well as deburrers and sweepers. The operator was expected to keep himself busy while a part was being machined—it was company time—which sometimes involved operating a second machine. There was certainly no reading of newspapers on longer batches, of which one British manager complained. Conscious attempts were being made in the British factories to extend operators' tasks and reduce the number of full-time inspectors—and deburrers and broom pushers. These attempts had met with limited success. Most operators did some debugging of the systems or software and many were involved in at least some inspection work. When it came to preventative mainte-nance and sweeping, though, some were more conscientious than others. Managers expected them to take on these tasks if they could, but their first priority was to ensure that their machine was running smoothly.

In brief, there were differences between the countries concerning operators' task ranges, mostly in the realm of related tasks, as one would expect from the flexibility debates. Batch size and factory size were important influences, although batch size was more important in Britain and factory size was more important in Japan, per-haps explainable by the following hypothesis. Taylorite—or Babbage—principles have penetrated British factories more than Japanese. Craftsmen retained the skilled parts of their jobs, and the rest were performed by semiskilled or unskilled workers, with only recent attempts at reversing this process. This situation is most clearly seen in large-batch production. In Japan, on the other hand, the nature of employment relations leads to less significance—in terms of pay and control—placed on task ranges. Operators may still be required to perform a wide range of tasks, or operate several machines, where batch sizes are large, and factory size rather than batch size exerts a greater influence on task ranges.

Unfortunately, many discussions of CNC use end with work organization and task ranges. What is more striking about CNC use in the eighteen factories, though, is who was doing the tasks. Differences here are symptomatic of a qualitatively dif-ferent approach to CNC in the two countries.

Programmers and Operators

Characterizations

Different types of workers were involved in CNC work in the two countries, indi-cating different qualities for which managers were looking. Although somewhat more operator programming was carried out in the Japanese factories, there were specialist programmers, and their backgrounds were very different from those of the British programmers. We might expect specialist programming to be slotted into the upper end of an operator's career ladder in Japan in order to utilize knowledge of the machining process, tools, and materials gained on the shopfloor, and in order to give a promotion to office work. Table 7.3, however, suggests a different arrange-ment.

In all the British factories at least some of the programmers had started off as operators; in most of them, all had. Exceptions were those involved in experimental DNC work, and two who had moved from technician to drafting and tool drafting to work study in production engineering, and then to programming. Most of the programmers were time-served (had done apprenticeships), and had done other production engineering jobs such as work study before programming.

By contrast, in only one of the five Japanese factories that used programmers were any of the programmers recruited from the shopfloor, and there the practice had been discontinued. Not only had most not come from the shopfloor, but pro-gramming was their first job in the company after their initial orientation and train-ing. Rather than traditional machining skills, their managers were looking for youth, adaptability, and mathematical skills. In the factories where traditional skills

TABLE 7.3 Backgrounds of Programmers

Factory	No. of CNC	No. of Programmers	No. from Shopfloor	Average Years on Shopfloor
J1	2	0	NA	NA
J2*	6	0	NA	NA
J4	7	0	NA	NA
J9	28	4	0	0
J45	15	1½	0	0
J50	3	1	0	0
J66	10	0	NA	NA
J140*	181	6	0	0
J180	100	20	13	5
B4	3	½	½	20
B8	4	½	½	14
B11	3	1	1	4
B12*	17	4	4	6
B39	6	2	2	8
B71	18	2	2	5
B145	39	7	7	5
B80*	16	5	3	15
B120	30	23†	13	15

Note: NA means "not applicable" as they did not use programmers.
*Large-batch factories
†Thirteen spend only 25–30% of their time programming

were valued most, programming was kept on the shopfloor, except for one instance, where it was done by a graduate engineer. The general trend, however, was of using less machining-experienced programmers. In some cases, young women (so-called office ladies) were assigned to programming. If the programmers had a question, they could ask their supervisor, and they were expected to look up speeds and feeds in manuals if necessary.

Similar differences were evident in the backgrounds of the operators (Table 7.4). In seven of the British factories, all CNC operators had prior experience on manual (conventional) machines. In the two factories which had taken workers directly onto CNC without prior operating experience, the practice was considered exceptional and had been discontinued. In six of the factories, the majority of operators were time-served (two of the exceptions being the large-batch factories), and in five the average length of operator experience on manual machines prior to being assigned to CNC was at least ten years.

By contrast, in five of the Japanese factories, workers had been taken directly onto CNC without prior machining experience, and in two others, after their "probationary" period of three to six months. In only one of the factories was the average prior experience on manual machines more than ten years. Two of the larger factories stressed that their operators needed to have machining experience, and one other said that machining experience was important, but they had been forced to compromise because of rapid growth. Even the more cautious of the factories,

TABLE 7.4 Years of Operating Experience on Manual
Machines Prior to NC/CNC Assignment and Average Ages

Factory	Minimum	Maximum	Average	Average Age
J1	0	6	3	28
J2*	0	4	1	27
J4	0.4	2	1	20
J9	0.4	27	3	35
J45	0	12	6	34
J50	3.5	9	7	31
J66	6	29	14	32
J140*	0	—	—	23
J180	0	5	2	27
B4	4	38	15	35
B8	6	37	22	41
B11	2	20	11	34
B12*	0	8+†	4	30
B39	0.5	20	6	31
B71	3	23	9	30
B145	3	30	7	28
B80*	3	35+	10+	42
B120	3	35+	15	41

Note: British figures do not include the first year of apprenticeship.
*Large-batch features.
†"That question is irrelevant because those skills are not needed now."

though, were now requiring less experience. Said one manager: "At first we had very skilled operators working on them [NC/CNC], now, not so skilled. We've got a combination now." At the large-batch larger factory (J140), where the production manager said questions about prior machining experience were "irrelevant because those skills are not needed now," experienced operators had also been assigned at first.

While Japanese managers were opting for less experienced operators, many British managers were opting for more. Early purchasers had at first accepted the vendor line that "trained monkeys" could operate NC (and, it should be noted, very early NC machines—drills and certain mills—were "semiskilled" machines), but quickly decided otherwise, and assigned more experienced operators to protect their expensive investments. Managers of the smaller factories—later purchasers—often visited larger factories to see how they used CNC, and heard that skilled, if not time-served (i.e., with apprentice training) operators were best. Abolition of the operator–setter distinction in the factories introducing module production was resulting in more qualified operators. As one manager said: "We want people now with a bit more savvy, who have had proper apprenticeship training."

In principle, managers look for a combination of general intelligence, sense of responsibility, and machining skills and knowledge in choosing CNC operators, but the proportional contribution of skills may differ. In the large British factories, the managers stressed machining skills and knowledge, and there was a strong tendency to identify these with apprenticeship qualifications. In the large factories making small batches—where there were setter-operators—at least 80 percent of the CNC operators had done apprenticeships and were time-served. In the smaller factories, managers were more equivocal about the necessity of formal qualifications, partly because they found it difficult to keep qualified craftsmen anyway. In some, managers stressed that anyone who came in and worked hard with the right attitude could be "on top" (i.e., on CNC) within a couple of years. In others, however, lengthy machining experience was stressed, as was the desirability of craft training.

The managers in many of the Japanese factories, on the other hand, were looking more for general intelligence and adaptability, which they associated strongly with youth. Young workers, it was thought, can learn machining basics quickly. Even if they have not mastered more advanced machining skills, they can combine basic skills with programming knowledge—which they can also learn quickly—and produce parts on CNC machines where it takes much more experience to produce on conventional machines: "After a year they're turning out parts it took our skilled operators years to be able to do." Moreover, younger workers trained on CNC were to be the core work force in the coming age of microelectronics-based production.

Older (craft-skilled) workers were supposed to have a CNC "allergy," to mistrust anything that smacked of binary numbers or digital computation. This "allergy"—and problems of older workers adapting to new technology in general—is widely discussed in the media, and most managers who mentioned it accepted it without first trying their older workers on the machines. The older operators were to continue doing their skilled work on manual machines until they retired, when their "skills [would] be replaced by science," to quote one manager.

In the British factories, age was associated more closely with machining experience and knowledge, and also with a sense of responsibility, which was assumed in the Japanese factories. In some, an adaptability factor was acknowledged. Younger operators did take to CNC quicker, and did better on external training courses. Such operators were still time-served, though, usually with at least one or two years on conventional machines after their apprenticeship. Older workers might not take to programming, but that did not stop them from at least operating the machine. In some cases an age factor was explicitly denied, as if it were a form of discrimination like race or creed.

The average age of CNC operators was less than 35 in all of the Japanese factories, and less than 30 in five (Table 7.4). It was over 40 in three of the British factories and less than 30 in only one. Only one Japanese operator had been assigned to CNC after the age of 35; several British operators had been assigned over 50. There were regular CNC operators less than 20 years old in four of the Japanese factories, but in none of the British factories. This difference was partly due to the higher average age of operators in Britain, but apprentices or finishing apprentices who could have been assigned were not. They still had some "rough edges" to wear off.

Explanations

To what extent was the emphasis on craft and machining skills in the British factories the result of union pressure, overt or covert? Managers might indeed have assigned time-served operators for the sake of industrial harmony. There had been disputes over pay differentials, with CNC operators claiming more (e.g., in factories B71 and B120), and if change was to be paid for it would make sense to assign skilled operators anyway. It should be noted, though, that the disputes were not over downgrading or dilution. Moreover, supervisors and managers were forthright about the merits of having experienced operators who had a "feel" for machines, which they associated with craftsmen. Most were themselves time-served. Their view of the desirability of craft skills was more important in their selections than industrial relations considerations. Even in the smaller factories, where unions were not recognized and managers were more equivocal about the need for craftsmen, the uncertainties in getting the machines up and running efficiently prompted them to select them. One or two managers did think that craftsmen might eventually become bored on CNC and ask to be taken off, but they were not going to encourage it.

A further question is if the British managers were so convinced that skilled operators were necessary, how were so many of the Japanese factories able to manage with young and inexperienced operators? At least three reasons may be advanced.

First, supervision was closer in the Japanese factories. In the large factories there were group leaders for five to seven operators, whose job was partly to train their subordinates and supervise them in new tasks. There were also assistant group leaders to help them. In the smaller factories there was one leader for every three or four young workers. In at least one of the factories, closeness of supervision was cited as the reason it was possible to assign inexperienced operators, while in one of the British factories, sparseness of supervision—one foreman to fifteen operators—was cited as a reason for having skilled craftsmen. (Leading hands where they existed were being phased out to give operators greater responsibility for their work). The young Japanese operators were expected to acquire the necessary skills on the job under close supervision rather than prior to it, whereas prior training is necessary where supervision is sparse.

Second, there were differences in the operators' educational backgrounds. The Japanese operators had spent twelve years in school, and more hours per year than their British counterparts, who had spent a maximum of eleven years. It is likely that their mathematical—and technical—skills acquired during the course of school education were higher than those of the British operators. Prais (1987) argues that Japanese 15-year-olds attain higher math levels than their British counterparts. and that graduates of technical high schools, from which many of the Japanese operators were recruited, have acquired vocational knowledge on a par with the old Ordinary National Certificate (ONC) in Britain. This knowledge is not particularly applied, but according to Prais forms a critical base in a world of advancing technology. While none of the operators would have been at the top of the academic achievement scale, Dore and Sako (1989) argue that differences between the two countries in education levels are most pronounced in the lower quartile, and that the Japanese system provides industry with workers who have a good numerical skill base for training, and who can follow detailed written technical instructions. Indeed, the Japanese operators were expected to learn from manuals, and were expected to acquire the basics of machining and programming more quickly than their British counterparts. British managers who were looking for broader or more theoretical knowledge in their CNC operators, as some clearly were, logically chose craftsmen. Apprenticeships are supposed to provide that knowledge, and entry requirements ensure levels of general academic accomplishment.

A third factor, though, was the attitude of managers towards CNC: a "technical" approach versus a "craft" approach. In a sense, and expressed in extreme form, the two approaches could be described either as viewing CNC as a computer with a machine-tool attached or as a machine-tool with a computer attached, with various shades in between. In the former case, if programming was correctly carried out and basic machining rules not transgressed, machining would proceed smoothly. In order to ensure this, young, adaptable operators, or operators with "a bit of math ability," as one Japanese manager put it, were selected. In the latter case, CNC has acknowledged advantages over conventional machine tools, such as reducing setting up times, but introduces a new dimension of uncertainty because the program acts as an intermediary between the operator and the machine. In such a situation, operators who "can tell by the sound of the machine" or "spot potential problems over the horizon" must be present to ensure smooth functioning. This difference in attitude was apparent not only in the selection of operators, but in attitudes toward unmanned operating.

Unmanned and Parallel Operation

A CNC machine may be programmed and left to run unmanned. This possibility was a major attraction of CNC for Japanese managers, but less so for British managers. "What would you think about leaving this $250,000 machine to run unmanned?" the production engineering manager of one large British factory asked a trusted operator on my behalf. The operator replied, "I wouldn't think much of it at all. I'd get more ulcers than I already have." Other British managers agreed that the machines were too expensive an investment to be left running unmanned, that diagnostics for unmanned operating were expensive, and that "you can still get the most out of a machine by having a skilled operator there." Again, this belief was only partially due to industrial relations considerations. In the large-batch factory one or two CNC machines were left running at lunchtimes or between shifts, "when it is safe to do so." The same applied for another factory (B145) when revisited in 1990. But none of the managers were as forthright about the merits of unmanned operating as were some of the Japanese managers during the initial interviews.

Owners (or their sons) of small Japanese factories with on-site residence *(machi koba)* often left machines running in the evening while they were watching television, checking on the machines during commercial breaks (Mori 1982). The two smallest factories here were no exception. The managing director of the third smallest cited unmanned operation as a major factor in his decision to purchase CNC: "First . . . the old operators were skilled and the young ones weren't, so we had to make up for that shortage of skills, and besides we wouldn't have been able to attract younger workers without CNC. The second reason was I wanted to increase productivity by getting a few extra hours out of the machines after everyone had gone home." (He was having only limited success because the operator of his new machining center was reluctant to leave it running unmanned. He, in fact, was taking medicine for ulcers). Among the larger factories, unmanned operation was also being carried out, particularly in the factory with the mini FMS and FMCs. In the two factories where there was no unmanned operating, small batches were cited, or it was a goal that had not been reached yet.

CNC is often difficult to justify on a single shift. Six of the British factories had a second shift, but only three of the Japanese factories. There was a resistance to introducing shift work in the others, summed up by one manager who said: "The biggest reason for not having shift work is because the workers are against it. Also, we don't have so many CNC machines, and if we had operators who came for those, there would have to be managers there as well. Then there are problems of rest, of night meals and what have you. . . . We're trying to increase our unmanned operation time instead." To some extent unmanned operating was a substitute for a second shift.

The possibility of unmanned operation, however, also reflected a different attitude toward the machines. The potential for trouble was often mentioned in the British factories. The expensive investments could easily spring a nasty surprise on the unwary. This fear was seldom mentioned in the Japanese factories. If the machines were programmed right, as they should be by adaptable programmers or operators, there should be no trouble, and automatic cut-off switches would prevent "pile-ups." Thus the machines were considered more reliable, and there seemed to be less concern over human error.

Such thinking also dominated attitudes toward parallel operation—having operators work on more than one machine simultaneously. In some Japanese factories, a manual machine had been placed beside the CNC machine to facilitate this approach. Operators ran more than one CNC machine in the large-batch factories, and also in some of the others. While there were instances of bar lathes being operated in parallel in British factories, none of the CNC operators were involved. One manager—at a large-batch factory—could foresee it happening. He thought the unions would assent to two machines being operated in parallel, but no more. In another, two machining centers had been placed together to allow parallel operation, but according to a supervisor "company policy" was one operator to one machine. Operators were being urged to use machining time to do other tasks such as inspection, but their primary responsibility was to make sure that nothing untoward happened to their machine and the parts it was machining, and operating a second machine would have been too distracting. Again, the possibility of parallel operation was not seen by the British as an especially attractive or even desirable feature of CNC.

Ethos of Change

These approaches to CNC use—technical versus craft—should be seen in the context of overall orientations to change. Change was a more natural phenomenon in the Japanese factories, captured in the words of one managing director: "Innovation, innovation, life is innovation." That change was a natural state rather than a necessary evil is related to the "catch-up" mentality that has been pervasive in Japanese industry, the nature of competition in domestic markets, pressure from "parent" companies in the case of subcontractors, and employment relations, which I elaborate on shortly.

Change is often referred to in Japanese media in terms of "hardware" and "software," with the latter exercising important constraints on the former. New technology such as CNC (hardware) requires new skills (software). Both are evolving in the direction of a greater application of scientific and technical principles to the production process. In one factory, this evolution was expressed in the slogan "From KKD [*keiken,* experience; *kan,* inspiration or knack; and *dakyo,* compromise] to NTT [numerical, technique, and time]." In another, the president's new slogan was "From hand work to head work." In a third, the skills of the older workers would in time be replaced by "science," and so on. Thus, the very skills that British managers valued, the feel for the machine that the craftsman acquires through years of experience, were the skills that were to be replaced in Japan by technical and numerical skills learned not through the hand but through the head. Slogans, of course, are not necessarily a reflection of reality—and may even concur with comments about the necessity of conventional skills—but there was less skepticism in Japan about this alleged evolutionary trend than in the British factories. (A vendor's trainer was thrown out of one British factory for his "programming first" approach).

One vehicle in Japan for the acquisition of these new skills was another "soft" form of innovation—quality control (QC) circles, which all of the larger factories operated. The diagnostic skills that workers were supposed to learn through their involvement in QC circles—identifying problems, logically analyzing the work process, and devising workable solutions—were new technical skills that would help achieve greater rationality of the production process and facilitate "hard" innovation.

Quality circles raise another point, that the Japanese shopfloor workers were seen as important agents in the process of change. Young operators, especially, were seen as leaders-in-training for future innovation and microelectronics-based production. The call for all employees to be involved in the process of change is related to employment relations. Companies try to harness employee cooperation and effort by focusing attention on change and future goals. If managers fail to do this, there is a fear that flagging morale and declining performance relative to competitors (also busily innovating) will reinforce each other in a vicious downward circle. Thus general slogans call for change and progress toward future goals: "New J9 in 10 years," "New J66 for 70th Birthday," "AR 2000" (all round skills by the year 2000), "SKY" (*shoshudan,* small group activities; *kaizen,* improvement; *yakushin,* progress), and so on, with concrete associated programs. All "members"—managers and regular employees—are urged to involve themselves.

It is unlikely that employees will respond if they feel they are not members, or are second-class citizens. Thus it may be argued that the success of these exhortations and programs depends on earlier innovations in employment relations, including thoroughgoing harmonization, as well as practices that emphasize company before occupation, rates-for-the-man rather than rates-for-the-job (or ability to do the job), which reward loyalty through seniority pay (thereby discouraging exit), and cooperation through evaluations.

I am not suggesting that all the Japanese factories were following clearly elaborated strategies for hard process innovation linked with soft. Neither purchasing decision making nor training programs support such a contention. Responding to immediate needs is common in Japanese factories as elsewhere. And often the alleged long-term direction of change derived as much from themes popularized in the business media as from strategic planning. But certainly there was an ethos of change, which should involve soft as well as hard innovation.

In the British factories, particularly the larger ones, change did not have the same prominence and was more often the subject of dispute, particularly for soft innovation. Attempts at QC introduction in three of the large factories illustrate the problems and differences. They had foundered in two cases partly because workers resisted what they viewed as attempts to force them to do manager's jobs, and in the other allegedly because the workers "felt responsible for their own work and did not like being told by groups or other people what they should be doing in their jobs." Far fewer resources in terms of time and money had been spent prior to introduction on awareness promotion, idea soliciting, and training, and there was much less attempt to infuse QCs with several dimensions of meaning such as individual worker development and group interaction as well as quality improvement and increased productivity. They were certainly not viewed as a means for transforming workers' skill bases.

The module production factories were attempting to reintroduce the circles under a different name and foster an ethos of change, but success would be compromised if "Us–Them" attitudes were not ameliorated. The removal of obvious status differences and companywide productivity bonus schemes was a step in this direction, but had not been markedly successful. At these factories, too, ongoing skill acquisition was being promoted, but the craft base was being strengthened rather than weakened. As elsewhere, change was not perceived in terms of hard and soft elements of an evolutionary application of science to the production process, and was not pushed by employment relations.

Conclusions

Clearly this account runs risks in emphasizing differences between the two countries and downplaying differences within them. Differences within the countries did, of course, exist. For small Japanese factories, labor costs were more significant in decisions to select young workers for CNC than in the larger factories. They used CNC to attract younger workers and taught them programming right from the beginning, even before they knew much about setting. Managers in some of the larger factories (which did not have the same recruiting problems) were dubious about the "programming first" approach, and more conservative in their views of skill requirements. Some assigned operators with experience on conventional machines to CNC, although they were also looking for youth and adaptability. Some relied on operators to program, others had specialist programmers. Some factories fell short of the "innovating enterprise" image, some had more success in QC activities than others, and so on.

There were differences among the British factories, too, especially between large and small. In the large factories the skilled equals craft-trained equation was strong, and craftsmen were chosen for most CNC work (except "semiskilled" work such as drilling and sometimes milling), while managers in some of the smaller factories declared their willingness to promote anyone with initiative. Operators did little programming in some, extensive programming in others. Some were moving toward more advanced forms of automation and unmanned operating, others were not contemplating it. And there were differences by batch size, particularly in the organization of work and selection of operators.

It is equally clear, though, that there were significant country differences in the use of CNC. Some of the factors that influence CNC use are national in scope. Education is one important example, as are "media climates." The strength of craft training and organization in Britain, and their relative weakness in Japan are critical. As well as some organization-specificity, employment practices have a national element (see Chap. 2).

The differences constitute what I have termed a "technical approach" in Japan, and a "craft approach" in Britain, described in terms of the selection of programmers and operators, attitudes toward the skills the machines require, attitudes about unmanned and parallel operating, and attitudes toward the machines themselves. The technical approach was linked to an orientation to change, in the direction of greater application of scientific and technical knowledge in the production process, and attempts to mobilize regular workers for this, particularly younger workers.

The craft approach also recognizes the necessity of innovation, sometimes as a necessary evil, and of learning new skills for new machines. Craft skills are still necessary, however, in view of the uncertainties that arise when installing the new machines as well as after. New skills are added to craft skills. Concepts such as the "intellectualization of blue-collar work" are treated with greater skepticism. In general, CNC operators are not seen as agents of transformation of their own workplace or their own skills, even though they are among the elite on the shopfloor, and though there may be individual "CNC champions."

Competitiveness is becoming increasingly linked to the ability to innovate, which suggests an advantage for Japanese factories. Innovation itself is no guarantee of success, though. "Window display" CNC machines can sometimes be found in Japanese factories, the result of managers rushing to purchase for fear of getting left behind, or because of pressure from parent companies without due consideration to production requirements. Some managers made an early initial purchase, and based on that experience, decided how—or whether—CNC was really useful for them. Most CNC machines were operational, however, and practices such as unmanned and parallel operating would suggest higher productivity even without taking into account soft factors.

Other contributions to this volume have documented constraints on the diffusion of new organization principles. Given worker educational backgrounds and other nationally embedded differences, it would be neither advisable nor feasible for British factories to adopt wholesale a technical approach to CNC. Building on strengths is a more viable option, and Sorge and Warner's (1986) Anglo-German study suggests that a thorough application of craft skills to CNC in German factories may also be associated with competitiveness. This was not, however, the laissez-faire management variety that Japanese observers sometimes note of British factories. This account suggests a need for evolving training programs throughout factory organizations. It also suggests that British managers have some way to go in tapping—and building—the innovative potential of those nearest the work process. To this end, more fundamental reforms in employment relations are probably necessary. Such reform, however, will continue to be shaped by supra-organizational influences found in British society.

References

Braverman, H. 1974. *Labor and Monopoly Capital.* New York: Monthly Review Press.

Dore, R., and M. Sako. 1989. *How the Japanese Learn to Work.* London: Routledge.

Mori, K. 1982. *Machi koba no roboto kakumei* (The Robot Revolution in Street-Corner Factories). Tokyo: Daiyamondosha.

Prais, S. 1987. "Educating for Productivity: Comparisons of Japanese and English Schooling and Vocational Preparation" *National Institute Economic Review* **119**(Feb.):40–56.

Senker, P. 1986. *Towards the Automatic Factory: The Need for Training.* Berlin: Springer-Verlag.

Sorge, A., and M. Warner. 1986. *Comparative Factory Organization: An Anglo-German Comparison of Management and Manpower in Manufacturing.* Hants: Gower.

Sorge, A., M. Warner, G. Hartman, and I. Nicholas. 1983. *Micro-Electronics and Manpower in Manufacturing.* Hants: Gower.

8

The Shaping of Software Systems in Manufacturing: The Implementation of Network Technologies in British Industries

JULIETTE WEBSTER

In Britain, currently, much attention is being paid to a postulated sea change in production practices and to the use of integrated production technologies to support a new approach to manufacturing. New methods imported from Japan, coupled with the use of software systems such as computer-aided production management (CAPM) originating in the United States, are seen as being the significant means by which British manufacturing competitiveness can be improved. The Department of Trade and Industry (DTI), industrial practitioners, management consultants, academics, and journalists have all contributed to this idea.

This chapter considers the promotion of CAPM technologies as "plug-in" solutions to current British industrial problems and examines the expectations of accompanying shifts to "Japanized" methods of production that have been generated by suppliers, consultants, and government agencies. The popularity of this new ideology of manufacturing has to be seen as part of a more general reorientation of British capital toward regaining some competitive advantage in the international marketplace. While these manufacturing methods and technologies are also gaining currency across Europe and America, in Britain this rhetoric of manufacturing is also strongly rooted in the political culture of Thatcherite (and Majorite) society. In Britain, the new manufacturing ideas have been accompanied by a powerful emphasis on the resurgence of capital, the growth of the private sector, the primacy of market forces, and the renewal of enterprise.

The chapter then investigates the reality of the implementation and diffusion of these systems within British industry. The ways in which companies from several industries have introduced such systems, and how they have had to configure them according to their individual production circumstances are examined. This reconfiguration raises questions of the appropriateness of attempting to directly import technologies and techniques from foreign, and quite different, production systems. In the course of learning to shape CAPM systems to their particular requirements, companies have undertaken a significant experiment in technological innovation: systems arising from the large-scale data processing approach to production control characteristic of early U. S. CAPM technologies, but being marketed in a manufacturing climate characterized by an emphasis on decentralized, flexible production organization utilizing Japanese methods, have been adapted to suit the circumstances and problems of British manufacturing industry. In the light of this experiment, concepts of work organization are inseparable from those of technology, because the former shapes, as well as is shaped by, the latter. The fact that technologies are strongly shaped at the site of implementation has significant implications for our understanding technological development. The chapter concludes by offering a reconceptualization of the innovation process, in which patterns of work organization at the implementation stage play just as crucial a part as do the intentions and visions of technology designers.

The British Manufacturing Climate

The new ideology of manufacturing in Britain posits major changes in the location of markets and a significant growth in international competition, and calls for increased business responsiveness to these factors. It suggests that highly designed, high value-added product markets will replace the old ones for basic commodities, that Europe will be a site for significant market growth, and that the Pacific Rim producers will join the Japanese as the key competitors against British manufacturers (see particularly DTI/PA Consulting Group 1989).

This industrial ethic advocates the development of manufacturing excellence, involving "continuous improvements" in production processes. Companies are encouraged firstly to reevaluate their business and manufacturing strategies and their corresponding utilization of technologies (Ohmae 1988). They are advised to systematically review their product lines and product changes, to review their competitive position, to work more closely with their suppliers, to attend more closely to the needs of their customers, and to develop new products and processes to cater to increasingly sophisticated and fast-moving markets for customized, high quality, reliable goods with shorter life cycles (ACME 1990). This approach constitutes what has been labeled "competitive edge manufacturing."[1]

There are a number of specific practices that commentators argue companies will adopt in implementing this general approach. To meet new market demands, a growing flexibility in production is predicted and, indeed, advocated. Responsiveness to markets will be achieved by speedy product changeover; slashing lead times, batch sizes, and stock levels; rapid detooling and retooling; and stringent quality control (Dear 1989; Wheatley 1989). Manufacturers will have to adopt a new philosophy of production, making only what is needed for sales rather than amassing large amounts of finished goods stock.[2]

The Place of CAPM in the New Philosophy of Production

It is argued that information technologies like CAPM will be pressed into the service of these productive innovations. As straightforward, cohesive systems of planning and control, they will be critical for supplying up-to-date management information to enable companies to develop responsive and flexible production methods (Bessant and Lamming 1984; Macbeth 1985). According to their advocates, if implemented correctly, they will rapidly bring about greater efficiency of production and utilization of plant and materials. For example, stocks can be monitored, materials can be ordered only when necessary, priority ratings for orders can be modified, and machines and labor utilized optimally. Increasingly sophisticated information systems will cross functional boundaries, will demand the integration of activities across departmental lines (information on sales, for example, being used to determine production patterns), and will lead to decentralized decision making and the consequent flattening of company hierarchies (Applegate, Cash, and Mills 1988).

The manufacturing organization of the future, then, will apparently be the "integrated organization"—integrated not only internally in terms of information systems that draw together previously separate activities and islands of automation, but also increasingly externally across the supply chain. Manufacturers will intervene much more closely in the practices of their suppliers, while simultaneously using direct electronic links for quotes, orders, and invoices in order to lock their customers in to their products (Houde 1990). This transformation in manufacturing practice is made explicit by Arthur Andersen & Company in its sales brochure for MAC-PAC:

> The systems that support this dynamic manufacturing environment are changing as old practices and approaches give way to new concepts and methods. Many companies are moving to MRPII, Just-in-Time (JIT), Distribution Requirements Planning (DRP), Computer Integrated Manufacturing (CIM), and to a new generation of systems that can combine all of these methods. To survive in this volatile marketplace, forward-thinking companies need mission-critical operations support systems that share information throughout the entire organization. As a manufacturer moving into the 1990s, you need to have all aspects of your manufacturing process integrated, sharing information, and changing as the industry changes.

The widespread adoption of CAPM in Britain has coincided, then, with that of a strong ideology of the transformation of manufacturing. What began as a U. S. technical import, has become reengineered toward a philosophy of production associated more with Japanese industry.

Underlying the prescriptions for increasing technological and corresponding organizational integration and flexibility, lies an unquestioning adoption of methods such as just-in-time and total quality control. These methods are now being more or less explicitly promoted for by significant industrial groups in Britain. While the practices promoted are not always pure applications of the Japanese approach (particularly where the stress is on technical solutions that are antithetical to the Japanese emphasis on organizational methods of structuring manufacturing), they are nevertheless representative of an attempt to spread an alternative orientation to production based on quality, flexibility, and simplicity.[3] Thus, CAPM systems are sold on the basis of playing their part in helping companies to reduce stock; increase visibility of parts, processes, and problem areas; facilitate product variation and a general orientation toward customers; and, in general, promoting dynamic manufacturing:

> FCMS (Factory Control and Management System) creates a manufacturing environment that can pull—as well as push—products through your shop. . . . With FCMS, you direct the factory and maintain total visibility of your manufacturing operation. . . . FCMS facilitates the implementation of just-in-time production and zero-inventory programs. . . . FCMS provides optimized plant scheduling to help you shorten lead times and reduce work-in-progress. [MSA sales brochure for Factory Control and Management System)

> MAC-PAC weaves the "pull" orientation of just-in-time (JIT) manufacturing with the "push" of MRPII. . . . No matter what your combination, MAC-PAC coupled with JIT techniques can help you achieve faster throughput and lowered work-in-process inventory. These improvements can help make sure your schedules are met on time, every time. MAC-PAC can help you not only boost customer service through on-time production, but also improve your bottom line with reduced inventory and more efficient, paperless processing. [Arthur Andersen sales brochure for MAC-PAC]

> The basis of the MCC (Manufacturing Control Code) system is a detailed model of the manufacturing operation. The simulation output provides information for all the functions involved in the manufacturing process. These key departures from previous computerized production control systems allow the user to aim for stockless production, and where appropriate, Just-in-Time practices—improving the efficiency and profitability of the entire business. [Davy Computing brochure for MCC system]

The American Production and Inventory Control Society (APICS), one of the most influential professional production management organizations, was, until recently, instrumental in promoting the diffusion of large-scale centralized CAPM systems. Now its literature abounds with articles advocating the adoption of Japanese pull systems (Clark and Staunton 1989), and it has played a vital part in popularizing the Japanese approach in the West. APICS literature is reproduced wholesale in *Production and Inventory Management,* the quarterly journal published by the British counterpart, BPICS, which is now completely concerned with promoting the use of one or another of the techniques previously described. Though BPICS has historically not been as influential in Britain as APICS has been in the United States, its messages to industry can be nevertheless seen as part of a dominant trend set in motion by a whole range of industrial practitioners promoting "flexibility" in manufacturing.

More influential in Britain has been the Department of Trade and Industry that, under the aegis of the Enterprise Initiative (a government program to improve practice in industry), has published an entire series of reports and handbooks under the umbrella title "Managing into the 1990s." These aim to raise business consciousness on a number of subjects that are clearly seen as elements of a putative new approach to industrial production in Britain—the Deming philosophy, just-in-time, computer integrated manufacturing, and manufacturing resource planning, for example. Also influential, management journals contain frequent articles advising companies on the principles and application of so-called Japanese flexible production approaches, so that, overall, companies in Britain are receiving clear messages on the ideal ways in which to organize their activities for the 1990s.

These images of the new production concepts being disseminated, as just described, are not unimportant. In Britain, they have been highly influential in shaping companies' expectations of technological offerings and their consequent implementation practices. British firms have been exhorted to implement CAPM software systems in conjunction with new production methods. They have attempted to transfer technologies that were developed in the United States and to apply them wholesale. Many have also tried to imitate Japanese approaches to the organization of production.

This has not been a simple process of technology transfer, however. The ideology of CAPM systems as a uniform collection of tightly specified packages is problematic and glosses over the uncertainties surrounding their application and implementation. In reality, they are a plethora of loosely bundled packages that have been constantly evolving both over time and in scope. They are subject to constant modification and renewal by suppliers, and old systems very quickly become outdated and difficult to maintain. They also vary from simple materials handling to multisite management information systems. The process of CAPM implementation is, as a result, often greatly oversimplified as one of merely installing a piece of "kit" that will provide the purchasing company with clear solutions to its manufacturing problems. The expectation of instant solutions that this simplified model generates has created great difficulties for user companies when they come to implement these systems. Moreover, given the significant differences between the Japanese and the British institutional, manufacturing, and industrial relations contexts (Oliver and Wilkinson 1988), the importation of Japanese industrial methods to Britain has not been a simple exercise. British users have found it necessary to modify and adapt these practices to meet local circumstances and traditions. In this process, the technologies and techniques have been substantially altered, as I show in the next section. This process might thus best be described as one of technology transformation rather than technology transfer.

The Implementation and Diffusion of CAPM in U.K. Industry

As a means of codifying and keeping track of a range of components and subassemblies, the original generic CAPM systems were clearly applicable to standardized batch manufacture and assembly. Just as in the United States, it was the automobile industry that spearheaded the development of production management technologies (with, for example, the early adoption at twenty-two General Motors' sites of optimized production technology (OPT), so in Britain it was the aerospace, engineering, and electronics industries that were the initial users of these systems. Lucas Aerospace, for example, was one of the first U.K. companies to introduce an IBM materials requirements planning system, MAAPICS. However, it quickly became apparent that CAPM technologies were unsuitable for many productive conditions. Their application to process industries, for example, was problematic because they tended to be designed to handle multiple components and multiple products rather than the serial processing of few materials. Early CAPM systems were also not ideally suited to contract industries where production was one-off rather than repetitive, and where individual components had to be strictly tracked at every stage in the production process. Industries have been faced with the task of developing customized software in order to meet their requirements; consequently, adaptation, tweaking, mixing and matching of modules, wholesale rewriting of code or even system specification have been the practices of almost every user company. Following are some examples of these innovations in the industrial arena of implementation and use.

Furniture Manufacturing

McKnight,[4] a Scottish furniture manufacturing company, was until 1988 a small division of a large and disparate corporate empire, Halls, when it was the subject of a management buyout. Consequently, it is still a small company. It is involved in the manufacture and assembly of domestic and educational furniture, such as dining suites and living-room shelving units on the one hand, and desks, chairs, and science lab furniture on the other. Domestic furniture is made largely to stock and educational furniture is made to order. There is no separation of the two lines during the actual production process, which consists of machining of raw materials into piece-parts, storing, and finally assembling the piece-parts into the end product. The process is relatively labor-intensive, involving skilled machinists and polishers, and unskilled laborers. Historically, production scheduling within the company was done informally. Raw materials were simply pushed through the shop until they reached the assembly stage, at which point a home-grown "fit" system matched domestic product components to sales orders and called them up for assembly in large batches.

   The CAPM system that Halls installed across the group in 1987 was an elderly product, a twenty-year-old batch system. It had originally been bought because it ran on Wang hardware, to which Halls had for some time been committed. When McKnight's management took over the company, it set about getting the CAPM system up and running. To do so, it decided to interface the CAPM system with a sales order processing system. Despite the fact that both packages were written for Wang hardware, the interface between them was poor and therefore they both had to be heavily customized by consultants to make them work together. Once they were installed, it quickly became clear that other modifications were needed to make the resulting system cater to existing production conditions. For example, the production forecasting techniques in one of the modules that scheduled production were inappropriate; McKnight would therefore use the package's standard forecasting up to a certain point, but would then manually delete the quantities generated by the machine. The company was planning to write its own version of that part of the system at some point.

Similarly, the computer system presumed that labor and work center statistics—standards, set-up times, run times, transit times, queue times—were recorded. McKnight, being now small and under-resourced, maintained no such records, and was faced with the need to start keeping records to exploit the CAPM system. To overcome this immediate problem, the company wrote its own capacity planning element that uses sales values instead of time study data, and it added a program that made the system work according to the actual rather than the calculated location of manufacturing orders. The systems administrator told me a familiar story when he said:

> The MRP package we have is very rigid. It relies on a very very good database and a good production planning team, full of expertise. As I say, we don't fully have that. We've trained and retrained and tried to train, but with the volume of the product going through, we still have mistakes cropping up. These small errors will result in MRP failing totally, so we run MRP over a weekend and it fails, so we are left without it. We fix up the problems, try to run it again. So we will have to rewrite that section of the MRP program.

Clearly, the behavior of this company in removing the precision from its CAPM system is far from the rational, purposive, strategic technological development that management consultants hope to encourage among user companies.

This situation is also the result of attempts to import the characteristics and approach of American large-scale data processing into small British companies with limited management data or resources for its collection, no system development, and no training. However blinkered McKnight's behavior seems to be, and however counterproductive this particular reconfiguration activity, it does show that the wholesale grafting of technologies and their operational principles, as solutions which can simply and instantly be transferred from one productive environment to another, can be highly problematic. The company could not get away just with tailoring the CAPM system to its informal methods for managing production. Innovations in the company's production practices themselves had to be made in line with the workings of the new system. Moves toward formal monitoring and data collection had to be instituted, and systematic sales forecasting practices had to be developed in order to make use of the system's facilities. The domestic furniture line could now be made on the basis of forecast or actual orders, eliminating the need for stocking final assemblies prior to dispatch, and as a result the dispatch area was closed down.[5] However, the move toward formal production control was an extremely slow process, during which time scheduling disasters continued to take place and production management actively resisted the encroachment of a computer system into its domain of hitherto personalized control.

Printing

Shore, a manufacturer of diaries and address books, provides another example of a company reconfiguring a CAPM system to suit its particular needs, only this time in a more constructive fashion. The company makes a standard product for sale in stationary retailers, and customized products that are commissioned by companies or organizations. Diary production is highly seasonal, and the cycle of manufacture is surprisingly long. The process of production of a 1991 diary, for example, begins in April 1989. Thus, at any one time there are always a number of years' diaries in production, and stock levels in the plant are consequently high.

Shore had been doing production scheduling manually before buying its CAPM system. Due dates for components and final product would be calculated roughly, working backwards from the due date of an order to initiate various stages in the production process. In practice, the company was invariably under pressure to complete orders in time, particularly at the year's end when work was rushed, and it was often late with deliveries. It introduced a CAPM system to help it improve its delivery record, to reduce its inventory, and to increase its utilization of plant and people. Like McKnight, Shore had to undertake a significant degree of software customization to match the CAPM products on the market to its particular circumstances and requirements. In fact, it took two different packages from different suppliers and combined the appropriate elements of each. While the shell and format of the first package, Impcon, suited Shore and provided almost all the functions it required, it did not include a finite capacity scheduling module that was suitable for the company's seasonal business, which was offered in another package, 4W. So the company "ripped the guts out" of Impcon, and embedded 4W within it. The scheduling facility needed further customization, however; it was more suited to an engineering environment with a low number of annual products, whereas Shore has about 2,000 orders annually. Moreover, it was written in a relatively old version of FORTRAN; Shore rewrote its system in a more modern version, and reconciled it to the Impcon part of the system, which was written in COBOL.

Shore also added a number of customized features: an enormous data base that contained bills of materials, and machining and routing details for each component of its products—pages of different sizes and colors, jackets, ribbons, page edging, and so on—and customized the reports generated by the system. Adding the data base alone took two years of extracting knowledge from craft workers and doing the necessary programming. Owing to the amount of customization that was necessary to get an appropriate system for this company, the implementation process was very protracted, to the extent that the company subsequently felt that it had not been cost-effective.

As this account suggests, Shore was not like McKnight, a small company with few resources to devote to the systematization and formalization of production. It employed around 1,400 people in facilities on both sides of the Atlantic. Its Edinburgh plant boasted both industrial engineering and data processing departments, and during the CAPM development phase, had a small team of staff working full-time on the project.

Despite having these resources and in-house expertise, the prevailing organization of production, as in McKnight, was highly ad hoc. The use of CAPM required a shift to a much more systematic production culture. Planning and shop-floor activities alike had to be more rule-based than of old; for example, informal practices such as the uncontrolled borrowing of materials from one job to finish another had to be ironed out. Stock control became more formalized: expensive materials (such as leather and gold leaf) were controlled separately from cheap ones (such as rivets and paper) and reordered on the basis of manual deduction from stock records. The latter were deducted automatically from stock records on the basis of what was known to be going through the shopfloor. Ironically, therefore, manual data updating was regarded as more reliable than automatic processing with respect to expensive stock items.

Yet, the overall system of production remained very much as before, with the same timetables for production and problems of scheduling for "special" customized products—features inherent to the process of producing for a seasonal and variable market. And, indeed, the company still carried significant levels of inventory, in particular large amounts of work-in-process around the factory. Meanwhile, the closure of the London-based order-taking office meant that still only 65 percent of orders were being met on time, so the system did not appear to be achieving the gains for which the company had hoped. In fact, the company's industrial engineer confirmed that the system's biggest asset had been in helping to confirm the existence of bottlenecks in the production process, of which he was already aware anyway.

Engineering

One of the most dramatic examples of the implementation of raw CAPM technology is that of BEC, a large engineering company with sites all over Britain, including one in Edinburgh, Scotland. BEC is a part of a large worldwide group with twenty-two U. K.-based companies and thirty-three overseas subsidiaries. It constructs capital plant equipment for the energy conversion and materials handling industries: turbine generators, steam turbines, and transformers on the energy conversion side; cranes, winches, valves, gearboxes, and the like on the materials handling side. Recently it was taken over by a major U. K. engine manufacturer.

The production process at the company's Edinburgh site involves manufacturing and assembling urban distribution transformers to contract. This process has particular implications for materials handling and production monitoring. Materials are generally bought on a contract-by-contract basis, while the delicate nature of the company's products dictates that it carefully tracks the origins and progress of each component that goes into them, in case of later equipment faults whose source needs to be identified. There is very little in the way of production automation in the plant, and in fact, the production process of making transformers is highly labor-intensive, involving the manual assembly of sheet metal and wire into transformer cores, which are then lowered into fabricated metal shells.

The company has historically suffered from problems of poor work scheduling, with contracts characteristically being completed as much as six months late. This record has partly been the result of the slowness of the drawing office in designing and developing each product prior to each contract being agreed, and in generating bills of materials so that raw materials could be ordered. In the early 1980s, the company began to think about addressing its scheduling problems by means of data bases that would capture bills-of-materials generation, and assist ordering and production scheduling. It had vague plans to develop some kind of PC-based network to handle these data bases. Honeywell was a long-standing systems supplier for the BEC group. In 1973, BEC headquarters had imposed upon its subordinate companies a Honeywell business system, and all the constituent companies continued to use Honeywell systems of various kinds. Consequently, when the Scottish site came to consider a system to improve its production management, it was taken for granted that Honeywell would again be the supplier. Instead of a PC-based network, however, Honeywell offered the company a "package deal" solution, consisting of a new mainframe, an MRPII system called Honeywell Manufacturing System (HMS), which had been principally marketed in the United States, a CAD system called Anvil 4000, and an accounting system called MSA Ledgers. The idea was that the CAD system would be used to generate bills of materials, which would be sent through to the MRPII system, which, in turn, would generate financial data for the ledger system. Thus, the company would have a sophisticated, fully integrated production control and financial system.

The experience of the system was quite different from the theory. The three packages—Anvil 4000, HMS, and MSA Ledgers—had not originally been designed by Honeywell to fit together at all, so that when they came to be installed at BEC, the interfaces between them had to be written from scratch. During the implementation and interface development process, however, a number of the systems developers left Honeywell, with the result that the promised integration never happened and BEC was left with three discrete systems.

Even the individual CAPM package, HMS, did not live up to its initial promise. HMS is a large, data-hungry system used by companies with high levels of computing resources, and predominantly in the United States. Honeywell does market a smaller system, Honeywell Distributed Manufacturing System (HDMS), more geared toward the U.K. market, which runs on mini- rather than mainframe computers and is more user-friendly. BEC, however, acquired HMS as part of its integrated package. It proved to be inappropriate for the level of computing resource at BEC's Edinburgh site, but also to have the barest of user support and system maintenance in Britain. Furthermore, the system turned out to be geared toward make-to-stock production, and, unlike HDMS, to have no special version for production to contract. The reports that it generated had to be heavily customized to make them useful to BEC. In all, because the choice of system had been imposed from the top down as a generic technological acquisition, it had not been made with reference to the actual resources and levels of expertise necessary to benefit from the system within the individual BEC companies, including the Edinburgh plant.

BEC was ill-equipped to handle a system implementation that involved writing software for the package interfaces, on top of learning how to use these new technologies from scratch and changing working procedures accordingly. Despite being part of a large enterprise, the company was left to its own devices and did not have the in-house expertise for a complex project of this sort. Nor did it have the organization to collect and maintain the data required to run these three systems. As far as production control was concerned, it had hitherto relied upon "finger in the air" methods—the personal surveillance of the shopfloor by the production manager. The design process was similarly vague: drawing office staff were not in the habit of specifying to shopfloor or store workers the materials required for their designs, which had to be identified through guesswork. So there was no communication of this information and no records of the materials needed or at what rate they were consumed.

The company found itself unable to tackle all these areas of inefficiency at once, particularly given the nonexistent nature of the linkages between the different parts of the computer system. It therefore ultimately decided on a much less ambitious system development strategy in which the three packages would be implemented gradually and completely separately. The CAPM system was implemented cautiously and selectively, one module at a time, and only in this way has it begun to give BEC the sought-for control over materials. The addition of a contract traceability function by Honeywell also made the CAPM system more appropriate to BEC's need to monitor the origins and destiny of each individual component material.

The Realities

Across these cases, therefore, two major impediments to the implementation of CAPM have been the imprecise and inaccurate nature of production control and the nonexistence of manufacturing data collection. These circumstances have resulted in an incompatibility between a production culture based on "ad hocery" and a set of technological offerings that rely critically on painstaking, systematized, and uniform information collection and production control practices in order to work properly. The transition that most British companies therefore need to make to create the right conditions for CAPM to even be implemented is downplayed by systems suppliers who portray the process in much more simplified terms. And, as shown, even if companies are able to successfully adopt a more structured approach to production management, there is still often a significant gulf between their particular practices and the facilities offered by off-the-shelf CAPM systems, which tend to be geared toward very standard needs. The organizational innovations required to utilize these systems have to be accompanied by significant technological innovations to make systems work in localized, unique conditions of production.

Conclusions

CAPM systems, then, rarely take a form that ideally suits the conditions of the user company. The notion that CAPM systems could simply be bought by a user and "plugged in" has been shown by experience to be oversimplified and too technically oriented. In fact, as well as the organizational innovations user companies have had to make to use CAPM, they have also invariably reconfigured, rewritten, knitted together, amended, and otherwise transformed CAPM packages into systems that are unique technological solutions. These individual initiatives have been attempts to overcome the deficiencies of the highly standardized CAPM system, which is geared to the manufacture and assembly of multiple components into multiple products, and they have contributed to the continuing evolution of CAPM technologies. System suppliers have in their turn begun to refine their technological offerings by developing special versions of CAPM systems that can be bought off-the-shelf rather than having to be specially and individually constructed.

In response to the initiatives and innovations set in motion by frustrated user companies, therefore, CAPM product development has progressed to involve a range of packages that can cater to most industrial situations generated by size of company, sector of company, and, most important, industrial process. Examples are process industry systems (Drive Computing's "Bliss" system), clothing industry systems (Kewill's "Xetal" system for the production of apparel), and repair and refurbish industry systems (see Panisset 1988). Increasingly, the trend in Britain has been toward developing a range of packaged CAPM products, and away from wholesale in-house CAPM development by users.

CAPM systems have often been portrayed as stable, cohesive technologies that would offer a number of solutions to current industrial problems, heighten the overall efficiency of British industry, and take us further into the era of advanced manufacturing. The importation of what were initially American technologies into the British industrial environment has been seen not only as unproblematic but as positively desirable. Alongside the selling of this "technological fix," a number of Japanese industrial methods have been suggested to enhance the competitiveness of British industry. The implication has been that these two innovations are connected, part and parcel of an overall change in orientation to industrial production in the late twentieth and early twenty-first centuries, and that their implementation in British industry is imperative. New systems and methods have had a great deal of promise attached to them.

This promise has not, on the whole, been fulfilled. A conference held in March 1990 for the British CAPM-supply industry noted that most CAPM systems conspicuously failed when implemented in British companies.[6] User industries in Britain have witnessed a phenomenon that Freeman (1988) has labelled "the productivity paradox," in which, despite high investment in systems designed to cut production costs and heighten efficiency, little or no economic growth has been evident. Instead companies have had to dramatically reshape their manufacturing technologies to make them fit CAPM conditions and yield the sought-for improvements. The idea that a technology or a technique can simply be imported wholesale from one country to another without reference to different industrial conditions, traditions, and practices has thus been shown to be mistaken and misleading; CAPM systems in Britain are not so much a case of technology transfer but more one of technology transformation.

This transformation of technologies raises the issue of how we conceptualize technological development. Most analyses of technological development employ a traditional linear model, in which invention–innovation–diffusion are conceptualized as separate "stages" (Fleck 1988b). In this model, it is at the invention stage that technologies emerge and become "fixed." Analyses using this model therefore tend toward "black box" technologies, seeing them as essentially autonomous and immutable, or at least open to scrutiny only at this early point in their development. According to this model, too, the marketplace operates a process of natural selection on those arbitrary offerings, choosing those which most fit its requirements.

These established artifacts are then diffused, where they have "impacts" on society, work organization, production systems, skills, and so on.

The CAPM case suggests the serious limitations of this model. It suggests that technological development, rather than being fixed at the design stage, continues through into the implementation stage of these systems, involving continuous efforts toward developing new solutions in the light of user needs and methods of working. In this conceptualization, the site of application and implementation of technology is also a site for innovation. Based on this recognition, Fleck's alternative model of technological development stresses

> . . . the possibility of the development of technologies which are at the outset intrinsically constituted in terms of user needs and requirements—that is, in terms of the characteristics of demand. This is achieved, not through some esoteric, arbitrarily plastic, "black box" of technology which responds to market signals conveying information about demand, but through determinate processes of technological design, trial and exploration, in which user needs and requirements are discovered and incorporated *in the course of the struggle to get the technology to work in useful ways, at the point of application.* [1988b, 3; my emphasis]

According to this approach, technological development is a spiralling rather than a linear process, in which crucial innovations take place both at the design and implementation stages, and are continually fed back into future rounds of technological change. Once the critical role of implementation becomes acknowledged, then the technologically determinist position whereby autonomous technologies have specific impacts is no longer sustainable. Their social settings shape technologies just as much as vice versa (Edge 1988; MacKenzie and Wajcman 1985). It is therefore clearly not helpful to treat technologies and their social contexts as separate phenomena in the way that traditional conceptions have tended to do; the definition of technology itself must incorporate the social arrangements within which it emerges and becomes embedded (Webster 1988a). As far as production technologies are concerned, this redefining means abandoning the preoccupation with hardware, or even software, alone. We require instead a scheme that acknowledges all those institutions, artifacts, and arrangements within which the adoption, configuration, and use of those technologies takes place. (This scheme includes the knowledge and expertise that have created technologies and are embedded within them [Dosi 1982], and the processes of learning and experience that inform innovative activity [Sahal 1981].) Joan Woodward (1958) was one of the first writers to suggest this unity of technology and social organization when she emphasized the divisions of labor, control systems, and structures of work organization associated with certain technologies. Similarly, Hill (1981, 86) has drawn a useful definition:

> In the first place, technology embraces all forms of productive technique, including hand work which may not involve the use of mechanical implements. Secondly, it embraces the physical organization of production, the way in which the hardware of production has been laid out in a factory or other place of work. The term therefore implies the division of labor and work organization which is built into, or required for efficient operation by the productive technique.

Production technologies, therefore, are inclusive phenomena. Their development proceeds through the interaction of various social and technical elements. These different components of technology cannot be separated from one another or treated as distinct variables; they are in constant mutual tension. Just as there is no linear effect of technologies upon society, so too the conditioning of technologies by social factors is not a simple one-way process. Technologies, once developed and implemented, react back upon their environments to generate new forms of technology, but they also generate new environments (Webster 1988b).

This relationship is of considerable policy significance. It suggests a great deal of scope for proactivity in the design of future production technologies. Recognition of this point enables us to intervene in the development process to secure the kinds of technologies and work organization structures best suited to each other and to the traditions of production in particular industries and places. In Britain this consideration may mean that more emphasis should be put on developing manufacturing software systems that can, if necessary, work in the context of highly unstructured and usually poorly resourced manufacturing milieux, rather than putting all the pressure on user companies to sweep aside their established practices and culture of production.

While it would be wrong to assume that production systems cannot be transferred at all, it is important to recognize that foreign systems cannot simply be imported, but must be transformed. Even Japanese companies, possibly the archetypal successful innovators, adopted and modified a range of manufacturing techniques that were themselves imports from elsewhere (Graham 1988; Oliver and Wilkinson 1988). The diffusion of particular, country-bound manufacturing practices across international boundaries is a process riddled with complexity, and adopting countries rarely take on foreign systems in their pure form. Different countries are forced to develop their own national systems for manufacturing, appropriate to local conditions. In attempting to do so, they set off a learning process that can yield novel and valuable innovations. Instead of advocating the wholesale mimicry of production practices that have been successful elsewhere, policy should be aware of how innovations may be rooted in certain socioeconomic contexts, and how they therefore need to be transformed to be useful in a different locale.

Notes

This paper draws on research into the organizational shaping of integrated automation carried out at Edinburgh University, in collaboration with James Fleck and Robin Williams. The project is funded under the Economic and Social Research Council's Program on Information and Communication Technologies (PICT). I am most grateful to Ian Graham and Robin Williams for their very helpful comments on earlier drafts of this paper.

1. See *British Business,* 10 February 1989, pp. 20–24.
2. See *Financial Times,* 14 November 1989, p.21.
3. This is a necessarily crude dichotomy between American and Japanese production

characteristics. Some so-called Japanese practices, such as total quality control, actually originated in the United States with Edwards Deming, while many American companies have recently embraced just-in-time with a vengeance. Nevertheless, insofar as we can draw a crude American–Japanese dichotomy of large-scale information systems versus simple, flexible manufacturing, the dichotomy is also characterized by the opposition of centralized control over production and decentralized operational flexibility (Jones 1987).

4. All user company names appearing in this paper are pseudonyms.

5. This is perhaps best thought of as an "exnovation" (Clark and Staunton 1989).

6. Department of Trade and Industry/Engineering and Science Research Council, application of computers to manufacturing engineering (ACME) conference on "Computer Aided Production Management," London, March 1990.

References

ACME (Application of Computers to Manufacturing Engineering Directorate). 1990. *Project Summaries.* CAPM Supply Industry Research Conference. Swindon, U. K.: ACME.

Applegate, L. M., J. I. Cash, and D. Q. Mills. 1988. "Information Technology and Tomorrow's Manager," *Harvard Business Review* **66**(Nov./Dec.):128–36.

Bessant, J., and R. Lamming. 1984. "Making IT Fit: The Design of Integrated Manufacturing Systems," *Design Studies* **5**(2):106–12.

Clark, P., and N. Staunton. 1989. *Innovation in Technology and Organization.* London: Routledge.

Dear, A. 1989. "Ideal Practice," *Management Today,* January, pp. 87–89.

Dosi, G. 1982. "Technological Paradigms and Technological Trajectories: A Suggested Interpretation of the Determinants and Directions of Technological Change," *Research Policy* **11**:147–62.

DTI/PA Consulting Group. 1989. *Manufacturing into the Late 1990s.* London: HMSO.

Edge, D. 1988. *The Social Shaping of Technology.* Edinburgh PICT Working Paper No 1, University of Edinburgh.

Fleck, J. 1988b. *Innofusion or Diffusation? The Nature of Technological Development in Robotics.* Edinburgh PICT Working Paper No 4, University of Edinburgh.

Freeman, C. 1988. *The Factory of the Future: The Productivity Paradox, Japanese Just-in-Time and Information Technology.* PICT Policy Research Paper No 3. London: Engineering and Science Research Council.

Graham, I. 1988. "Japanization as Mythology," *Industrial Relations Journal* **29**(1):69–75.

Hill, S. 1981. *Competition and Control at Work.* London: Heinemann.

Houde, J. 1990. "How to Use Strategic Communications Networks to Gain Competitive Advantage." Seminar organized by Network Resource Center, London, March.

Jones, B. 1987. "Flexible Automation in Britain." Paper presented at Social Aspects of Flexible Automation workshop, European Center for Coordination and Documentation of Research in the Social Sciences, Turin, September.

Macbeth, D. 1985. "The Flexible Manufacturing Mission—Some Implications for Management," *International Journal of Operations and Production Management* **5**(1):12–15.

MacKenzie, D., and J. Wajcman, eds. 1985. *The Social Shaping of Technology.* Milton Keynes, U. K.: Open University Press.

Ohmae, K. 1988. "Getting Back to Strategy," *Harvard Business Review* **66**(Nov./Dec.):149–56.

Oliver, N., and B. Wilkinson. 1988. *The Japanization of British Industry.* Oxford: Blackwell.

Panisset, B. 1988. "MRPII for Repair/Refurbish Industries," *Production and Inventory Management* **29**(4):12–15.

Sahal, D. 1981. *Patterns of Technological Innovation.* Reading, Mass.: Addison-Wesley.

Webster, J. 1988a. "Technology and Social Shaping." Presentation to Program on Information and Communication Technologies (PICT) national network meeting, Edinburgh, August.

Webster, J. 1988b. "Theorizing Technology," Edinburgh PICT internal mimeo.

Wheatley, M. 1989. "Variable Factor," *Management Today,* February, pp. 94–98.

Woodward, J. 1958. *Management and Technology.* London: HMSO.

9

A French-style Sociotechnical Learning Process: The Robotization of Automobile Body Shops

CHRISTOPHE MIDLER
FLORENCE CHARUE

Within a decade of the experimental introduction of the first robots in industry in the 1970s, robotics rapidly became the subject of national discussion in France, involving government,[1] organized labor, and management (Bayart 1985). Media attention fell along two axes. Some commentators claimed that robotics would rapidly encompass all industry—an assertion not supported by any valid economic analysis. The profitability of these new machines, which involve heavy investments, was assumed. Another media focus was on robotics' "social consequences," including massive reduction of employment, expansion of swing shifts, uncertainty regarding future qualification requirements, and difficulty in reconverting the existing labor force.

After local experiments and much discussion, the 1980s saw the introduction of robotics on a massive scale in France, mainly in the automobile industry.[2] This development bore out previous prophecies that manual labor would find it difficult to adapt to robotics. But the capacity of traditional industrial practices to use robotics in economically sound conditions had been grossly overestimated (GRAP 1988). Therefore, robotized industries began to investigate new learning processes in connection with new production practices: new organizations, management principles, control equipment, and know-how at all levels of qualification in the shops. Because the two French automobile manufacturers, PSA and Renault, were undergoing a major crisis at this time (Roos and Altshuler 1984; du Tertre 1989), high-speed apprenticeships were considered crucial.[3]

This chapter examines the experience of PSA and Renault to see how this learning process was handled. We look specifically at automobile body shops, the sector in which over 85 percent of the robots in the French auto industry are concentrated.[4] Despite the similarity of products, uniformity of welding techniques, industrial concentration favoring standardization, same equipment suppliers, and similarity of technological points of departure (manual Taylorian shops), the sociotechnical patterns of robotized body shops show significant diversity. Far from disappearing over time, these differences have solidified, thereby disproving the classic theory of the effect of similar environment on forms of production. These findings lead us to develop a theory of *process determinism:* the different learning processes of the new technologies induce irreversible effects (or "path dependencies") that strongly constrain change (Charue 1990).

The Robotic Technology: A Permanent and Cumulative Learning Process

We begin with an analysis of the technical evolution of body shops, which were the leaders in this process of change. In the following section, we analyze the organizational developments.

The body construction stage in car manufacturing starts downstream of the metal stamping shop, where the shaped metal components are assembled to make up the finished shell. Next, the doors and engine hoods are fitted, before the completed assembly is passed on to the painting shop. During the 1950s, these operations were performed manually. Workers fixed the stampings in jigs, adjusted them to correct fit, and then welded them into one piece using manual spot-welders. In the 1960s, automatic multispot welding machines fitted, adjusted, and welded the stampings into a complete subassembly. The machines proliferated and were integrated into large-scale production lines; by 1970, some shops performed more than half of each car's spot welds using this technique.

With the introduction of the assembly robot in the early 1970s, the process of integrating the adjusting and welding functions was reversed, returning to systems more reminiscent of the old manual shops: the robot taking on the positioning function (a robot arm with a handling grip) or the welding function (arms with spot-welding) as required. The newest PSA and Renault shops are about 80 percent robotized, and the number of robot installations has increased rapidly. Figures 9.1 and 9.2 illustrate the rates of robotization at the PSA and Renault factories, respectively (Pélata 1988; Grégoire 1988).

This considerable increase in the number of robots is a part of the overall evolution of the global technical system, from mechanized automation to flexible manufacturing systems. A closer analysis of robotization policy reveals that planning engineers regard each project not as an end in itself but rather as an opportunity to test the feasibility of introducing robotics to a new phase of manufacturing by drawing on cumulative experience. The following is an analysis of this policy of cumulative learning.

Differences Between Workshop Models

The technical options of the two manufacturers differ in three respects: plant layout and the human–machine relationship; production flow constraints; and flexibility and production capacities.

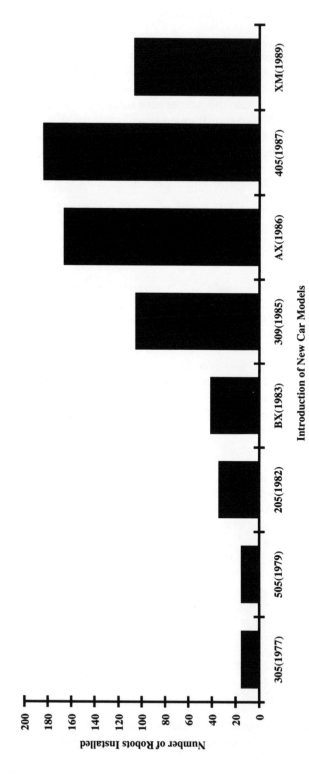

Figure 9.1 Expansions of robotics application in car body shops at PSA.

158

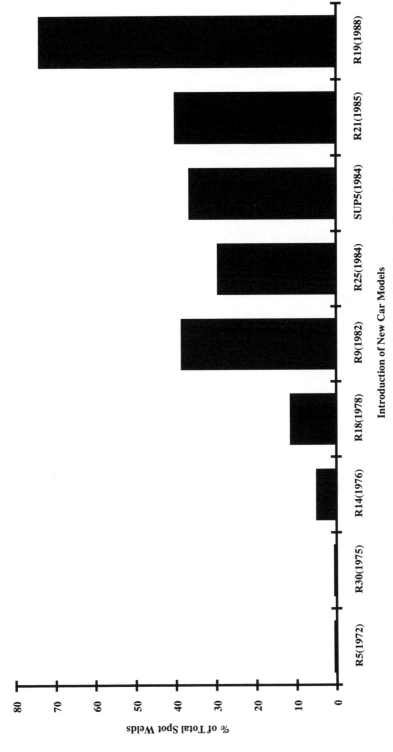

Figure 9.2 Expansions of robotics application in car body shops at Renault.

PLANT LAYOUT AND THE HUMAN–MACHINE RELATIONSHIP

With the introduction of robotics, what role remains for manual work stations, which load components onto robotized production lines, weld small parts, and perform operations not suited to automation? Different types of layout result from different organizational responses. In some shops, the manual stations (upstream preparation of parts) are kept separate from the robotized sections, so that a sharp division exists between the semiskilled workers on the one hand and the line operators and maintenance specialists on the other. Elsewhere (for example, at the Renault R19 factory), this separation is not imposed so that the manual work and the line-operating activity remains associated. In both cases, buffer stocks are provided to isolate the work rate of the manual workers from that of the robots and thus to avoid the inevitable delays caused when manual activity interacts directly with automatic processes.

PRODUCTION FLOW CONSTRAINTS

How can the plant management deal with the contingencies? What buffer stocks need to be available to nullify the effects of temporary shortages of input to the production lines? Are there ways to cut out of and back into the lines so that downgraded line stations can be brought into play? Does the workshop have the manual resources (semiskilled workers) needed to substitute for an automatic station that has broken down? Do the production control rules impose strict observance of a given rate of flow of output, or is the plant management allowed room for improvisation?

Our analysis of French body shops revealed a number of differences. For example, the Citroën shop initially had no way to provide manual replacements or to cut out of the line. The Peugeot shop at Poissy, in contrast, corrected any omissions by establishing manual spot-welding at the exit from the automatic production line.

In general, the shops tend to put up with production flow constraints and eliminate manual replacement resources. However, there usually exist "downgraded" production systems that deviate from the flow processes initially planned by the production engineers; on-line stocks are definitely lower than they were ten years ago but generally remain higher than had been anticipated. As an example, consider the on-line levels of vehicle floorboard components at one body shop. In 1980, the actual stock was 3,000 units; the projected on-line inventory for a new body shop started up in 1985 was 40 units; the present effective inventory was 40 units plus 150 held off-line. In summary, the trend is strongly toward automation, but manual intervention and maintenance of buffer stocks remain critical.

FLEXIBILITY AND PRODUCTION CAPACITIES

Going beyond the standardization of basic technical elements (robots and automatic systems), PSA developed the concept of a standard body shop configuration, with fixed specifications for capacity (1,000 cars per day in two shifts) and flexibility (able to produce three different models with several versions of each) (Grégoire 1988). Thus far, five body shops of this type are in service, and three others are near completion.

This option implies some features that may appear inconsistent with achieving economies of scale. For instance, the Peugeot plant at Sochaux comprises two polyvalent body shops working side by side, and Citroën's Aulnay site is about to follow suit. Yet the aim for a high degree of flexibility has not yet been attained. All the polyvalent body shops of the PSA group are still producing a single model, with the sole exception of the one at the Poissy plant, which assembles both the 205 and 309 Peugeot models using the same equipment. The principle of compensating for market irregularities by switching between models is still only a theory at all the other plants.

A concept of a global technological model does not exist in the Renault company. The only standardization is found at the earliest stage of body-shop activity, in the production of subassemblies. Beyond this stage, the emphasis is more on tailoring the technological configuration to suit the specific features of the production program (expected production level, special site conditions, etc.). Each Renault site is dedicated to a specific market segment (bottom end, lower-middle and higher-middle ranges, top end), and each segment is itself carved up into model options (saloon cars, hatchbacks, 2- or 4-door versions, and so on). Inter-model capability is featured mainly in more manually operated factories elsewhere, each producing several models simultaneously.

This difference between the two manufacturers' strategic options is due to their different model ranges and their respective industrial traditions. Since the mid-1970s, Renault has had four market segments; PSA produces two quite distinct ranges (Peugeot and Citroën) with a total production volume slightly higher than that of its competitor.[5]

The Manufacturers' Main Strategies

The industry's principal advocate for robotics has been corporate services for process engineering. What was their strategy, and how did it compare with that of the rest of automobile management?

The dream of the totally automatic factory preceded the introduction of robots. But automatic mechanization was incompatible with the major changes in the automobile market in the 1970s as the "economy of variety" led Renault and PSA to increase their model ranges. Robotics seemed the only way to reconcile a purely technical strategy (maximum automation) with new marketing strategies.

Another plausible option, the evolution of modern but manual body shops, was totally ignored. The lack of interest in this option is somewhat surprising considering that Renault was a pioneer in experimenting with new organizational patterns in the 1970s. Two factors explain this neglect (Midler 1984). First, the specificities of body shop tasks limit the potential for improving work conditions without significant technical assistance. Organizational innovations in the 1970s essentially concerned assembly lines and mechanical plants. Second, production managers were not prepared to undertake considerable and lasting efforts to promote the manual option because they faced serious problems with labor unrest. The "factory without workers" seemed attractive, especially given the technicians early optimism. Ultimately, of course, the arrival of robots did not circumvent a crisis in labor relations but in fact precipitated it.

Industrywide labor problems resulted in uniform technical developments across the two companies. The only (minor) differences were the compromises resulting from overall constraints (maximum production capacities) and the particular demands of production managers (layout, flow management).

Development of Organizational Patterns in Robotized Body Shops

Organizational choices involve not just a single learning process, but rather a number of different processes. There are several different plants with the same parent company involved, each facing specific local industrial conditions. In addition, factories are not accustomed to communicating with each other.

The lack of communication among plants has made the introduction of robotics not a gradual and continuous process of transformation, but a series of technological shocks interspersed with long periods of stability during which the successive impacts had to be absorbed and mastered. Unlike the central engineering departments, at least until quite recently, the local factories did not benefit from other plants' experience and saw no reason to pass on their own experience to others.

Consequently, each body shop (PSA and Renault) has evolved somewhat differently. Here we set out the key stages in the development of new organizational models and the ways in which the broad questions raised by robotization have been tackled.

The Pioneering Generation—Revealing the Inadequacy of Traditional Working Systems

In 1982–1983, Renault (at the Douai plant), Peugeot (at Mulhouse), and Citroën (at Rennes) moved from pilot-testing a few robots installed in odd corners to the robotization of complete production lines. This move meant that the working practices of whole workshops had to be thoroughly overhauled.

First there was a steep reduction in the volume of manual welding and handling tasks. Over a period of twenty years, the direct manual labor input fell from about 10 hours to 2 hours per unit. Second, new tasks related to automatic line control were created. These included start-up and shut-down operations, machine supervision, contingency diagnosis, emergency breakdown repair, and "downgraded" replacement stations. Finally, there was need for more advanced maintenance skills and a transformation of maintenance duties, because maintenance was divided into two very distinct phases. During the production phase, machine performance has absolute priority and stoppages must be avoided at all costs; during a stand-down phase, the machinery is fully available for inspection and maintenance. As a general rule, two day-shifts are reserved for production, and one night shift is given over to the maintenance crews.

The launching of the robotized production lines proved to be a painful experience; production targets were far from being attained. The unaltered work organization of the body shops was soon found incapable of coping with the new production requirements (GRAP 1988).

Design of Organizational Objectives

To overcome these problems, organizational experiments, often involving only one section of a body shop, were carried out from 1982 to 1984. These were designed and promoted by innovators who were in most ways unlike the average production manager.

After this stage of local experiments, the period around 1985 was devoted to elaborating normalized organizational patterns at the firm level at Renault, Peugeot, and Citroën. The initial innovators were generally involved in these processes, as were management, both line and staff (Renault and Citroën) consultants to set up and promote new methodologies (Peugeot and Citroën) and labor unions, and French administration (Renault and Peugeot).

The objectives for normalization differed for the two groups (PSA and Renault). In 1982, Renault's "MIDES" (Mutations Industrielles et Dynamique Economique et Social) program first sought to set up an internal think tank in partnership with the labor unions; it did not aim to establish precise organization norms. The program was considerably affected by the change of chairmen in 1985 and all the turbulence that followed during the next three years.

At Citroën, precise organizational patterns were formalized in the frame of an ambitious company project, the Mercury Plan, with which the general management was deeply involved. In all the Citroën body shops we analyzed, the Mercury organizational norms appeared to be obligatory but, in practice, there was considerable deviation.

At Peugeot, the "ISOAR" (Impact Social et Organizational des Automatismes et de la Robotique) program from late 1983 to 1985 institutionalized job definitions and career plans in a labor agreement but was not concertized for the entire company as it had been at Citroën. These new organizational patterns were all characterized by the institution of a new operational function—the "line controller"; formal integration within the roles of both individual operatives and whole work shifts of formerly distinct functions (production, maintenance, and supervision); and a shortening of the chain of command.

The Remaining Diversity of Production Patterns

As early as 1984, field surveys revealed differences in the degree to which traditional forms of organization had been revised, the content of the new job definitions, and the level of qualification and vocational profiles corresponding to the new functions (Freyssenet 1984). Our current survey shows that the position has hardly changed. Three broad principles continue to figure prominently in corporate discourse: (1) differences in the degree to which traditional forms of organization have been revised, (2) the content of the new job definitions, and (3) the level of qualification and vocational profiles corresponding to the new functions. However, actual shop-floor conditions differ considerably in four respects.

First, the two shops differ in the degree or rate of organizational integration of the various functions contributing to a robotized production line. Up to a high level of management, the old-style division of responsibility between production and maintenance continues to prevail in some plants. Elsewhere, by contrast, the maintenance department as such no longer exists, and there remains—apart from the semiskilled manual workers—only a single category of shopfloor operatives, all of whom come under a single production department.

Second, the separation between two phases—production during the day, maintenance overnight—remains subject to the dictates of the body shop's production objectives. If the production rate is too high, output takes priority over maintenance, even at the expense of entering a vicious circle of breakdowns. A variety of arrangements aim to avoid the danger of overspecialization that leads, for example, to day-duty line controllers being unable to inform night-shift technicians because they are not responsible for breakdown repair or to maintenance technicians whose ignorance of production line procedures causes them to disrupt morning starting operations.

Third, the shops differ in the length of the chain of command and the role of each link. The usual hierarchy has four levels: a member of the plant management team responsible for coordinating the body shop activity with that of the other production departments; a workshop manager and an assistant manager ("AM2" grade in the French industrial job classification); a foreman ("AM1"); and the shopfloor workers. In body shops where functions are more integrated, the AM2 is often either a technician with supervisory experience or a young qualified engineer, and plays a key coordinating role within a general area of responsibility. In less integrated shops, the AM2 acts more like a traditional production supervisor. At the lowest level, there are various kinds of shift supervision, sometimes involving assistant technicians and tool setters and sometimes even with a division between the production and the maintenance sides.

Fourth, the shops' line controllers have different backgrounds, qualifications, and assignments. In the PSA group (formed by the merger of Citroën and Peugeot), the line controllers are all former maintenance technicians, whereas some of the Renault plants rely on former semiskilled workers who have received intensive training to the required level. In the latter case, the line is operated by a joint system involving different levels of qualification and a large degree of collective control.

The New Industrial Doctrine and Its Managerial Apparatus

Just as the period from 1980 to 1985 gave birth to new job designs, organizations, systems, and career configurations in France, the years 1985 to 1990 saw the widespread introduction of new management methods and tools, many following the Japanese example.[6] During that time, central technical engineers and plant managers visited Japan in droves.

The messages they brought back supported the organizational options already introduced into many body shops. Many of the early innovations were undertaken jointly with the union organizations, who at the time were closely studying the future of the industry. In line with a dichotomy firmly entrenched in French managerial thinking, the unions' advocacy of these new methods was thought to be directed more toward social betterment than toward improving industrial and business efficiency. However, when technical engineers joined in promoting such ideas as the need to give shopfloor workers greater responsibility and higher qualifications—all in the name of learning from Japanese achievements—this attitude was modified considerably.

This period did not merely give lip service to the new industrial doctrine; it also furnished the methodological basis for making the new job configurations effective. It is not enough to appoint production controllers and to proclaim the virtues of teamwork. If the new configuration is not to remain an empty shell, it must be backed up by individual and collective working instructions.

The effort toward greater reliability is a good example of this necessity. From 1987 to 1989, all the body shops considered here instituted "zero breakdown." But the mere introduction of new organizational patterns failed to significantly improve equipment serviceability ratios. The shops lacked the kind of skills, instructions, and instruments needed to focus energies on breakdown diagnosis and fault analysis, to implement preventive maintenance procedures, and to rationalize breakdown repair action. In the late 1980s, robotized body shops were given the necessary methodological assistance with massive interventions of consultants, including some Japanese specialists.

The doctrine being pushed at that time advocated an overall approach to factory management. The ultimate target was "zero fault, zero defect" and the means of attaining it was total reliability (a permanent drive to improve plant performance; an accent on preventive, rather than remedial, maintenance; and the rationalization of repair and maintenance action). The criterion of success was the assurance of maximum equipment serviceability during manufacturing time.

Although they converted to high-tech systems later than other factory departments such as parts machining shops, the body shops attained the new performance standards more quickly. They were forced to keep up with the rate of output from the assembly line immediately upstream, which worked on a two-shift schedule.

The management used a number of tools and methods to back up the reliability drive. They introduced plant monitoring systems that enabled them to keep breakdown records, to determine the performance of a given department, and to compare different factories. They also introduced a system for collectively evaluating the action taken to promote reliability ("Total Productive Maintenance" meetings), designed to secure the spontaneous participation of all workers in the common effort. Finally, they introduced individual monitoring systems that enabled the line controllers to follow the implementation of preventive maintenance action, to keep abreast of progress, and so on. These monitoring systems were developed after determining the parameters related to overall performance: quality index cost of rejects, availability time cycle, maximum hourly throughput, production rate, and so on.

Three Typical Robotization Models in French Body Shops

Beyond this diversity in production practices, is it possible to formalize different typical organizational models of French robotized body shops?

A "model" may mean a management method that can be circumscribed in terms of time and space ("a management package" like the quality circle); or it may mean a vast field of institutions and social entities encompassing market identifi-cation, business organization, training institutions, pay and promotion systems, and collective bargaining arrangements. Here our definition falls between these two extremes. Because we are primarily concerned with the management practitioner, we focus on *management models,* sets of procedures and ground rules that govern the interaction of agents in the undertakings concerned. This parameter does not mean, of course, that we discount the importance of such social institutions as training schemes and codes of industrial practices. These are external to the specific model but must be taken into account.

The management model comprises the following elements:

- The technical system.
- The structure and definition of roles.
- The specific tools within which those roles are implemented (indicators and sys-tems of evaluating performance and organization and assessing skills and actions) (Berry 1983).
- The system for replicating the conditions of implementation—the social mech-anisms that can ensure the durability of a particular form of management (train-ing, recruiting, and career development schemes).

Using these elements we can formalize models that typify the variety of body shops analyzed. All three models obey the same general production doctrine. Over and above the convergences due to fashion effects (Midler 1986), this doctrine is the result of a general—albeit somewhat belated—strategic recognition of and recep-tiveness to the facts of a competitive market.

The *fusion-exclusion model* features a maximum integration of the mainte-nance and production functions (the single key job of line controller, a single chain of command and systematic alternation of daytime production with overnight maintenance), on the basis of a strong geographical breakdown (the concept of each body shop as an autonomous undertaking). The methodological approaches are more personalized than generalized, allowing discretion not only by the workshop manager but also by the line controller in charge of running and maintaining each set of installations. The semiskilled manual workers are not involved in running the automatic production systems.

In the *neoclassical model,* the skilled technicians are split into two categories. One of these, broken down into teams, operates the production lines; the other, under a common command structure, carries out maintenance and repair opera-tions throughout the body shop. The methodological systems (quality circles and the like) provide a communications link across the functional dividing line. As in the fusion-exclusion model, the semiskilled workers are confined to performing what manual tasks remain.

The *Integrative Model* combines, within the same production unit, varied levels of qualifications, and the allocation of tasks is made at the team level; the produc-tion line is operated by retrained semiskilled workers with the support of mainte-nance technicians allocated by sectors. The emphasis is on teamwork principles, self-apprenticeship, and the joint monitoring of overall team performance.

Such a wide diversity of organizational patterns, cannot be attributed solely to the dispersion of plant locations or to an early trial-and-error experimentation process. In the next section we focus on the causes.

A Theoretical Learning Process Framework for Analyzing Industrial Changes

Diversity as the Result of Irreversible Learning Processes

Contingency theories seek to relate industrial configurations to environmental variables such as technology, product characteristics, and the social and institutional environment of the firm (or plant). Such adaptation theories presume that, sooner or later, modifications will either bring the different systems closer to each other or select among them.

These theories do not fit totally with our data. The product and technological similarities lead us to seek causes for the observed diversity in more sociological variables: the specificity of the local labor environment, the human relations in the different firms, and the corporate capital structure. On this basis, we can differentiate the analyzed body shops in two ways.

First, labor qualification is variable, in particular among semiskilled workers. Although the integrative model might seem more readily applicable to the plants where the semiskilled qualification level is higher, our data contradict this hypothesis. Curiously, this model was designed in the plant whose semiskilled workers were an older immigrant population that had been working on highly Taylorized tasks since the beginning of the 1960s.

Second, Renault is nationalized, but PSA is a private capital group. We would expect Renault body plants to be more affected by central labor policies reflecting the firm's social responsibility (regarding employment, cost externalization, etc.). Our data confirm this hypothesis. The integrative model, which implies an internal solution to the problem of retraining semiskilled workers, fits only Renault. But the model is not yet generalized within Renault plants, nor is it the most frequent case there. Other Renault body plants are run on the neoclassical model, as we describe later.

Our methodology (Midler 1986–1987) favors long-term action research that permits us to analyze how problems are dealt with *ex ante* and how decision-making processes shape current industrial changes. In the past, dynamics have been considered the result of strategies or determinism that require only decoding. In our approach, dynamics appear as complex, collective learning processes; we focus on the uncertainty and fuzziness of actors' perceptions of situations, objectives, and possible responses. As the dynamics progress, knowledge increases concerning what to do and how to do it. However, at the same time, decisions are already affected by previous options taken, therefore producing irreversibility. The observed diversity can be attributed to this phenomenon.

Two factors of the learning process (Thévenot 1985) have been underestimated by past approaches. The first is the time frame of the learning process. Industrial timing is not homogeneous. With the acceleration of product replacement, plants must adapt to the life cycles of the products. If the production of a mature product is not utilized to introduce innovative production practices, it will be too late to do so when the new product is maturing and all energies are focused on immediate production (Midler 1989).

The second underestimated factor is the adequacy and availability of knowledge to face a problem as soon as it appears (Hatchuel 1988). A proper theoretical apparatus is a prerequisite to collectively think out a problem and to design, negotiate, prepare, and implement the necessary changes. The preexistence of credible organizational patterns to guide the changes is essential (Midler 1988, 1989). In the body shops we studied, those who did not have the tools fell into short-term reactive processes with drastic consequences for their evolution.

The Restructuring of the Labor Force

With the development of robotics, automobile manufacturers faced two problems: a shortage of technical competence in the entire production staff and a surplus of semiskilled workers. The general employment policies of the two French groups' policies—which are the central topic of labor negotiations—influenced how they handled these problems.

THE IMPACT OF EMPLOYMENT POLICIES

Since 1983, Renault has been reducing employment. Even during the most difficult period of 1985–1987, this reduction was handled without layoffs, exclusively through normal departures, incitations to voluntary departure, and, to a much greater extent, anticipated retirement at age 55. This last measure was included in the government's plan for handling unemployment (the National Employment Funds); Renault's employment policy is clearly related to nationalized status.

Employment reduction based on the age criterion had two consequences. First, it was impossible to solve the problem of the excess of semiskilled workers by massive layoffs of this category. Second, it was impossible to solve the inadequacy of technical competence through the massive hiring of young technicians, since the flow of departures, too small to result in the necessary reduction of jobs, led to a hiring freeze until 1989.

PSA adopted a different employment policy. The necessary reduction was handled exclusively in the framework of the National Employment Funds. Layoffs were made in the semiskilled category, but hiring was maintained for more qualified personnel. As a result of this overall employment policy, PSA handled the labor restructuring problem by resorting to the labor market.

HOW THE BODY SHOPS HANDLED UNANTICIPATED RESTRUCTING

Restructuring decisions—relocating individuals to new tasks, hiring, layoffs, and so on—imply knowledge of the proper functioning of robotized body shops and an appreciation of the adequacy of previously existing qualifications.

When the Renault and Peugeot innovators formulated their plans, the robots had already arrived, and the new key function (automatic line controllers) had to be explained to the operatives then best qualified to perform it—the maintenance technicians. This is a typical example of determinism in the learning process: all restructuring scenarios that required a significant period of preparation were excluded because of uncertainty about the problems and design responses. After that first step, the gap between the remaining semiskilled workers and the others actually *increased.* The line controllers and maintenance crew developed their technical know-how on the job, while the semiskilled were excluded from this education. This learning process configuration, typical in the pioneer or "isolated" plants, leads to the fusion-exclusion or neoclassical models.

PEUGEOT: BRIDGING MAINTENANCE AND QUALIFIED WORKERS

Converting maintenance workers into line control technicians raised two problems: (1) how to get qualified maintenance technicians to accept a switch to production line work, which they regarded as less prestigious (Coffineau and Sarraz 1985), and (2) how to evaluate the new qualifications required for line control jobs.

The job classifications applying to production line jobs, based on proficiency in a given trade (electrician, mechanic, etc.) as confirmed by a highly formal test, were totally inadequate to describe the functions of the line controllers in the new setup. Automatic line controllers must be proficient in all the techniques needed to ensure continuity of performance along the lines they control. They must demonstrate on the job, not merely in the classroom.

To tackle this problem, management of the Peugeot Mulhouse plant set up the ISOAR program (already described), which ended in 1985–1986. The solutions stressed the links between maintenance and production, and provided equivalent rates of advancement.

The choices implemented in the PSA body shops after 1985 were shaped by practices that had been institutionalized in labor agreements (Peugeot) or supported, in general, by top management (e.g., Citroën's "Mercury Plan"). These choices advanced the original decision to no longer distinguish between maintenance and production workers. Line controllers were appointed from among former maintenance technicians, and new entrants now needed a certificate of secondary technical education (*bac technique*). Semiskilled workers had no future in the PSA body shops.

RENAULT: RESPONDING LOCALLY TO THE RETRAINING OF SEMISKILLED WORKERS

Unlike the case at PSA, the body shop management at Renault embarked on a scheme to convert semiskilled workers to line-controller functions. This scheme, developed at the Flins plant in 1982–1983, and similar to one devised in mechanical shops, attempted to meet production requirements while simultaneously accelerating the training process by on-the-job exchanges of experience and knowledge. Production line workers were upgraded by receiving intensive training, while the line controllers were incorporated within operational units comprising different levels of skills and qualifications.

The policy stressed training programs, followed by heavy and continuous involvement of plants before new equipment is launched. These factors led Renault to modify its project development procedures at the end of the 1980s (Midler 1989).

Until 1989, when a convention signed with labor unions framed these programs in a precise central human-relation policy, local initiatives had more autonomy to respond exactingly to the semiskilled problem. Unlike Citroën's central program, which had earlier achieved a more homogeneous policy, significant variations remained within Renault at the end of the 1980s.

This analysis of the transformation of the work force shows how successive choices, far from contributing to a cohesiveness of the three different models, in fact exacerbated their differences by freezing their idiosyncracies into institutional forms.

The Transformation of Production Supervisors

The appointment of new production supervisors raises similar problems to those already described: the shift foreman's qualifications become irrelevant when the number of workers per shift falls to such low levels and when the ability to manage workers becomes less important than a proficiency in keeping the machines running. Furthermore, the maintenance crews are not too small to fill all the gaps in the new production units.

The French auto manufacturers have handled the problem without resorting to hard redundancy measures. Their usual solution is a mixed supervisory system: appointing a shop supervisor from the maintenance side and line controllers from the production side, or vice versa. The production supervisors, lacking the technical competence to supervise their crews, are often by-passed by maintenance programs on which engineers and maintenance or line control workers directly interact.

Production supervisors, then, appear to play the key role in the diffusion of the new industrial doctrine. Two scenarios are possible: requalifying the existing supervisors, with massive and diversified training programs; and addressing the problem over time through the effects of newly hired and highly qualified people (young engineers or high level technicians) on production supervision.

A "French-style" Sociotechnological Learning Process

Did other European automobile manufacturers adopt sociotechnological patterns in their body shops that are similar to those of the French approach? Or, conversely, can we identify aspects of change in the Renault and PSA body shops that appear to be uniquely molded by the French institutional context? Our study was limited to the French case, but other works, especially those of Jürgens, Malsch, and Dohse (1989), permit us to understand the French case in a comparative light. In particular, the French characteristics can be isolated by considering the role played by labor and management.

The Role Played by the Labor Organizations

Our analysis gives little consideration to the part played by the trade unions in this process of assimilation. Their relative absence from the scene requires some comment and explanation.

As we pointed out earlier, during the first half of the decade considered, the redefinition of jobs and the restructuring of labor representation were at the heart of union preoccupations, feeding discussions with the employers' organizations (CNPF, confédération generale du travail [General Confederation of Labor]) and leading to legislative measures and collective agreements. Through the MIDES (Renault) and ISOAR (Peugeot) programs, the automobile industry was in the forefront of this movement, in which unions, management, and government together assessed the implications of advanced technology.

The largest union in the automobile industry—the communist-led CGT (confédération nationale du patronat française [National Confederation of French Employers])—was then committed to a strategy of participation in industry, an attitude obviously influenced by the "Union of the Left" government's being in power. This outlook was not to survive after the switch to a more austerity-oriented policy.

Another major, though related, factor was disagreement over how to respond to the wave of unemployment that hit the French car industry in the 1980s. The Citroën disputes, centered around the labor unrest in the Talbot plant acquired from Chrysler, ended in defeat for the union, as was the failure of the deal negotiated with Renault that hastened the departure of then CEO Bernard Hanon and led to the adoption of policies much more severe than those heralded by the abandoned draft agreement.

All these events were to spark a profound and lengthy union crisis that is still gravely affecting the French industrial relations climate. Since then, union membership in the automobile factories has declined substantially, and its weakened representatives have clung to basic claims focusing on job security and preserving vested rights. The partnership system that had marked the earlier experiments in labor relations was in most cases reduced to compliance with the statutory requirements for providing information to the union representatives, while the rank-and-file workers contributed more directly to its implementation at the shopfloor level.

The Role of Management

The specifically French features of robotics assimilation must be sought by examining the characteristics of the management tradition in the car-manufacturing industry. Forty years of development on Taylorist lines have resulted in production management for the most part failing to enhance their technical or managerial proficiency. The reliance on technical solutions, and on the authority of technicians, is founded primarily, in most cases, on the inadequacy of the alternatives proposed.

The rapid and coherent introduction of robotics conflicts with the traditionally slow and uncoordinated approach to developing appropriate organizational models. When innovative systems were devised locally, they were seen not as contributions to factory management experience but merely as the personal exploits of the local innovator, who was regarded by some as brilliant and by others as an opportunist upstart. This bipolarity explains why such "experiments," however successful have found difficulty in being accepted and exploited more widely.

Also, despite all the rhetoric about the importance of the human factor in the workplace, the French car-manufacturing industry remains profoundly characterized by a technocratic ideology that equates technology with efficiency and sees the human factor merely as a problem of redeployment. In this context, it is difficult to promote a more integrated concept of the social and organizational policies that would result in greater effectiveness.

The extension of robotization has not been founded on any spectacular demonstration of its economic superiority over more labor-intensive systems, but on a consensus among technocrats and company managers according to whom, for example, labor-intensive workshops can no longer be managed to meet high standards of quality while avoiding industrial conflict, and so on. The concept of an alternative based less on technology and more on human relations has hardly been voiced since the "Swedish model" of the mid-1970s lost its attractiveness.

From this standpoint, the car industry represents an extreme case of French managerial practice, contrasting sharply with policy at companies like BSN, where CEO Antoine Riboud has taken up arms against the technocrats as obstacles to market success. Beyond these positions, can we foresee a long-term evolution in French managerial general attitude? During the past few years, various trends seem to suggest it.

There has been greater interplay between headquarters and local management regarding both production planning, where the factories are becoming involved in increasingly earlier stages of decision making and factory organization, where the centralized departments are going beyond their purely technical-administrative function to assist the factory managers in designing operational methods in various areas (diagnostic exercises, pilot workshops in which high-ranked engineers are temporarily seconded to production functions, the use of outside consultants, etc.). Job profiles have been enhanced at the factory management level, with a greater number of young engineering graduates being appointed to workshop assignments for significant periods. Finally, there have been changes in the training programs in French engineering schools, with an effort to develop social sciences.

Conclusions

What are the prospects for each of the three current organizational models (fusion-exclusion, neoclassical, integrative) in French robotized body shops? Are some less likely to survive than others? The questions are particularly relevant to body-shop operations because these models aim to establish and sustain a process of ever-greater machine reliability. The problem is clearly stated by the shopfloor workers when they ask: "What will happen to us after all breakdowns have been eliminated?" If no satisfactory answer is found, the targeted objective may cease to be pursued, with the Taylorist rationale retaining the upper hand.

The Importance of Technological Obsolescence

New factory organization models emerged in response to the need to exploit new and sophisticated technologies. At the start of 1990, the robotization of body-shop operations is virtually completed, in technical terms. The completion of this phase does not mean, of course, the end of technical enhancements, but with the ongoing introduction of new generations of robots and automatic systems the changes are likely to be less brutal than previously experienced.

After all, the main argument in favor of robotization is that it enables much of the investment outlay to be recovered when a new car model is put into production to replace an existing one. What happens to this argument if technological obsolescence reaches the same rapid pace on the tooling side as on the end-product side? Even if the technicians do not themselves object, the paymasters of the automobile industry will not fail to do so: throughout the last two decades, the shops have made heavy demands on capital investment resources.

Stabilization via Increased Production Volume

Body shop workers are being asked, in effect, to saw off the branch they are sitting on. But this problem has thus far been kept in the background, because productivity gains have resulted in a greater volume of output rather than in job cutting. Following a serious crisis, the recent period has seen regular expansion of the European car market (up by 30 percent over the past five years) and increased output by the two French firms, even though their relative share of the total market was declining at the same time. Our survey identified various processes relating greater reliability of machine performance to increased volume of output, first during the general upsurge of demand and then in the stabilization phase (harnessed to the launching of new models). Conversely, we also saw the extent of the difficulties in justifying an emphasis on equipment availability during periods of overcapacity, when the sales of a given car model fell below expectations.

It could be unwise to rely on further market expansion. Nevertheless, there are grounds to justify pursuing the reliability drive, even when overall market volume stabilizes. Existing models will have to be replaced and the policy of multimodel production using a common production line will have to be fully implemented.

Stability of Organizational Models Versus a Dynamic Process of Job Development

How will the three models stand up to the change from a strategy based on expanding demand to one emphasizing cost reduction?

The most vulnerable of the three seems to be the fusion-exclusion model, because of its use of sectional divisions, the stereotyped nature of its line-control personnel, and its strict segregation of semiskilled workers. It relies strongly for its continued survival on external factors: an outside labor market able to absorb its surplus manual workers, and being able to retain the service of line controllers whose employment profile is higher than that corresponding to a function beneath their level of qualification, and in which the tasks required of them are becoming mere routines. Furthermore, the future will bring the problem of training those more qualified technicians who must always be available to launch new production series and to deal with particularly difficult breakdowns. The line-controller function demands constant attendance on the job and is thus hardly compatible with taking advantage of a more profound knowledge of nonroutine technology.

In contrast, the integrative model leaves considerable scope for internal reconstruction, owing to the heterogeneous composition of the operating teams. The problems it poses are related to the need for major retraining of its personnel—both the semiskilled and supervisory—in terms of cost, delay, and feasibility. We provided a number of examples of the difficulties in this model raises. In particular, there is the need to efficiently build and consolidate a new style of factory management without resorting to large-scale outside intervention. In many cases, replacing a high-level manager, or making a decision under the pressure of immediate contingencies, has been sufficient to disrupt a program under implementation. Also, in the Renault model, the role played by the maintenance technicians is both vital and insecure: they provide the essential means of making progress (by tuning up the equipment and by initiating the semiskilled charges, who can progress without moving from their place of work).

Falling between two models, the neoclassical model leaves the maintenance side as a coherent whole under its own management structure, but offers no development prospects to the semiskilled personnel. This model may appear as less satisfactory than the integrative model to those who hold the Japanese model as the paradigm. But this model corresponds well to the particular institutional context that informs the sociotechnical learning process in French plants. The capability of each of these body shops to adopt new patterns of work is constrained by their inherited practices, as well as by the larger corporate, educational, government, and union institutions. It is this interaction between the unique characteristics of each plant and the national institutional environment that generates variety in practices and yet also a conformity to a French pattern in the evolution of the organization of work.

Notes

1. A "Robotic Commission" in the Ministry of Research and Technology submitted its conclusions in June 1982 (French Economic and Social Council 1982). Generally speaking, government authorities at this time strongly promoted the expansion of robotics in France as a new force in the international economic competition.

2. According to annual statistics in *Axes Robotique,* there were 1,280 in 1983, 2,714 in 1985, and 4,890 in 1987. The automobile industry accounts for about 50 percent of this total volume and considerably more when only more sophisticated robots are included.

3. The 1970s saw considerable concentration in the French automobile industry. Peugeot took over Citroën in 1974 and Chrysler France (which became Talbot) in 1977. In 1980, only two groups remained: Renault, which was nationalized just after the Second World War and which developed through internal expansion (in 1982 Renault was the first European manufacturer); and PSA, with two major makes, Peugeot and Citroën.

4. There are eight main body assembly plants in France: three for Renault, three for Peugeot, and two for Citroën—the latter two makes being integrated, as previously noted, in the PSA group.

5. Private car sales in Europe in 1989 were as follows: PSA, 1,697,400; Renault, 1,384,461. Production of private cars in 1981 was as follows: PSA, 1,862,000; Renault, 1,590,000.

6. Publications widely read in French car manufacturing circles included Shingo's *Maîtrise de la Production et Méthode Kan Ban* (1984) and Béranger's *Les Nouvelles Régles de la Production* (1987).

References

Bayart, Denis. 1985. *Mise en oeuvre et réalités de la robotique*. Research report. Paris: Centre d'Etude des Systèmes et Techniques Avancés (CESTA).

Béranger, Pierre. 1987. *Les nouvelles règles de la production*. Paris: Dunod.

Berry, Michel. 1983. *Une technologie invisible*. Paris: Centre de Recherche en Gestion.

Charue, Florence. 1990. "Apprentissage organisationnel et mutations industrielles. Le cas de la robotisation des tôleries automobiles." Ph.D. diss., Ecole des Mines de Paris.

Coffineau, Alain, and Jean Paul Sarraz. 1985. *ISOAR: Peugeot Mulhouse*. Rapport de recherche IECI, October. Strasbourg: IECI éditeur.

du Tertre, Christian. 1989. *Technologie, Flexibilité Emploi*. Paris: Editions L'harmattan.

French Economic and Social Council. 1982. "The use of robotics in production, and its perspectives for the future," Rapport du Conseil Economique et Social, Paris, February.

Freyssenet, Michael. 1984. "La requalification des opérateurs et la forme sociale actuelle d'automatisation," *Sociologie du Travail* **4**:422–33.

GRAP (Groupe de Réflexion sur l'Automatisation de la Production). 1988. "Une chaîne robotisée au concret" in "Pour une automatisation raisonnable de l'industrie," a special issue of *Annales des Mines,* January, pp. 12–18.

Grégoire, Michael. 1988. "Robots at automobiles Peugeot: From a tool to a system," in *Actes du congrès AFCET automatique 88,* pp. 605–15. Paris: AFCET.

Hatchuel, Armand. 1988. "Les savoirs de l'intervention" communication au colloque de Cerisy: "Les métiers de l'organisation," Research paper, June. Paris: Centre de Gestion Scientifique Ecole des Mines de Paris.

Jürgens, Ulrich, T. Malsch, and K. Dohse. 1989. *Moderne Zeiten in der Automobilindustrie. Strategien der Produktionsautomatisierung im Laender- und Konzernvergleich*. Berlin: Springer-Verlag.

Midler, Christophe. 1984. "L'amélioration des conditions de travail comme enjeu organisationnel," *Revue des Conditions de Travail* **13**:22–27.

Midler, Christophe. 1986. "Logique de la mode managériale," *Revue des Annales des Mines, série Gérer et Comprendre* **3**:74–85.

Midler, Christophe. 1986–1987. "Une expérience de recherche en gestion," in *Rencontres Pluridisciplinaires,* pp. 47–57. Séminaire de Sociologie du Travail 1986–87 Paris, Publication CNAM-CNRS.

Midler, Christophe. 1988. "De l'automisation à la modernisation; premier épisode: une expérience novatrice chez Renault," *Annales des Mines, série Gérer et Comprendre* **13**:(dec.):4–16.

Midler, Christophe. 1989. "De l'automisation à la modernisation; deuxieme épisode: vers de nouvelles pratiques de gestion des projects industriels," *Annales des Mines, série Gérer et Comprendre* **14**(march):26–34.

Pélata, Patrick. 1988. "How to get robots busy: Problems to get a good reliability of the automatised body shops in RENAULT," in *Actes du congrès AFCET automatique 88,* pp. 669–78, Paris: AFCET.

Roos, Daniel, and Alan Altshuler, eds. 1984. *The Future of the Automobile,* Report, MIT.

Shingo, S. 1984. "Maîtrise de la production et méthode Kan Ban," in *les Editions d'organisation.*

Thévenot, L. 1985. "Les investissements de forme," in *Conventions économiques,* pp. 21–71. Paris: CEE-PUF editeur.

III

DIFFUSION OF NEW WAYS
OF ORGANIZING

10

The Diffusion of American Organizing Principles to Europe

BRUCE KOGUT
DAVID PARKINSON

The slow productivity growth of the United States during the 1970s and 1980s has all but eradicated the remarkable esteem in which its industry was held in the years immediately following World War II. In Europe, wartime destruction left little doubt that economic structures had to be remade in accordance with two seemingly mutually exclusive models of the United States and the Soviet Union. Yet, though they were widely different, it was hardly coincidental that both models encouraged the growth of mass production run by large organizations. It had been the American example in the earlier part of the century that was the target of Soviet emulation. It was the American model, even if emulated only indirectly, that dominated the ideas of best practice in Europe, and elsewhere, at the midpoint of this century.

To a large extent, the postwar competition between the United States, Europe, and Japan was driven by a dynamic of the American exploitation of techniques of mass production and their diffusion to other countries. These techniques are the most pronounced expression of what can be called the dominant "organizing principles" of American corporations. These principles consisted of rules by which to rationalize work and to increase the volume and throughput of production and distribution.

Despite the importance of these principles to postwar competition, they did not emerge as sudden innovations, but evolved through a long period of trial and error dating back to the early 1800s. By the late 1800s, they were sufficiently advanced to allow such American firms such as the Singer Sewing Corporation and the Westinghouse Company to invest successfully in European operations. These early examples were harbingers of the rapid expansion of American exports to and investments in Europe.

The slow evolution and development of the techniques of the rationalization of

179

work and mass production are important indicators of the difficulty facing even innovators to understand the implications of new organizing principles. The problem is not only the difficulty of understanding, but also, of course, of changing social relations among classes and individuals. To a large part, these early innovations spread first in the United States because of its unique conditions: the large flow of immigrants with diverse skills, the scarcity of labor, and the demand created by an expanding population.[1] This wave of change overwhelmed the traditions of craft workers, as well as the social institutions that supported such traditions.

In Europe, however, strong craft institutions reflected hundreds of years of development. The new American principles of organization could only be contemplated from the perspective of their challenge to the well-entrenched social relations of class and status. The economic challenge posed by the United States beginning at the turn of the century created tremendous interest in how the United States organized its work. But the dilemma facing European firms was how not only to understand these organizing principles, but how to adapt them to indigenous conditions.

This chapter sketches a brief history that examines the diffusion of two related, but different, sets of organizing principles that have characterized the American economy. The first set includes those principles that appertain to the rationalization of work in a broad sense. These principles were identified as the "American System of Manufactures" by the mid 1800s. Their most well-known expression are the ideas associated with Frederick Taylor at the turn of the century. The second set includes the principles by which American corporations came to be organized. The most distinguishable principle of this sort was to divisionalize authority by product line—what is called the multidivisional structure.

The history of these principles and their diffusion illuminates the obvious point that their adoption in Europe was accompanied in no small degree by indigenous adaptation. But a more important observation is that these adaptations varied depending on the nature of the existing social order. To highlight this issue, we focus primarily on the case of the United Kingdom where Taylorist ideas were only partially accepted, but the multidivisional structure, at least in name, was widely adopted by the leading corporations.

To a considerable degree, our argument bridges the recent work of Lazonick (1990) and Chandler (1990).[2] Lazonick has detailed the strong argument that the United Kingdom failed at the shopfloor level to adopt new methods of organization that had been developed in the United States. Chandler, in an ambitious study, has argued that the U. S. dominance can be attributed to its development of large corporations that generated the "organizational capabilities" to manage large investments in production, distribution, and marketing.

The contribution of our argument is to clarify by a comparison among countries and kinds of principles how the concrete social conditions influenced the adoption and adaptation of new methods of organizing. The British lead in adopting the multidivisional structure was the outcome of the control of management over corporate organization; its lag in rationalizing work was an outcome of management's weak position in the operation of the shopfloor.

We begin first with a discussion of the historical roots and development of the multidivisional structure in the United States. Then we recount the case of the spread of this practice to Europe, focusing particularly on the United Kingdom. The contents of this chapter, though historical, are obviously of contemporary interest insofar as the current period is characterized by a new wave of organizing principles stemming from Japan. Our concluding remarks address, briefly, the implications for understanding the diffusion of Japanese methods of organization.

The history we trace is not adequate to the task of establishing precisely the adaptations made to the adoption of American methods. Yet, it is clear that the principal difference was that standardization in the United States was motivated, to a great extent, by the shortage of skilled labor, whereas in Europe, the challenge was to combine in some way the indigenous craft organization of work with these new methods. To this extent, this history has a striking parallel to the description given in Whittaker's chapter on the current grafting of Japanese practices onto the traditional organization of work in British industry (Chapter 7).

The American Organizing Principles of Work

The American System of Manufactures

The organizing techniques frequently identified with Taylorism are to be found in the changes occurring in the early part of the 1800s. By the mid 1800s, the "American System of Manufactures" had become a widely discussed form of organization. Starting in the armories of New England, it gradually spread throughout related industries. The primary property of this system was the use of standards and gauges to achieve the interchangeability of parts. Clearly, if progress was to made from reliance on the craft skills of workers operating individually, the evolution of the division of labor required standardization of the components of the final good.

There did not seem to be any recognition that interchangeability would itself permit mass production and that it even required a different organization of work. Rather, the early goal was to produce weapons whose parts could be easily replaced in battlefield conditions. The Springfield and Harper Ferry armories took over twenty years to reach a semblance of interchangeability (Smith 1977). Critical to this achievement was the invention of "go–no go" gauges to establish standardization. Once standardization had been identified as the key element, demand grew for accurate machinery.

The relationship between standardization and mass production itself was not established until the Civil War. Prior to 1850, in fact, the American factory grew very slowly in size; economies of scale were neglible (Atack 1985). It was the achievement of a modicum of standardization with less skilled labor that was the contribution of the early history of manufacturing in the United States.

After 1850, however, plant size grew rapidly. In part, this growth reflected the introduction of electricity that allowed factories to be freed from the constraints of a single belt driven by a large steam engine (Nelson 1980). For the first time, significant scale economies were achieved (James 1983; Atack 1985). Standardization laid the groundwork for the evolution of mass production systems.

This link between standardization and mass production was recognized early on by the Singer Sewing Corporation. Benefitting from the diffusion of the armory technology, Singer, founded in 1851, took thirty years to achieve interchangeability in parts.[3] The diffusion of the Singer method was not only international, but also interindustry, for it was Singer that introduced a systematic high-volume approach to manufacturing the woodwork inputs into its sewing machines.

Taylorism and Mass Production

The implications of standardization for mass production were limited, however, by the absence of control over the workplace. In the United States, the battle for control was fought in the later part of the 1800s and this struggle was no greater than in the mechanical engineering industries. In these industries, as elsewhere in the United States, the predominant organization was the inside contracting system, which delegated the hiring of workers to a contractor. In other industries, such as textiles, a supervisor was employed, but the role to drive the workers was largely the same.

It was in this environment that the piecework system began to develop. Taylor's proposals were among many during this time, but they differed by establishing a so-called scientific method by which to measure productivity and, hence, pay of the individual worker, and by delegating responsibility to a central office rather than to a foreman or boss. In this sense, Taylorism was a method by which management took direct control over the workplace and gained, or so Taylor eventually argued, the cooperation of workers by setting a fair wage based on objective standards.

Introduced into several Philadelphia factories, Taylorism diffused slowly. By 1909, it had been tried, to varying degrees, by 172 firms, representing only 1.2 percent of all plants (Thompson 1914). Though the majority of these firms were industrial, 23 of them were in services, transportation, and government work. It is particularly important to note that Taylorism diffused most rapidly in labor-intensive and emergent industries (Nelson, 1980, 57). In fact, the spread of Taylorism was especially effective in public services and in offices. The height of this expression can be seen in the idea of secretarial pools, as it developed in the 1920s and 1930s (Davies 1982).

The widespread use of Taylorist methods is evident in the data collected by the National Industrial Conference Board in the 1930s and 1940s (see Baron, Dobbin, and Jennings 1986; Kochan and Cappelli 1984). By 1935, 34 percent of firms with more than 250 employees used time and motion studies; by 1949, this rose to over 50 percent; among firms with less than 250 employees, the percentages are 13 and 26 for 1935 and 1949, respectively. Though these percentages by sectors favor manufacturing (especially rubber, electrical manufacturing, and automobiles and parts), insurance and other services also engaged in time and motion studies and the majority used some form of job analysis.

By the end of World War II, Taylorist ideas of management had been fully routinized in the American economy. Accounting and evaluation systems also came to reflect the emphasis on measuring direct labor costs (Johnson and Kaplan 1987). The only major element dropped in the American practice was piece-rate pay. With the advent of assembly lines, the intensity of work was driven by the pace of machinery. In the office place, it was driven by increasing norms of professionalism.

A development closely affiliated with Taylorism was the further evolution of mass production systems. Whereas Taylorism was oriented toward the creation of functional departments and efficient incentives for individual work, mass production, and its most pronounced expression in Fordism, concerned the transformation of individual work into a coordinated flow. Though Fordism is frequently associated with large fixed capital investments and mechanization, the early applications were to labor-intensive operations. The first application was to convert the assembly operations of Ford from batch to flow production. Except for inventory and manual tools, the capital investment was minor. If demand increased, additional lines were simply formed adjacent to one another, sometimes spilling into the parking lot (Lewchuk 1987).

From the history of Hounshell (1984), the diffusion of standardization can be traced from the armories into a broad number of industries by 1900. The commonality of these industries were their newness and reliance on capital goods, as stressed by Rosenberg (1969). The early industries that dominated the U.S. economy, principally housing, furniture, and textiles (all needed for the westward expansion), decreased in importance over time.[4] Increasingly, the American economy favored industries where large firms predominated: railroads, chemicals, automobiles, rubber, and electronics. And these were the industries where the new methods of organization, including the multidivisional structure to be discussed later, were rapidly adopted.

Diffusion to the United Kingdom

The transformation of the American economy from agriculture to industrial products had a major impact on Europe, especially on the United Kingdom. In the early part of the 1800s, a principal concern of Great Britain was the loss of technology and know-how, not only through the exportation of capital goods but also through the emigration of workers. Indeed, the development of the textile industry in the United States benefitted considerably from the violation of British patents and the hiring of skilled workers (Jeremy 1981).

The growing strength of the U.S. machine-tool industry transformed the debate on the outflow of British technology and the controlling of exports to concern over import competition. By the end of the 1800s, the importation of American machinery was seen as critical to sustain a number of export industries in the United Kingdom. The bicycle industry is a stunning example of the success of this policy (Harrison 1969). Prior to the turn of the century, the American bicycle industry expanded overseas to Europe and Japan on the basis of standardized manufacturing techniques. Its dominant export position was lost to British companies, which adopted American machinery, lowered costs, and maintained a higher level of quality. The U.S. firms never successfully consolidated; standardization without mass production was not sufficient to compete in world markets.

In the 1890s, the loss of export markets to the United States caused a first recognition of the "labor problem" in the United Kingdom as an issue in international competitiveness. A common call was for increased management control over the shopfloor. The influential Colonel Dyer (who set up the Engineering Employers Association) argued, for example, for "the freedom to manage their own affairs which proved so beneficial to the American manufactures as to enable them to compete . . . in what was formerly an English monopoly" (Lewchuk 1987, 70).

As a solution to this problem, the United Kingdom employers experimented with various forms of the piece-rate system, much like the experiments in the United States. Yet, a critical difference was that these piece rates were introduced without a radical change in management's control over the shopfloor. While, in the United States, machinery was increasingly used to replace labor, this process was rejected in the United Kingdom due to the entrenched position of skilled labor. Though skilled labor in America also objected to Taylorism, the influx of immigrants provided manufacturers with a pool of capable but unskilled workers suited for the new methods of production. In Britain, the craft tradition of skilled workers remained a formidable obstacle to effective management control of the workplace.

These differences are transparent in the history of the British auto industry and the arrival of American firms. Concomitant with, and even prior to, the British experiments with piece-rate wages, American firms began to arrive in the United Kingdom with these new methods of production. Singer opened its first factory in Glasgow in 1867, being reputedly the largest one in the United Kingdom and producing 65,000 machines a year (Hounshell 1984, 95). The success of the Singer Glasgow operations is a clear example of how the growth of American multinationals rode on the back of these changes in the organization of work.

Yet, the most stunning extension of American principles of work to the United Kingdom was the establishment of Ford's factory in Manchester in 1911. Within a few years, both the assembly line innovations and the $5 dollar a day wage were transferred to the Manchester facility. By World War I, Ford was the leading firm in Europe.

The response of the British industry was slow. Prior to World War I, only one firm was reported to have experimented with Taylorism (Lewchuk 1987, 89). Except for the policies initiated by General Motors following its acquisition of Vauxhall, the British-owned competitors to Ford remained committed to essentially craft methods of production. Though the World War I experience led to a growth in the rationalization movement, it also introduced the shop steward as a negotiator between labor and management. Scientific management principles, however, began to diffuse widely throughout the 1920s and 1930s, as seen in the large consultancy practice of an American, Bedeaux, who had devised a way to measure output. Bedeaux consultants were believed to have worked for more than 240 firms in this period (Littler 1982, 106ff.) Still, the effectiveness of these applications were limited by the lack of shopfloor control. Direct managerial control over labor was not achieved until the 1970s (Lewchuk 1987; Whipp and Clark 1986). By this time, the British auto industry was reduced to a single national firm, Rover.

Diffusion to Continental Europe

As a contrast to the British experience, it is useful to consider briefly the reaction of Germany and France to the new American methods. The relatively rapid response of the continental producers stands in interesting contrast to the British case. By the turn of the century, Germany had risen to rival the United Kingdom and the United States in the international trade in capital goods.

Attempts to introduce Taylorism were not widespread. As in France, Taylor first won renown through his invention of a high speed steel-cutting tool. Time and motion studies were first tried at Krupp in 1910 with a reported 25 percent saving in labor costs (Homburg 1978, 179). Its introduction at Bosch led to a prolonged strike in 1912 and 1913. Though the strike was crushed, the response of German labor was to seek to use the new doctrine of efficiency to bargain for better wages and working conditions (Homburg 1984).

In the postwar period, German industrial leaders expressed considerable interest in Taylorism and, increasingly, in mass production. German firms were decidedly smaller in comparison to those of the United States and the United Kingdom, with the exception of the electronic industry (Kocka and Siegrist 1979). In the 1920s, the burst of acquisitions and consolidations promoted acute interest in mass production and efficient organization.

The literature in Germany was rife with discussions of time/motion studies and aptitude tests (Devinat 1927). But the incentive system of Taylor was not widely adopted, nor did the Bedeaux system penetrate more than twenty-five firms (Homburg 1984). As in the United States, wages were increasingly defined in reference to organizational norms and a growing interest in social welfare benefits. Rather, Taylorist ideas were gradually subsumed in the rationalization movement, under government support, that swept Germany in the mid-1920s. This movement not only influenced work organization in industrial sectors (above all in electronics), but also in the office place (Fridenson 1978). Taylorism succeeded in name because of a strong indigenous development in methods of efficient production.

It was in France, however, that the diffusion of Taylorism and mass production was the most pronounced. Although the level of French managerial administration generally lagged behind the British and the German in the late 1800s and early 1900s, France dominated the European auto industry. The intense home competition led to an interest in new machines and methods of production. French firms quickly moved to import, for example, the most advanced capital equipment from the United States in order to improve their productivity (Laux 1976).

Auto companies were also quick to understand the advantages of the American system. Taylorism had been introduced into France through the singular efforts of a prominent engineering academic, Henri Le Chatelier. Le Chatelier saw in Taylorism the practical applicaiton of engineering to design more efficient organizations. As Maier (1970) has argued, the strong engineering tradition in France, as well as in Germany, established favorable conditions for the reception of Taylorism.

However, the early experiments with Taylorism were failures. In 1912, Berliet hired time-study experts in his plants without considering to persuade workers of the benefits (Moutet 1975). The recommended cuts in piecework led to a strike. Renault, who had already introduced some aspects of Taylorism in his plants in 1908, visited Taylor and Ford in the United States in 1911. In 1912, time-study was extended to several Renault plants. Following the publication of unfavorable American union reports, a strike broke out, though as with Bosch it was crushed.

It was only during World War I that Taylorism was recognized to achieve productivity gains in a handful of munitions plants (Moutet 1975). Following the war, the competitive effect of Ford's production out of its Manchester plant incited French auto companies to adopt mass productions systems. Citroën adopted the assembly line in 1919, Berliet, in 1920, and Renault and Peugeot, two and three years later, respectively. The only major German producer to adopt mass production was Opel in 1924, shortly before its acquisition by General Motors (Fridenson, 1978).[5]

But France also strongly stressed the indigenous roots of Taylorism. The rationalization movement, which also gained prominence in France during the 1920s, emphasized the work of French authors, especially Fayol regarding the organizaiton of the firm. Due to the support of the state and unions in the postwar period, French employers entered the 1920s in a strong position following the successful breaking of a number of major strikes. Time/motion studies expanded rapidly; only in the United Kingdom was the Bedeaux system more widely spread than in France. As in Germany, Taylorism became part of the emergence of an engineering ideology that reinforced the penetration of managerial control over the shopfloor.

Discussion

In his study of the diffusion of scientific management in Europe, Devinat (1927) noted that Taylorism had spread widely throughout the continent, including the Soviet Union. Its greatest success, however, lay in those countries marked by similar indigenous efforts. In each country, its diffusion was strongly influenced by the existing institutional structure.

These institutional influences were of two kinds. First, the ability of management to control the shopfloor strongly modulated the introduction of new Taylorist ideas. Yet, the experiences of the United Kingdom, Germany, and France suggest that the most conductive environment was one where management had neither dominant nor weak control. In the United Kingdom, the failure by management to gain control over the shopfloor, as had occurred in the United States in the earlier part of the century, rendered it difficult to introduce new techniques of production, as well as new capital equipment (Lewchuk 1987). In France, the power of the employers after the breaking of the postwar strikes reduced the necessity to build further on the early initiatives of the rationalization movement; the initial interest in Taylorism floundered in the postwar period (Moutet 1975).

In Germany, the growing cooperation of labor and employers led to a gradual transformation of the German economy. This transformation did not occur under the label of Taylorism. Indeed, the rationalization movement in Germany self-consciously stressed the German roots of the programs to standardize production, consolidate industry into fewer firms, and to diffuse best practices in the economy.[6] However, the conflict between the tendency of rationalization to lead to mass production and the tradition of craft workers led to a tension in the organization of work in Germany that has persisted to current times.

The second institutional factor was the support of political and ideological institutions. The diffusion of new methods of production was strongly supported by the

German government, especially through its contribution to numerous trade associations and technical centers.[7] Furthermore, the emphasis on productivity was reinforced by the technical training of German workers and managers. In France and in the United Kingdom, the educational institutions worked to separate the shopfloor from management. The debate over Taylorism was, as Maier (1970) argued, indeed an ideological struggle to extend managerial control over the workplace.

An interesting possibility, to which we can only allude here, is that the failure of the British efforts resulted from the lack of an engineering managerial class that could legitimately make this argument. In Chandler's (1990) words, the United Kingdom developed an economy characterized by "family capitalism." Notwithstanding whether this claim of the greater importance of family control in Britain will bear up against comparative evidence, what is clear is that British management did not develop the administrative control over the shopfloor to introduce quickly new methods of organizing the factory and to build the appropriate incentives.

The Multidivisional Structure

The multidivisional structure was one of the most significant management innovations of twentieth century, and was crucial in the growth of industrial firms beyond the limits of single product lines (Chandler 1962; Fligstein 1990). Originating in the United States in the 1920s, it was a direct outgrowth of the emergence of large American firms, competing on mass production and large volume distribution. It coincided with the "marketing revolution" of the 1920s and led to a reordering of both the industrial structure of the United States and the power structure within many firms.[8] The functional structure and single industry focus was gradually replaced in the top American corporations by a new emphasis on growth and sales through diversification and the allocation of functional authority to product divisions (Chandler 1962; Williamson 1975; Fligstein 1990).

To illustrate the development of the multidivisional structure, we draw primarily on the well known history of Du Pont discussed by Chandler (1962, ch. 2). The modern Du Pont was created when Pierre and Coleman Du Pont consolidated the explosives industry into a single, tightly controlled and functionally organized firm in 1902. With a monopoly in military explosives, Du Pont underwent tremendous growth, growing by 54 times during the First World War. However, with the end of the war, Du Pont faced an urgent need to find a use for its vastly expanded productive capacity. The solution was to enter the paint, dyestuffs, and artificial leather industries, partly because the dominant firms in these industries had been German and were thus removed from competition by the war, but largely because these industries could make use of Du Pont's basic raw material, nitrocellulose.

Du Pont's new businesses required a new set of capabilities. Its traditional product (high explosives) was sold by tonnage but many of its new businesses required merchandising. Faced with fierce competition in these new markets, Du Pont soon was experiencing serious losses in its new product lines (although the explosives operations continued to be profitable). It took several years and several studies that all came back proposing the radical idea of the multidivisional structure, and a deep recession before structural change actually took place.

This radical innovation involved splitting the company into product divisions, each with relative autonomy in day-to-day operations. A new general office was created to hold the individual divisions accountable, ensuring that they were managed efficiently. The general office also would focus on the broader strategic issues of the enterprise as a whole. While this structure assured accountability and control, it freed up the time and attention of upper management for strategic issues at the corporate level (Chandler 1962; Williamson 1975). Du Pont was soon again profitable and growing.

Meanwhile, at General Motors, Alfred Sloan independently created a similar structure to gain control over the far flung empire William Durant had built. Not long after implementing the new structure, General Motors gained the lead over Ford in sales (Chandler 1962). Perhaps because of its central role in the turnaround efforts of such pioneering companies as Du Pont and General Motors, the new organizational structure was widely believed to contribute to the success of these corporations and, particularly after World War II, the form was widely adopted by other large American corporations.[9]

It is curious that Pierre Du Pont was involved in the development of the new organizational structure at both Du Pont and GM, and yet he seemed to make no connection between the structural problems of the two companies. While this might seem strange, we should note that Du Pont was struggling with a diverse but tightly controlled and rationalized functional organization, while Alfred Sloan at GM was struggling with a far-flung holding company. It is also an indication that the multidivisional structure was not yet recognized as an organizing principle, much as in the case of the slow recognition of the principles of standardization (Chandler 1962, 114–115).

The success of the new structure in addressing the management problems of the time was striking. Throughout the 1920s and 1930s, firms with the new structure grew faster and were more profitable than firms without it (Fligstein 1990, chaps. 4 and 5). The combination of factors leading to the origin of the new organizational structure—complexity, customer diversity, and competition—is reflected in the industry distribution of the multidivisional structure in 1960. In some industries, notably mining and metals, firms tended to grow and diversity but stuck to products that were sold largely to their traditional customers. Few of these firms adopted the new structure. At the other extreme were the electrical, electronics, and power machinery industries, where technological complexity led to diversification into products that served diverse customers. In these industries, 90 percent of firms adopted the new structure (Chandler 1962).

The diffusion of the multidivisional structure in a sample of large American firms is well illustrated in Figures 10.1 and 10.2. Figure 10.1 shows the proportion of adopting firms by industry in 1960, 1970, and 1980. Figure 10.2 shows the diffusion of the multidivisional structure in 150 large American firms.

The hypothesized performance advantages driving the diffusion of the multidivisional structure are best articulated by Williamson's (1975) "M-Form Hypothesis." Williamson argued that as firms grew more complex they suffered from

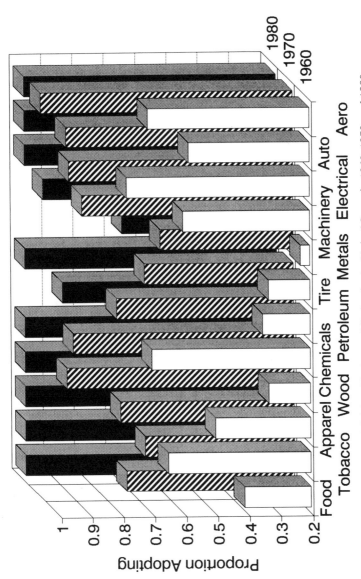

Figure 10.1 Multidivisional industry diffusion in the United States in 1960, 1970, and 1980.
Source: Based on data from Bhargava (1973).

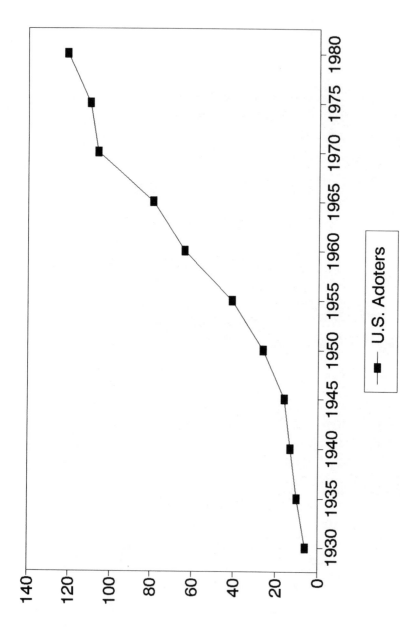

Figure 10.2 Diffusion of multidivisional structure in 150 U.S. firms. *Source:* Based on data from Bhargava (1973) and additional research by the authors.

U.S. Adoters

cumulative control loss including the confounding of day-to-day and strategic decisions resulting in poor performance. He hypothesized that the multidivisional structure more nearly approximates neoclassical profit maximization than does the functional structure for large, complex firms. Empirical work has largely confirmed this claim (see Armour and Teece 1978; Teece 1981; Hill 1988).

Diffusion to the United Kingdom

The forces driving the divisionalization of European firms during the postwar years were the same as for American firms: administrative complexity caused by diversity and inefficiency in the face of competition. An important difference, however, was that this competition was frequently from the United States, which was perceived as a leader in the adoption of new management practices such as the multidivisional structure. These factors of growing administrative complexity and the demonstration effect of the American adoption prompted the rapid diffusion of the multidivisional structure by European firms, especially in the period 1960–1970 (Channon 1973; Dyas and Thanheiser 1976; Pavan 1972).

One of the major contrasts between Europe and the United States is the later adoption of the multidivisional structure in Europe. In the three major European industrial countries—the United Kingdom, France, and West Germany—there were few (if any) firms adopting the multidivisional structure prior to 1950. This lag is widely attributed to the less competitive environments in these countries in the inter-war years (Channon 1973; Franko 1976). In the British case, joint stock companies were relatively less common than in the United States. In 1914, 80 percent of U.K. companies were still private family companies and by 1950 a remarkable 50 percent of the top British firms were still family dominated (Channon 1973), lending support to Chandler's (1990) description of the United Kingdom as being a case of family capitalism. The prevalence of privately held firms, protected markets and the restrictive practices and cartels that flourished in Britain during the 1930s (there were no significant antitrust laws in Britain until 1948) led to a less competitive environment in British industry than the United States.

The changes in the United Kingdom are well documented by the data collected by Channon (1973). For 1950, he found only twelve of ninety-two (13 percent) firms in his sample had adopted the multidivisional structure and of these, eight were foreign owned or controlled. The four domestic multidivisional firms represented only 5 percent of the domestic firms in his sample. However, throughout the 1950s and 1960s British firms rapidly adopted the new structure so that by 1970, 72 percent of all firms in Channon's sample were multidivisional.

The Spread to Continental Europe

The history of the diffusion of the multidivisional structure Germany and France is similar to that of the United Kingdom's. In these countries, companies traditionally enjoyed relatively protected environments. This protection often had government approval (if only tacitly) and was embedded in the financial and banking structure. Companies were tightly controlled, often by single families, or linked through financial arrangements, and publicly traded companies were rare.

Consequently, the widespread adoption of the multidivisional structure in these countries did not get into full swing until the 1960s. The spread of the multidivisional structure in these countries was primarily due to the development of market, technological, and legal environments similar to those that prevailed earlier in the United States (Alford 1976; Chandler and Daems 1980). Principal among these developments were the rapid growth in gross national product and the rise of mass consumer markets, the adoption of large-scale, capital-intensive production technology, and significantly stronger antitrust laws. The emergence of a more competitive environment forced many of the holding companies to rationalize and consolidate their operating units.

The emergence of greater competition also explains the earlier adoption by British firms because the United Kingdom enacted antitrust laws earlier than the other European countries. The United Kingdom first enacted tough antitrust laws in 1948, while Germany, which had affirmed the legality of cartels in 1897 did not pass any antitrust legislation until 1957, and then only under pressure from the United States and the other Allies (Channon 1973; Dyas and Thanheiser 1976).

A second factor leading to increased competition in France and Germany was the entry into domestic markets by American multinational firms in the postwar years and, after the Treaty of Rome, the increasing international competition among European firms. The American firms, with their modern technologies and management, were especially competitive and an important perceived threat to both European industry and political independence. The success of the American firms was overwhelming. By 1965 10 percent of the United Kingdom's industrial output was produced by American firms (Channon 1973). Many European firms explicitly imitated their successful American competitors. The Channon study found that twenty-two of thirty-two British companies employing a consultant on their structural change used a single American firm, McKinsey & Company (Channon 1973). McKinsey was also reported to be involved in more than a dozen German restructuring, which would roughly account for 25 percent of German firms adopting the multidivisional structure (Dyas and Thanheiser 1976). Some of the widespread imitation of American firms was driven by European firms' attempts to compete in the United States (Franko 1976).

The evidence from these studies is that the diffusion of the multidivisional structure among European firms was affected in important ways by the history, traditions, and structure of business in each of the countries. In the United Kingdom, these factors lead to a relatively rapid and widespread diffusion of the new form. In Germany and France these factors inhibited the diffusion.[10]

Comparison of Diffusion

Due to the important studies on the diffusion of the multidivisional structure in the United States and Europe, it is possible to compare roughly the rate of diffusion among several countries.[11] We should caution the reader that these comparisons are based only on the rate of adoption by those firms that implemented multidivisional structuring. The sample was, furthermore, restricted to the 150 largest firms in the United States and the 85 largest firms in Europe. The sample sizes for the individual European countries are relatively small. To avoid giving a false aura of precision, we present the data graphically and refrain from statistical testing at this juncture.

Despite these cautions, a number of interesting patterns emerge from the comparisons. In Figure 10.3, the pattern of diffusion for the United Kingdom, France, and Germany is broadly similar to that of the United States, with an initial lag of a few decades. Although few firms adopted the multidivisional in any of the countries before 1960, noticeable in the figure after 1960 is the earlier, more rapid diffusion in the United Kingdom compared with Germany and France. These patterns reflect the management and social factors previously discussed.

In contrast with the spread of Taylorism, these figures show that the United Kingdom did not lag behind in the adoption of the innovation. In fact, the United Kingdom shows an earlier incidence of adoption and a larger number of adopting firms compared to the rest of Europe. The differing degree of adoption among the top firms in each country by 1970 is striking. It ranges from a high (in 1970) of 76 percent in the United Kingdom (Channon 1973) to a low of barely 43 percent in Germany, with France at 47 percent (Dyas and Thanheiser 1976).[12]

These observations are reinforced by the industry distribution of the multidivisional structure given in Figure 10.4. Firms with the multidivisional structure tend to cluster in certain industries, such as power machinery, electrical machinery, and electronics, which are technologically complex. Few of the large firms in any of these economies are in industries such as textiles and apparels, lumber, leather

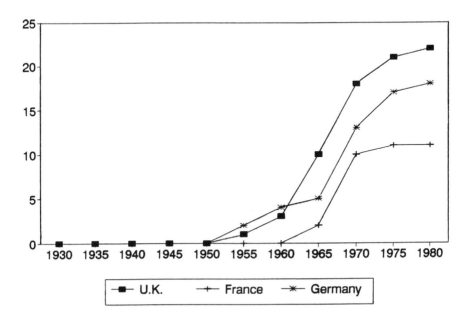

Figure 10.3 Multidivisional structure: European diffusion. *Source:* Based on data from Franko (1976) and additional research by the authors.

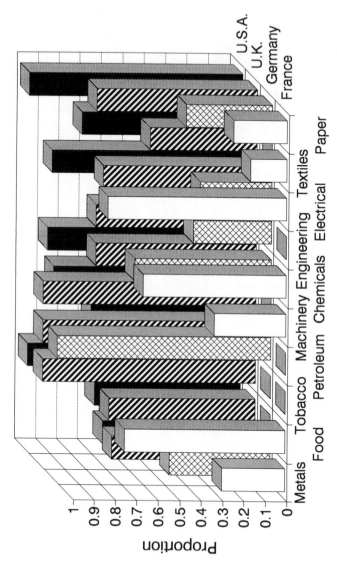

Figure 10.4 Multidivisional structure: Industry distribution by country. *Sources:* The industry classification is based on Channon (1973). There is some arbitrariness in the assignment of companies from other than the U.K. to Channon's industries. Data: U.S.A., Bhargava (1973); U.K., Channon (1973); Germany and France, Dyas and Thanheiser (1976).

products, or instruments. The few that are in these industries have a lower incidence of multidivisional structure than the other industries, which is in line with the American experience.

Adaptation and Graft

Most analyses of the advantages of the multidivisional structure focus on the role of the central office and its relations with the divisions. However, these relations are traditionally quite different in the European firms form those in the United States. In Germany, where the collegial system of management is prevalent, there are important differences from the American case. Among these differences is a lack of monetary incentive schemes tied to divisional performance.[13] The spread of new organizational charts across Europe in the 1960s was not accompanied necessarily by the spread of American style internal control and accounting systems.

In explaining the adoption of the external form of the multidivisional structure without much of the important internal substance, it is important to recall the conditions of the post–World War II debate in Europe. The success of the United States, and the relative weakness of Europe, led to a plethora of academic and government studies investigating the European problem. A large number of commissions and studies in the United Kingdom attacked domestic industry for their poor managerial capabilities compared to U.S. subsidiaries operating in Britain.[14]

In response to these criticisms, the rapid diffusion of the multidivisional structure among European firms in the late 1960s evolved in a heated politicized environment stressing the superiority of the American methods. The prestige attached to adopting an Americanized structure led to the "on-paper" adoption of a multidivisional structure that is not comparable to the typical American divisional firm. The internal operations of the divisionalized firm are as crucial to its efficiency as is its surface structure. In the American firms, there tended to be a clear distinction between the strategic or entrepreneurial responsibilities and the operating responsibilities. A substantial general office that appraises, controls, and plans is as important as is the actual separation of divisions with conflicting operational needs. This separation is frequently lacking in the European adaptation.

In the United Kingdom, this paper adoption was particularly easy. Many British firms had originated in the merger of smaller family owned and controlled firms. Most of these firms never rationalized or consolidated their operations. Mergers took place through the exchange of shares, and, perhaps, partly because of tradition and partly because of a less liquid stock market, control of these firms remained fractured. Each family continued to manage what was formerly its own firm, and the whole enterprise was managed usually in a collegial manner (Channon 1973).

Most of these newly merged firms adopted a holding corporate structure (Channon 1973; Hannah 1983). Consequently, it was perhaps particularly easy for these firms to superimpose the look of a multidivisional structure on their existing structure. However, little changed internally. This practice was widespread throughout Europe, and only one third of the European firms adopting a divisionalized structure between 1960 and 1970 even set up a general office (Franko 1976).

The missing characteristics of the multidivisional structure extend to more than just the nature of the general office. The use of collegial management in many of the U.K. and German firms has a distinctly nondivisional characteristic. In the collegial system, the same individuals that are division managers make up an executive committee, and there is only a small general office. The resulting management system does not effectively separate corporate issues from day-to-day operating issues. Given these differences in the American and European patterns of divisionalization, it is not surprising that the findings on the profitability of the adoption of the multidivisional structure have been different in the U.K. and European case than the American case. While the multidivisional structure has been found to contribute to profitability in American firms, the findings previously discussed are inconclusive for non–American firms.[15]

To a large extent, then, the multidivisional structure was not so much adapted to European conditions as it was simply grafted onto the presentation of the existing organization. Channon (1973, 213–14) writes in conclusion:

> British companies thus widely adopted the multidivisional structure during the past 20 years as the organizational form best suited to manage the diversified enterprise. However, the observations indicated that while companies accepted the need to divide their organizations into logical multifunctional units, many of the internal characteristics of the corporations adopting multidivisional structure reflected prior structural forms. In particular, there was little evidence of change in the reward system, especially as a mechanism to apply pressure and internal competition for divisional performance.

A Focus on the United Kingdom

Why did U. K. firms adopt the multidivisional structure so much more rapidly and extensively than they adopted Taylorism? What explains the paper adoption of the new corporate structure? The answer to both these questions, as suggested earlier, lies in the peculiar conditions of labor relations and business in Britain.

The roots of these conditions lie in the developments marking the early industrial history of labor relations in the United Kingdom. At the time of the first industrial revolution, the separation of ownership and control took place very early in some industries. Most important, this separation took place before effective means of administration were developed and widespread. In manufacturing, subcontracting was the dominant method of organizing work. Under this system—similar to the internal contracting method of early American industry—the owner provided the machinery and factory, but the actual production was under the control of subcontractors, who were free to hire their own help and arrange production as they wished (Gospel 1992). This system of labor organization invariably had problems of control, which were not abetted by the prevailing methods of accounting. It was not uncommon that accounts were completed only several years after transactions (Mee 1975). In contrast, modern methods of cost accounting began to diffuse widely in the United States by the close of the 1800s.[16]

But this difference in accounting practices is most likely linked to a more fundamental contrast between the United States and the United Kingdom, namely the

British deadlock to resolve the "labor problem"—which, afterall, had been experienced in all industrial countries at the turn of the century—by exercising more authority over the traditional craft organization. While shopfloor control in Britain and in the United States developed through the same stages of personal, technical, and administrative authority, the United Kingdom failed to extend this control effectively to the shopfloor (Fox 1985). Even as late as 1968, a government report noted that the system of national collective agreements to establish pay, but with local bargaining to establish piece rates and incentives, led to a stalemate at the shopfloor. Many companies, the report concluded, had "no effective personnel policy to control methods of negotiation and pay structures, and perhaps no conception of one" (*Royal Commission on Trade Unions and Employers Associations 1965–1968, Report HMSO;* cited in Channon [1973, 41–42]).

That the slow adoption of Taylorist and mass production methods is not an expression of a general failure of management to recognize the nature of the organizational challenge from the United States is evident in the diffusion of the multidivisional structure in the United Kingdom. The nature of British organizations made it extraordinarily easy to nominally adopt the multidivisional structure. Many of the large British firms were formed by mergers, sometimes involving scores of firms, and there was no widespread rationalization (Hannah 1983). Most of these firms adopted a holding structure with the constituent parts continuing to be managed independently. For example, after their merger in 1951 to form British Motor Holdings, Austin and Morris retained a high degree of competitive independence. Further mergers and attempts at rationalization in 1968–1972 were also largely failures (Clark 1987, 306).

The decentralized holding-company structures of many large firms made the nominal adoption of the multidivisional structure a simple matter. However, the true adoption of the multidivisional structure appears to have met the same difficulties as the adoption of Taylorism. This paper adoption left British firms with the form of modern management but not the substance.

It is a reasonable speculation that an additional factor accounting for the extremely rapid diffusion of the multidivisional structure in the United Kingdom was its value as a quick and easy response to the widespread criticism of British business in the postwar period. It allowed firms to easily solve their internal political problems by, ironically, reinforcing and legitimizing the existing decentralized structures. Thus, both by its appeal as a symbolic adoption of the perceived "best practices" of the United States and by the authority of British management to impose at least a semblance of structural change on the corporate organization, the multidivisional structure diffused in the United Kingdom at a rate comparable to that of other countries.

Conclusions

This history presents two sobering considerations, the first concerning the importance of national institutions on adoption, the second the simple difficulty of knowing what to adopt. The slowness of the diffusion of these practices within and among countries underscores the difficulty of altering institutionalized patterns of work. This difficulty is not only hampered by the resistance of traditional groupings, but also by the uncertainty about the potential modes by which work can be organized. It is not surprising, then, that the adoption of these new practices should therefore be grafted onto and transformed by the existing institutional structures.

The history of the adoption of the multidivisional structure points to the wide belief in the superiority of American practices in the postwar period. On the back of these practices, American multinational corporations and, later, American consulting companies extended their operations internationally. The emergence of the United States as an industrial power at the turn of the century and its extraordinary dominance after the Second World War led to the emulation of its principles of work.

Yet, the social and institutional context modulated the strict emulation of these organizational practices.[17] Though British managers were unable to successfully use the American example to gain control over the workplace as was done in the United States, they fared no worse than the American and continental European firms in their capabilities to nominally adopt the multidivisional structure. However, this emulation was imperfect and constrained by the social context in which U.K. firms operated.

In this regard, a second consideration is the simple difficulty in identifying new practices, even when the innovating firm is a competitor from the same country. These difficulties—of detecting practices, understanding them and their contribution to success, and transferring them—increase when we cross international borders (see Kogut 1991 for discussion). This consideration is more troubling, for it casts doubts on the conventional wisdom found not only in practice, but also in academic discussions. The recognition that firms from other countries are competing with superior productivity does not, in and of itself, indicate the source of this productivity. There is, therefore, the problem of what March and Olsen (1976) call "superstitious learning," that is, a false attribution of causality is made. That the adoption of the multidivisional structure is an example of a solution searching for a problem cannot, on the basis of the current evidence, be ruled out.

These issues are, obviously, not only of historical interest, because the current period is characterized by the process of identifying and adopting a set of organizing practices with their origin in Japan. In part, the adoption of such practices as just-in-time, manning of multiple machinery, and outsourcing of critical components stumble on differences in the institutional conditions of countries. As Whittaker (Chapter 7) shows, the experiences of Japanese and U.K. firms in adopting new product technologies of flexible and automated production are strongly conditioned by the training of workers and the prevailing system by which labor is organized, renumerated, and promoted.

Leaving aside the social capability and feasibility of adopting new practices, an especially troubling realization is how far short our understanding of the sources of the Japanese advantage falls in sorting fact from belief. Certainly, the many studies on Japan over the past decade, as reviewed by Lincoln in Chapter 3, have advanced the perspective that the organization of work at the shopfloor, across functions, and across the chain of suppliers is pivotal.

The issue in question is not, then, whether practices can be transferred across borders. The historical record of the diffusion of American practices, as well as that of the practices of other countries, shows that organizing principles can be adopted, though the varying extent of adaptation can be considerable.[18] Rather, the remarkable observation is that after so much study, the identity of the Japanese organizing principles responsible for the unquestioned productivity and quality advantages is still in dispute.

It is in the recognition of the difficulty of identifying these traits that the slow speed of the diffusion of organizing principles across borders can be understood. Of course, it is also this very difficulty that interacts with the social conditions and that allows for the shaping of interpretation to accord with the alignment of the prevailing social norms and distribution of power. What is transferred and how it is adapted is, in part, an outcome of the demonstration of economic advantage by the firms of leading countries; but it also a reflection of how these methods are interpreted in the context of the existing relations of class and group in a society.

Notes

We would like to thank Jim Lincoln for his comments on the conference draft.

1. These observations were forcefully argued by Habakkuk (1962).
2. Both of these books came out after the completion of the paper presented at the conference; their content confirms much of what we had written, and we would like to acknowledge their precedence even if we have failed to fully incorporate their findings.
3. Hounshell, however, argues that this claim was exaggerated (1984, 105ff.)
4. See Ferguson (1979) for the early history; Nelson (1980) for their technological stagnation.
5. The clearest indication of the spreading of American organizing principles was in Czechoslovakia, where the auto producer Skoda named its new plant the "America."
6. See Brady (1933) for a detailed account of the rationalization movement.
7. This importance of these institutions in contemporary Germany is outlined in Chapter 1 by Herrigel (this volume).
8. Fligstein (1990) discusses at length this reordering of industries and firms. In the 1920s and 1930s, firms adopting the multidivisional structure grew faster and surpassed those firms not adopting the structure. See especially his chapters 4 and 8.
9. A number of studies trace the diffusion of the multidivisional form through American industry. Among the most complete of these is Bhargava (1973) and Rumelt (1974).
10. Differences in the diffusion rate of the multidivisional structure in these European countries are consistent with the empirical studies of the relative efficiency of the multidivisional structure in these countries. For the United Kingdom, Steer and Cable (1978), Thompson (1981), and Hill (1988) find support for the superior performance of the multidivisional structure. However, Cable and Dirrheimer (1983) find a negative relationship between the MD form and profit in Germany. (There has been no French study).
11. We would like to thank Lawrence Franko for kindly sharing his data on the European diffusion with us. For a description of the data, see Franko (1976).
12. For continuity with the discussion on Taylorism, we have not included the data on Italy, where the multidivisional structure had only disseminated to 26 percent of the sample of the largest corporations. See also Pavan (1972) for a discussion.

13. For a discussion of the German system of management see Dyas and Thanheiser (1976, 106–108); for a discussion of weak incentives in British corporations, see Channon (1973, 210ff).

14. For a representative study, see Dunning (1958) and his chapter in this book (Chap. 11).

15. See our earlier comments, and Mahajan, Sharma, and Bettis (1988, 1188–1201) for an overall review.

16. Whereas it might be argued that modern accounting principles were developed the United Kingdom, the evidence appears to suggest that their diffusion was far greater in the United States. For a critical appraisal of the United Kingdom, see Pollard (1965); for a more positive view, see Edwards and Newell (1991). The developments in the United States are sketched in Chandler (1977).

17. These conclusions are similar to those of Westney's regarding the adoption of Western practices in Japan (Westney 1987).

18. The study by Westney (1987) is one of the clearest of the works that should have put to rest the naive question about whether practices may be transported.

References

Alford, Bernard. 1976. "The Chandler Thesis—Some General Observations," in Leslie Hannah, ed., *Management Strategy and Business Development,* pp. 52–70. London: Macmillan.

Aoki, Masahiko. 1988. *Information, Incentives, and Bargaining in the Japanese Economy,* Cambridge, U. K.: Cambridge University Press.

Armour, H., and David J. Teece. 1978. "Organizational Structure and Economic Performance: A Test of the M-Form Hypothesis," *Bell Journal of Economics* **9**:106–22.

Atack, Jeremy. 1985. *Estimation of Economies of Scale in Nineteenth Century United States Manufacturing.* New York: Garland Publications.

Baron, James N., Frank R. Dobbin, and P. Devereaux Jennings. 1986. "War and Peace: The Evolution of Modern Personnel Administration in U. S. Industry," *American Journal of Sociology* **92**:350–83.

Bhargava, Narottam. 1973. "The Impact of Organization Form on the Firm: Experience of 1920–1970." Ph.D. diss., University of Pennsylvania, Philadelphia.

Brady, Robert A. 1933. *The Rationalization Movement in German Industry: A Study in the Evolution of Economic Planning* (reprinted 1974). New York: Howard Fertig.

Cable, John, and M. J. Dirrheimer. 1983. "Markets and Hierarchies: An Empirical Test of the Multidivisional Hypothesis in West Germany," *International Journal of Industrial Organization* **3**:43–62.

Chandler, Alfred D. 1962. *Strategy and Structure: Chapters in the History of the American Industrial Enterprise.* Cambridge, Mass.: MIT Press.

Chandler, Alfred D. 1977. *The Visible Hand: The Managerial Revolution in American Business.* Cambridge, Mass.: Belknap Press.

Chandler, Alfred D. 1990. *Scale and Scope: The Dynamics of Industrial Capitalism.* Cambridge, Mass.: Belknap Press.

Chandler, Alfred D., and Herman Daems, eds. 1980. *Managerial Hierarchies: Comparative Perspectives on the Rise of the Modern Industrial Enterprise.* Cambridge, Mass.: Harvard University Press.

Channon, Derek F. 1973. *The Strategy and Structure of British Enterprises.* Boston: Division of Research, Graduate School of Business, Harvard University.

Clark, Peter. 1987. *Anglo-American Innovation.* New York: Walter de Gruyter.

Davies, Margery W. 1982. *Women's Place Is at the Typewriter: Office Work and Office Workers 1870–1930.* Philadelphia: Temple University Press.

Devinat, Paul E. 1927. *Scientific Management in Europe.* Geneva: International Labor Office.

Dunning, John H. 1958. *American Investment in British Manufacturing Industry.* London: Ruskin House.

Dyas, Gareth P., and Heinz T. Thanheiser. 1976. *The Emerging European Enterprises: Strategy and Structure in French and German Industry.* London: Macmillan.

Edwards, John, and Edmund Newell. 1991. "The Development of Industrial Cost and Management Accounting Before 1850: A Survey of the Evidence," *Business History* 33(Jan.):35–57.

Ferguson, Eugene S. 1979. "The Americanness of American Technology," *Technology and Culture* **20**:3–24.

Fligstein, Niel. 1990. *The Transformation of Corporate Control.* Cambridge, Mass.: Harvard University Press.

Fox, Alan. 1985. History and Heritage: *The Social Origins of the British Industrial Relations System.* London, Boston: Allen & Unwin.

Franko, Lawrence G. 1976. *European Multinationals: A Renewed Challenge to American and British Big Business.* Stamford, Conn.: Greylock.

Fridenson, Patrick. 1978. "The Coming of the Assembly Line to Europe," in W. Krohn, E. T. Layton, and P. Weingart, eds., *The Dynamics of Science and Technology.* Dordrect, Holland: D. Reidel.

Gospel, H. F. 1992. *Markets, Firms and the Management of Labour in Modern Britain.* New York: Cambridge University Press.

Habakkuk, H. J. 1962. *American and British Technology in the Nineteenth Century: The Search for Labor Saving Inventions.* Cambridge, U. K.: Cambridge University Press.

Hannah, Leslie. 1983. *The Rise of the Corporate Economy,* 2d ed. London: Methuen.

Hill, Charles. 1988. "Internal Capital Market Controls and Financial Performance in Multidivisional Firms," *Journal of Industrial Economics* **37**:67–83.

Homburg, Heidrun. 1978. "Anfaenge des Taylorsystems in Deutschland vor dem Ersten Weltkrieg," *Geschichte und Gesellschaft* **4**:170–94.

Homburg, Heidrun. 1984. "Le Taylorisme et la Rationlisation de l'organization du travail en Allemagne (1918–1939)," in *Le Taylorisme,* pp. 99–113. Paris: Editions La Decouverte.

Hounshell, David A. 1984. *From the American System to Mass Production, 1800–1932.* Baltimore: Johns Hopkins University Press.

James, John A. 1983. "Structural Change in American Manufacturing: 1850–1890," *Journal of Economic History* **43**:433–59.

Jeremy, D. J. 1981. *Transatlantic Industrial Revolution: The Diffusion of Textile Technologies between Britain and America.* Cambridge, Mass.: MIT Press.

Johnson, H. Thomas, and Robert S. Kaplan. 1987. *Relevance Lost: The Rise and Fall of Management Accounting.* Boston: Harvard Graduate School of Business.

Kochan, Thomas A., and Peter Cappelli. 1984. "The Transformation of the Industrial Relations and Personnel Function," in P. Osterman, ed., *Internal Labor Markets,* pp. 133–61. Cambridge, Mass.: MIT Press.

Kocka, Jürgen, and Hannes Siegrist. 1979. "Die hundert groessten deutschen Industrieunternehmen im spaeten 19. und fruhen 20. Jarhhundert. Expansion, Diversifikation und Integration im internationalen Vergleich," in N. Horn and J. Kocka, eds., *Law and the Formation of the Big Enterprises in the 19th and Early 20th Centuries,* pp. 55–122. Göttingen: Vandenhoeck and Ruprecht.

Kogut, Bruce. 1991. "Country Capabilities and the Permeability of Borders," *Strategic Management Journal* **12**:33–47.

Laux, James M. 1976. *In First Gear: The French Automobile Industry to 1914.* Montreal: McGill-Queen's University Press.

Lazonick, William. 1990. *Competitive Advantage on the Shop Floor.* Cambridge, Mass.: Harvard University Press.

Lewchuk, Wayne. 1987. *American Technolgoy and the British Vehicle Industry.* Cambridge, Mass.: Cambridge University.

Littler, Craig R. 1982. *The Development of the Labor Process in Capitalist Societies.* London: Heinemann.

Mahajan, Vijay, Subhash Sharma, and Richard A. Bettis. 1988. "The Adoption of the M-Form structure," *Management Science* **34**:1188–1201.

Maier, Charles S. 1970. "Between Taylorism and Technocracy: European Ideology and the Vision of Industrial Productivity in the 1920s," *Journal of Contemporary History* **5**(2):27–61.

March, J., and J. Olsen. 1976. *Ambiguity and Choice in Organizations.* Bergen, Norway: Universitetsforlaget.

Mee, G. 1975, Aristocratic Enterprise: *The Fitzwilliams Industrial Undertakings.* Glasgow: Blackie.

Moutet, Aimee. 1975. "Les Origines du systeme de Taylor en France. Le point de vue patronal (1907–1914)," *Le Movement Sociale* **93**:15–49.

Nelson, Daniel. 1980. *Frederick W. Taylor and the Rise of Scientific Management.* Madison: University of Wisconsin Press.

Pavan, Robert J. 1972. "The Strategy and Structure of Italian Enterprise." Ph.D. diss., Harvard University, Boston.

Pollard, Sidney. 1965. *The Genesis of Modern Management.* London: MacKay and Co.

Rosenberg, Nathan. 1969. "The Direction of Technological Change: Inducement Mechanisms and Focusing Devices," *Economic Development and Cultural Change,* **18**: 1–24.

Rumelt, Richard P. 1974. *Strategy, Structure and Economic Performance.* Boston: Graduate School of Business, Harvard University.

Smith, Merritt Roe. 1977. *Harper's Ferry Armory and the New Technology: The Challenge of Change.* Ithaca, N.Y.: Cornell University Press.

Steer, Peter, and John Cable. 1978. "Internal Organization and Profit: An Empirical Analysis of Large U. K. Companies," *Journal of Industrial Economics* **27**:13–30.

Teece, David J. 1981. "Internal Organization and Economic Performance: An Empirical Analysis of Principal Firms," *Journal of Industrial Economics* **30**:173–99.

Thompson, C. B. 1914. "The Literature of Scientific Management," in C. B. Thompson, ed., *A Collection of the More Significant Articles Describing the Taylor System of Management.* Cambridge, Mass.: Harvard University Press. (Reprinted in 1972 by Hive Publishing Co., Easton, Pa.)

Westney, D. Eleanor. 1987. *Imitation and Innovation: The Transfer of Western Organizational Patterns to Meiji Japan.* Cambridge, Mass.: Harvard University.

Whipp, Richard, and Peter Clark. 1986. *Innovation and the Auto Industry: Product, Process and Work Organization.* New York: St. Martin's.

Williamson, Oliver E. 1975. *Markets and Hierarchies.* New York: Free Press.

11

The Governance of Japanese and U.S. Manufacturing Affiliates in the U.K.: Some Country-specific Differences

JOHN H. DUNNING

In recent years, increasing attention has been paid to country-specific characteristics affecting the competitiveness and strategic behavior of multinational enterprises (MNEs) and their foreign affiliates (see, in particular, Dunning 1981, 1990, and Porter 1990). It has been found that as firms have increased the number and extent of their foreign operations,[1] their ownership-specific advantages have become more related to the coordination of cross-border production and less to the competitive strengths that may have prompted the investment in the first place (Kogut 1983, Dunning 1988). Nonetheless, research has revealed noticeable country-specific differences, not only in the industrial and geographical patterns of MNE activity, but in the ownership and organizational structures of that activity and its impact on the economic welfare of host countries.

This chapter examines how far home-country characteristics of firms may have helped shape differences in the organization, work practices, and decision-making procedures of Japanese and U.S.-owned manufacturing affiliates in the United Kingdom by drawing mainly on two surveys conducted by the author.[2] The first, which was undertaken in 1953, studied the decision-making practices of some 205 U.S. manufacturing subsidiaries, which accounted for an estimated 90–95 percent of the output of all such affiliates in the United Kingdom. The second was a similar survey of all the Japanese manufacturing affiliates in the United Kingdom in 1983 that at the time numbered only 261. The data obtained in these surveys has been supplemented by more recent information about both groups of affiliates and, in particular, by information obtained by Hood and Young (1983), and by Young, Hood, and Hamill (1985, 1988) in their analyses of the investment strategies of multinational affiliates in the United Kingdom.

The chapter opens with an economic theory of the management and control of decision making by foreign affiliates by their parent companies, based on the eclectic paradigm of international production (as set out in Dunning 1981, 1988). In particular, I hypothesize that the control and influence exerted over the competitive or ownership-specific advantages possessed MNEs, and their ability to transfer and utilize them efficiently in their subsidiaries, rests on the transaction costs of exercising alternative modes of internal governance. I proceed to apply this hypothesis in comparing and contrasting the control and influence exerted by U.S. companies over resource usage by their U.K. affiliates in the 1950s and 1980s with that of Japanese MNEs over their affiliates in the 1980s, both across and within a variety of functional areas. In conclusion, I give some attention to differences in the operating practices of Japanese and U.S. affiliates that may have little or nothing to do with their countries of origin.

An Economic Theory of the Management and Control of Foreign Affiliates

Why might the organization and operation of Japanese and U.S. affiliates in the United Kingdom differ from each other? The accepted theory of international production suggests that there are two main reasons. First, the two groups of affiliates may have access to a different set of intangible assets or competitive advantages that affect the way in which they organize their value adding activities. Second, the two groups may differ in the extent to which their parent companies deem it necessary or desirable to control or influence the way in which resources are allocated and functions are performed. Making comparisons of the two groups of firms at two different times adds the further possibility that the competitive advantages of the parent firms and, in this case, the competitive conditions of the host country may have changed so as to affect both the assets available to the affiliate and the extent to which the parent company wishes to control the use made of these assets.

The Comparative Competitive Advantages of the Japanese and U.S. Economies

It is not my purpose to describe in detail differences in the ownership-specific advantages of Japanese and U.S. firms. Many of these differences emerge in the discussion on individual areas of working practices.

CHARACTERISTICS OF SUCCESSFUL SECTORS
Studies of the revealed comparative advantages of firms located in Japan and the United States in patterns of patented innovations and in patterns of trade in goods clearly show substantial differences in the sectors in which the two groups of firms perform best. To give just one example, first, over the period 1978–1986, Japan's revealed technological (or patenting) advantage (RTA)[3] was greatest in photographic equipment, calculating and copying machines, radio and television receivers, office equipment, motor vehicles, typewriters, and semiconductors, and least in chemicals and pharmaceuticals, aircraft, tobacco, and mining equipment (Cantwell and Hodson 1990). By contrast, the United States had the most marked RTA

in aircraft, coal and petroleum products, mining equipment, and several kinds of food products and computers; while it recorded the least favorable ratios in precisely those sectors in which Japanese-based firms were the strongest (Cantwell and Hodson, 1991). These sectors broadly correspond to those identified by Porter (1990), and Archibugi and Pianta (1989) as those in which U.S.- and Japanese-based firms do relatively well or poorly in export markets.

The resource requirements, demand size and structure, structure of competition, and the role of government in affecting these advantages are very different in each country. Hence, the sectors in which Japan is strongest are the fabricating industries requiring a skilled or semiskilled, well-motivated, and disciplined workforce. Those industries produce for a demanding and sophisticated market and maintain close working relationships with their component suppliers. They exist in an environment where strong domestic rivalry provides competition among the main supplying firms. By contrast, sectors in which U.S. firms do particularly well are those based on natural resources in which the United States is comparatively well-endowed (e.g., petroleum, tobacco, and some food processing); those that receive or have received substantial government financial support (namely, defense-related industries such as aerospace and computers); those that are capital- and scale-intensive; and those that supply differentiated high-income consumer goods (e.g., health-care products).

Besides requiring different stimuli for the production of the various Japanese and U.S. commodities, the relative importance of different parts of the value-added chain and/or the functions associated with them tend to be different. Some of the most successful sectors of the United States are those that engage in processing activities, which tend to involve fewer transactions along the value-added chain and where the human element influencing quality control is rather less than in the fabricating sectors. Moreover, the United States no longer has a comparative advantage in supply of low-cost products, even in those such as motor vehicles where production involves substantial economies of scale. Instead, competitiveness has to be based on a continual process of product or process innovation and improvement and/or of product differentiation accompanied by intensive advertising (e.g., pharmaceuticals, food and tobacco products).

Generally speaking, processing activities are the sectors in which success tends to be determined by such variables as the vitality of entrepreneurship, the effectiveness of R&D, the willingness to employ the latest and most efficient machinery, and the emphasis given to effective marketing. In contrast, the sectors in which the Japanese appear to have had the most success emphasize the relative importance of the right kind of sourcing decision and relations with suppliers, the minimization of inventories, the avoidance of breakdowns or bad workmanship on the shopfloor, and the critical nature of good industrial relations.[4]

TRANSFERENCE OF STRENGTHS

The extent to which these features of competitive strength may be successfully transferred to foreign affiliates, and, when transferred, whether or not the transferring company needs to control or influence their use, is the final example of how the ownership advantages of Japanese and U.S. firms may differ. This point is discussed in more detail in the following section, but one general point should be made here. The ability of an importing country to absorb and disseminate new resources, technology, organizational methods, and entrepreneurship rests mainly on the availability of indigenous complementary resources and the ease with which these resources can be efficiently coordinated with the imported resources.

Broadly speaking, as Kogut pointed out in a recent paper (Kogut 1990), new organizational skills or systems are more difficult and costly, and usually take longer to transfer across national boundaries than new technologies. This condition exists primarily because the former are more likely to be country-specific in their origin and in their application factors than the latter. Put in a different way, the higher the transaction costs associated with either transferring or utilizing intangible assets across boundaries, the less likely they will be transferred or, if they are, the more likely control over them will be exerted by the transferring company. And, as demonstrated later in this chapter, the transaction costs associated with decentralizing decision making, as in the case of supplying products in which Japanese firms have competitive advantage, are generally different (and directed to different functional areas) than those in which U.S. firms are advantaged.

PATTERNS OF INDUSTRIAL ACTIVITY

To conclude this section, I briefly describe the industrial pattern of U.S.-owned activity in the United Kingdom in 1953 and 1982, and that of Japanese activity in 1982 and 1988. Table 11.1 sets out some relevant facts. Among other things, it reveals a much greater concentration of direct Japanese investment in the fabricating industries, particularly in the electrical and electronic equipment sectors, compared with U.S. investment, both in 1953 and 1982. By contrast, with the exception of the rubber tire industry, there is little Japanese participation in the major processing sectors which, in both 1953 and 1982, accounted for about one-fifth of the employment in U.S. affiliates. The major similarity between the employment dis-

TABLE 11.1 Percentage Distribution of Employment of U.S. and Japanese Manufacturing Affiliates in Selected U.K. Industrial Sectors

	U.S. Affiliates				Japanese Affiliates			
	1953	%	1983	%	1982	%	1988	%
Food and related products	16,500	6.7	56,500	9.6	0	0.0	123	0.5
Chemicals and pharmaceuticals	31,300	12.7	67,300	11.4	106	2.0	874	3.5
Electrical and electronic equipment	13,600	5.5	66,700	11.3	4,059	75.6	13,254	52.6
Nonelectrical engineering products	77,000	31.3	103,700	17.6	698	13.0	3,400	13.5
Motor vehicles	56,000	22.7	112,600	19.1	0	0.0	2,325	9.2
Industrial and precision instruments	16,200	6.6 ⎫			324	6.0	450	1.8
Textiles and clothing	3,900	1.6 ⎬ 181,400		30.8	42	0.8	98	0.4
Others	31,700	12.9 ⎭			146	2.7	4,681	18.6
Totals	246,200	100.0	588,200	100.0	5,375	100.0	25,205	100.0

Sources: Data from Dunning (1958, 1986), U.S. Department of Commerce (1984), and JETRO (1989).

tribution of the two groups of firms is that, in both cases, it tends to be skewed toward the technologically advanced and faster growing sectors of U.K. industry, and to those producing branded consumer goods with a high-income elasticity of demand.[5]

An examination of the competitive or ownership-specific advantages of U.S. firms in 1953 suggest these strongly reflected the ecostructure of the U.S. economy. Those particularly identified in my 1958 study were (a) the ability of U.S. firms to innovate capital or technology-intensive producer goods, and to successfully differentiate high-income consumer goods; (b) their managerial and marketing skills in producing and selling these goods; and (c) their capacity to exploit large-scale and fairly homogeneous markets. On the one hand, because of high real wage costs, U.S. firms were induced to engage in labor-saving production methods; on the other, its large and reasonably homogeneous home market and the high income of its consumers generated patterns of demand which, when emulated by other countries, gave U.S. firms a powerful competitive edge over their international rivals.[6]

The nature of the competitive ownership advantages of Japanese investors in 1981 was similar to that of U.S. investors in the 1950s, in as much as that they both resulted from the possession of particular rent-earning assets, rather than arising from the common governance of cross-border value-added activities. Since the early 1960s, Japan has been seeking to catch up with the United States and Europe in its manufacturing capabilities. To break into foreign markets dominated by its foreign competitors, its firms had either to introduce new products that, because of their limited innovatory capabilities, they found very difficult to do, or to tempt consumers to switch their purchases to their own products, for example, by lower price and superior product design, quality, and reliability. The latter strategy was, in fact, the one chosen by Japanese firms. Moreover, as might be expected from late entrants in the product cycle, the Japanese have sought to compete by differentiating their products, which they have done (especially in the motor-vehicle industry) primarily by providing additional features or by upgrading their sales or after-sales servicing. Coupled with aggressive marketing tactics, Japanese products have created a distinctive image for themselves that has often enabled them to outcompete their Western counterparts in U.K. markets.

The main difference, then, between the competitive strategies of U.S. affiliates in the 1950s and Japanese affiliates in the 1980s is that the former rested on the innovating capacities of the investing companies and on the more successful application of management and marketing skills; while the latter arose from quality control, product differentiation and cost advantages, an emphasis on good industrial relations, and efficient procurement policies.[7] The pharmaceutical and vehicles sectors in the 1950s, in which the U.S. affiliates were particularly dominant, were recipients of the first kind of advantage; the consumer electronics and the vehicle sector in the 1980s, of the latter.

By the 1980s, however, U.S. MNEs investing in the United Kingdom were also enjoying substantial sequential advantages and those that, inter alia, reflected the restructuring of their value-added activities in the European Community (EC). In the 1990s, there is some reason to suppose that Japanese MNEs, particularly in the electronics and vehicles industries, will generate both more innovatory and systemic advantages. Certainly, like the parent companies of American affiliates both in the 1950s and 1980s, they are among the most technologically progressive and fastest growing companies in Japan.[8]

The Management and Control of Competitive Advantages

Given the distinctive competitive advantages of U.S.- and Japanese-owned firms, why should parent companies wish to control or influence the extent to which these advantages are transferred to their affiliate, or the way in which they are used?

Economic theory suggests there are three main reasons why foreign affiliates may not be given full autonomy of decision making in both these respects. First, the MNE may perceive that, when viewed as self-contained profit centers, the objectives of (the management of) affiliates may not always be consistent with its global objectives. This conflict is particularly likely to arise if there are differences in the perceived goals of the affiliates and those of their parent company, or if there are costs or benefits arising from decisions made by, or on behalf of, the affiliates that are external to those affiliates, but internal to their owners. Second, the price of decision-making or related services may be greater in the host than in the home country. Third, for one reason or another, the higher efficiency of centrally organizing these services may not justify the delegation of decision-making authority.

The first and third reasons suggest that the choice both between centralization and delegation of decision-making within an organization, and the nationality of the main decision makers, may be likened to that between the hierarchical and market route of transferring competitive advantages. For example, it might be hypothesized that the more the ownership-specific advantages of an MNE stem from its common governance of geographically dispersed, interrelated activities, or from proprietary knowledge that is idiosyncratic, uncodifiable, costly to transmit, and in danger of being abused or dissipated, the more likely that either the top decision-makers of the affiliate will be expatriates of the home country, or that their decisions will be closely guided or controlled by the management of the parent company.

The second reason for not decentralizing decision making has more to do with the country-specific differences in the costs of decision-making resources. Given the same "output" where the (marginal) cost of decision making is less in the home country than in the host country, such decisions are unlikely to be delegated. Quite apart from the presence or absence of economies of scale in decision making, management and management support costs may vary across boundaries. In some cases, line management may require physical proximity to the market and decisions may need to be customized to local requirements; in others, line management may need to be near to the main center of decision making. Thus, while it may be more efficient for decision making on sourcing or industrial relations to be localized, those having to do with innovatory activities may need to be centralized.

Using the framework provided by these three reasons, it should be possible to predict the extent of and the areas in which decision making in U.K. affiliates is controlled by their parent companies. It should also be possible to identify country-specific differences determining the control and location of decision making. Why, for example, is production management in Japanese subsidiaries less autonomous in its decision making than used to be the case (and I believe still is) in U.S. subsidiaries? Why is a Japanese national more likely to head up the finance and accounting department in a U.K. subsidiary than an American expatriate is in the U.S. subsidiary? The answers to these and similar questions are attempted in the following paragraphs.

The Structure of Decision-making Patterns in U.S. and Japanese Affiliates

The way in which parent enterprises influence or control decision making in their affiliates tells us something about the nature of the hierarchical relationships within MNEs, and especially whether affiliates are viewed as independent entities or as part of a coordinated network of value-added activities.[9] As has been suggested, we would expect the competitive advantages of the latter type of MNE, and those associated with sequential investment, to be more of a transaction cost-minimizing kind, rather than those resting on the proprietary ownership of a specific asset, for example, a patent.

Table 11.2 summarizes our perception of the similarities and differences in the influence and control exerted by the parent companies of U.S. and Japanese MNEs over their U.K. affiliates. The table also attempts to identify the main changes in the governance of decision making in U.S. affiliates between 1952 and 1982. As was previously discussed, we would expect the influence of the investing companies to be greatest where their competitive advantages (vis-à-vis those of indigenous or other MNE firms producing in the United Kingdom) were perceived to be the most pronounced; and for parental control over the use of these advantages to be most in evidence where there was some danger of their being mismanaged by their affiliates.

Overall Managerial Philosophy and Attitudes Toward Decision Making

In general, Japanese affiliates in the 1980s would seem to have exercised a much closer influence on, and control over, general managerial philosophy and style than did their U.S. counterparts in the 1950s. At the same time, many U.S. subsidiaries—and particularly those utilizing an integrated product and marketing strategy in Europe—are now subject to more centralized control than they once were.

These country-specific differences in management ideology are partly a function of the type of activity, degree of multinationality, pattern of ownership, and age of the affiliate, but, perhaps most significant, of the more systemic approach adopted by the Japanese toward decision making. The attention paid to encouraging the right work ethic, group consciousness, and team support requires a cohesive and integrated policy toward decision making. Even in an area in which Japanese influence and control appears to be quite loosely exercised, namely employee compensation and industrial relations, the chief executive of the U.K. affiliate is likely to require that the policies of the personnel department toward recruitment, work organization and standards, discipline, wage and incentives, promotion, and

TABLE 11.2 Comparative Managerial Influence and Control Exerted by U.S. and Japanese Parent Companies over U.K. Affiliates

Area of Management	U.S. Affiliates (c. 1953)	U.S. Affiliates (c. 1982)	Japanese Affiliates (c. 1982)
Overall managerial philosophy and strategy	Affiliates mainly nationally responsive (Doz 1986) or part of multidomestic operations of parent company (though varies between sectors). U.S. nonnationals or expatriates, mostly a minority on board of directors of affiliates.	In some sectors (motor vehicles, pharmaceuticals, computers, etc.) U.K. affiliates part of the integrated network of European operations. Decision making more centralized.	Strongly influenced and moderately controlled by parent company. Chief executive of affiliate normally a Japanese national. Japanese nationals or expatriates comprise majority of local board of directors.
Product and pricing policy	Truncated range of products supplied by parent companies. Minor modifications and adaptations to U.K. customer requirements. Pricing policy mainly determined by local management.	Move toward more multisite rationalized and/or product specialized production and European branded consumer goods. Fuller range of products produced in Europe.	Affiliates supply only one major product line that, when adapted to local needs, is of the same quality as that produced by parent companies. Product policy decided centrally. Pricing policy also influenced by parent companies.
Production methods	Less automated, particularly in ancillary; e.g., mechanical handling equipment.	Increasingly approaching those of U.S. parent companies.	Mainly same as in Japanese parent companies, but in some cases scaled down to suit lower volumes produced.
Procurement policy	Left mainly to U.K. purchasing managers, but stricter tolerances and standards required compared to those demanded by U.K. firms.	More attention given to quality of intermediate products subcontracted, particularly where final product is destined for export market.	Strongly influenced and controlled by parent company. Very rigorous quality control procedures. Considerable help given by affiliates to suppliers in upgrading quality.
Wages and salaries	Loosely controlled: tendency to pay well above average rates; many incentives and bonuses.	Now more in line with practices and procedures adopted by U.K. companies. Employer compensation differences between U.S. subsidiaries and U.K. firms less than in 1952, but former still often leads U.K. industry in working conditions.	Moderately influenced and loosely controlled. Pay slightly above average rates. Few incentives. Time rates disliked.

Training industrial relations	A good deal of training given at all levels. Loosely influenced and controlled, but bargaining conducted at plant level. Majority of affiliates unionized; some just one union.	A movement toward one union.	Expected to conform to overall managerial philosophy; hiring and firing policy decided centrally. No, or only one, union preferred. Appointment of senior management personnel requires approval of parent company. Substantial training given at all levels.
Marketing	Strongly influenced and controlled by parent company. Marketing methods replicate U.S. practices. Much attention given to after-sales servicing.	For nationally responsive affiliates, less influence and control by parent company. Most integrated affiliates adopt a common European marketing policy. Advertising generally follows U.S. practices. Export markets generally controlled by parent companies.	Destination of output decided and controlled by parent company. Most output sold to separate marketing affiliates. Nothing especially noticeable in marketing methods, except Japanese are tough negotiators over price, and salesmen maintain more face-to-face contact with clients than in normal U.K. practice.
Innovation policy	Strongly influenced and controlled by Head Office (HO). Some R&D in U.K. mainly to do with machinery design, product and materials adaptation. Some development research in industrial instruments, pharmaceuticals, and vehicles.	As in 1952, but more fundamental or specialized R&D undertaken in U.K. by U.S. affiliates in pharmaceuticals, information, processing, and electronics sectors. Less R&D is now undertaken in tire and motor vehicle industries.	Strongly influenced and controlled by parent company. Little R&D in U.K., but some product design and research starting in color television sector.
Accounting and financial control	Moderately influenced, especially in new methods of production planning and control. Accounting usually standardized on U.S. lines. Dividend policy determined by parent company (Dunning, 1986a, 1986b).	As in 1952.	Strongly controlled by parent company. Usually a Japanese is in charge of this managerial area. All decisions relating to financial targets, choice of investment projects, and dividend remission determined by parent companies.
Organization of affiliates	Few regional offices (ROs). Most subsidiaries organized as part of an M structure of organization, either on geographical or product lines. Locational decisions taken at HO or RO.	More regional offices. Otherwise, as in 1952.	No regional offices. Some Japanese MNEs organize their subsidiaries on M lines, but many have not gotten further than setting up an international division.

Sources: Data derived from chapters 4 and 9 of Dunning (1958), chapter 4 of Dunning (1986b), Hood and Young (1983), and Young, Hood and Hamill (1985).

industrial relations are consistent with the overall philosophy and expectations of
the company, that is, the production of high-quality defect-free products at competitive prices.

By contrast, the emphasis of the U.S. managerial control in the 1950s was more
directed at ensuring that American product and process innovations, budgetary
control, and procedures and marketing methods were smoothly and efficiently
transferred to a U.K. environment; and, more generally, that in all branches of
management a degree of professionalism was injected.

The greater importance attached to the parent company's philosophy and techniques of management control by the Japanese compared to the Americans, and
the perceived higher costs of decentralizing decision making within Japanese
MNEs, is shown by the fact that whereas the chief executive of 40 percent of U.S.
subsidiaries in 1953 set up since 1940 were headed by American expatriates, the
corresponding figure for Japanese affiliates in 1983 was 85 percent. Moreover,
whereas all but three (i.e., 86 percent) of the executives interviewed in Japanese affiliates asserted that they were markedly influenced and controlled in their overall
management objectives and procedures by their parent companies, the corresponding proportion of executives in U.S. subsidiaries, who so opined, was 33 percent of
all subsidiaries and 55 percent of those set up within the previous twelve years.
More recent data suggest that in 1984, 14.3 percent of the chief executives of U.S.
manufacturing affiliates were U.S. nationals (Young, Hood, and Hamill 1985),
whereas in 1988 some 89 percent of the managing directors of Japanese subsidiaries
were Japanese nationals (JETRO 1989).

Linguistic and Cultural Factors

Linguistic and cultural differences between home and host countries also explains
why, in many areas of decision making affecting U.K. production, the Japanese
influence and control is greater than was, and is, that of the American. Consider,
for example, three kinds of communication channels in which the affiliates of
MNEs may be involved: (1) between themselves and their parent or other home-
based companies; (2) between different interest groups within the affiliates, for
example, management and workers, technical and sales staff, and so on; and (3)
between the affiliates and their local suppliers, customers, competitors, and government.

To avoid misunderstandings due to language or different ways of gathering,
monitoring, and presenting information (among other things), it is not surprising
that, in 1988 in the majority of Japanese affiliates, the heads of finance and accounting departments were Japanese nationals; and that, usually, Japanese production
managers and chief technicians are appointed to ensure a free exchange of knowledge and ideas between themselves and their counterparts in Japan or heads of
R&D departments. In contrast, efficient face-to-face communication within subsidiaries and among the subsidiaries and indigenous firms, customers, and government bodies, requires not only a proper understanding of the local language, but of
business customs, social norms, and commercial law. Consequently, a U.K.
national almost always heads both the personnel and procurement departments.

Even so, special attention is given to training these time managers in the Japanese way, while there is usually a senior Japanese manager on the staff of these departments.

In the case of U.S.-owned subsidiaries in the 1950s, such linguistic and cultural constraints were not as apparent, and neither are they in the 1980s. Rather it was (and is) in the functional areas in which the parent company considered indigenous management lacking in the required skills, experience, or entrepreneurial initiative that U.S. expatriates were (and are) most likely to be in charge. Foremost among these areas were sales, production management, marketing, and R&D capital expenditure and budgetary control.

In all U.K. affiliates, the number of Japanese nationals employed at the end of 1982 was 144 or 2.7 percent of all employees. By 1988, the number had risen to 553, or 2.2 percent of all employees. The majority of these expatriates were in senior managerial, technical, or professional positions. In a sample of 150 U.S. subsidiaries in the 1950s, I identified only 34 in which the chief executive was a U.S. national; and 15 in which Americans were employed in other managerial capacities. These differences are partly a reflection of linguistic and cultural factors; partly those of age, size, and experience; and partly due to the parent company's perception of the ability and willingness of local nationals to do the job required of them. At the same time, spokespersons of Japanese MNEs frequently emphasized that it was their companies' intent to indigenize the management of their U.K. subsidiaries as soon as possible.

Employee Compensation and Industrial Relations

While both groups of affiliates claimed that they conformed to local customs and norms, there is a good deal of evidence that, in rather different ways, they have actively influenced these, and that the way in which they have done so reflects their country of origin. This section points out some differences in personnel practices and wage policies.

Most U.S. subsidiaries in the 1950s adopted an aggressive philosophy to labor recruitment and were willing to pay well above the competitive wages to attract the right kind of labor; they also gave substantial monetary incentives to encourage productivity (Dunning 1958, pp. 254ff). Nearly two-fifths of American subsidiaries claimed they assimilated their parent plant's wages policy "in all major respects" and a further 22 percent that U.S. practices were "adopted and modified to suit the particular needs at had." All these firms stated that they aimed to pay their workers "above the minimum trade union rates" (Dunning 1958, p. 256). Several U.S. firms, for example, Kodak and Esso Petroleum, were renowned for introducing new incentive and profit-sharing schemes in their U.K. affiliates in the 1950s. At the same time, only 15 percent of subsidiaries were fully unionized and federated. Labor selection and training methods generally followed American lines.

By the early 1980s, there were less obvious differences between the wages and industrial relations policies of U.S.-owned subsidiaries and their U.K. competitors. In almost every area of decision making, apart from the recruitment of senior executives, the influence of the parent company was much less limited. At the same time, recent evidence indicates U.S. affiliates continue to introduce innovatory work practices, emphasize individual performance-related payment schemes, offer more generous employee fringe benefits, and follow more professional recruitment and selection procedures (Buckley and Enderwick 1985).

Japanese affiliates are currently inclined to adapt their labor practices to local needs. In particular, they are particularly sensitive to local criticism of their recruitment procedures. They appear to make every effort not to poach labor from other firms; they have broadly conformed to nationally agreed wage levels; they offer relatively few bonuses or monetary incentives; and, almost without exception, their labor force is fully unionized. Their distinctive impact is shown in the area of hiring policy, where they seek to recruit employees able and willing to work as part of a team; the adoption of a more open and consultative style of industrial relations; the widespread use of quality control circles; the provision of first-class working and social conditions; and their strong preference for negotiating employee benefits and working conditions with only one trade union. The fact that, up to now, most of their workforce is made up of is young, semiskilled, female labor, and is normally recruited in areas of high unemployment, has made it easier for them to adopt a home-country stance toward their workers. This stance, however, is in contrast to the friendly and informal style of management that was (and is still) a conspicuous feature of U.S. affiliates, and that, again, to quite a large extent, reflects the culture of the home country.

Innovatory and Production Activities

Decisions on the amount and kind of innovatory activities of both groups of affiliates were strongly centralized, as were those on major items of capital expenditure. In 1953, three quarters of U.S. affiliates in the United Kingdom undertook some R&D; and by 1981 such affiliates were accounting for about 15 percent of all R&D expenditure by British manufacturing industry. By contrast, only 15 percent of Japanese affiliates engaged in innovatory activities in 1982, and most of this took the form of product and process adaptation. However, the fact that there was much less R&D undertaken in Japanese than in U.S. affiliates is likely to be more a function of the age and product structure of affiliates than anything else. Several Japanese branch plants in the electronics and motor vehicles sectors have gone on record that they intend to engage in R&D activities in Europe within the next few years. Whether the United Kingdom succeeds in attracting these facilities remains to be seen.[10]

Both U.S. and Japanese affiliates aimed to replicate their parent companies' production methods as far as they could. However, in the 1950s, U.S. subsidiaries were forced to make the most adaptations, mainly because differences in Anglo-American market characteristics and the cost of factor inputs. Today, these differences are much less marked, partly because of the lower significance of wage costs in total production costs and partly because the United Kingdom is now regarded as part of an internal European market that has a total spending power at least as high as that of the United States. Both groups of affiliates tended to be more capital- and technology-intensive than their indigenous competitors. However, again mainly because of their more recent origin, Japanese affiliates were considerably less horizontally diversified or vertically integrated than their American counterparts. They were also more prone to engage in flexible manufacturing methods and pay more attention to minimizing inventory costs. Again, in part at least, these differences reflect home-country competitive priorities and interfirm relationships.

Product Policy

In general, the range of products produced by Japanese affiliates in the United Kingdom in the 1980s is much more truncated than that of their U.S. counterparts both in the 1950s and 1980s. Again, I believe this reflects more the more recently established presence of the Japanese in the United Kingdom than the nationality of ownership. Partly for this reason, too, U.S. subsidiaries were given more freedom to introduce new products or modify existing products, and, except for affiliates supplying internationally branded goods for the export market, there was less centralized control over product quality. In the latter area, however, there is absolutely no compromise by the Japanese. After all, it is product quality and reliability that the Japanese regard as their most important competitive advantage in penetrating the European market. Their insistence on a strict adherence to standards and inspection procedures is practiced at every stage of the value-added chain.

Until 1983, the majority of Japanese affiliates supplied only one major product. In the last decade, there has been a steady trend toward a wider product range and process integration. Examples include color television assemblers diversifying into video tape recorders, microwave ovens, steam irons, and food mixers; and industrial electronics subsidiaries integrating backward to produce semiconductors, microchips, and silicon wafers.

Procurement Policy

In most major respects, decision making on sourcing methods and policies was similar in U.S. and Japanese affiliates, though the Japanese more closely involved their parent companies in the fixing and monitoring of purchasing standards. Indeed, almost all the criticisms of U.K. suppliers by U.S. subsidiaries and the perceived impact of the latter's purchasing demands on the former were reiterated (with even more fervor) by Japanese firms thirty years later. Whether it is an inherent feature of foreign-owned companies to castigate their local suppliers and claim a beneficial impact on their performance is not known, but it is surprising that so little change had apparently taken place in the perceived capabilities of the supplying sectors over the intervening thirty years. I believe part of the explanation is that U.S. and Japanese affiliates bought, or buy, from different kinds of suppliers; and part, that the purchasing requirements of the two groups of firms reflected that fact that their end products were at different stages of the product cycle. For example, because in the 1950s U.S.-owned firms were more innovatory in the products they introduced into the United Kingdom, they tended to find their local suppliers lacking in experience, vis-à-vis their home-country counterparts. Japanese subsidiaries, on the other hand, are currently producing products similar to their U.K. competitors;

their distinctive impact is on the quality, price, and delivery timetables of the materials, components, and parts they buy.

PURCHASING STANDARDS

While in U.S. affiliates, the decisions on "make or buy" and "buy locally or import" were taken by local purchasing managers without approval by the parent companies, in the majority of Japanese affiliates, these decisions were centralized. Indeed, for the more important components and parts (e.g., a color television tube), the parent company of the buying subsidiary normally tested samples of the products of alternative suppliers and, more often than not, required a detailed cost breakdown of the product. It was the parent company, too, that made the final decision on whether a particular specification was up to standard or not. Since, too, unlike their American counterparts in the 1950s, Japanese affiliates were freer to import their inputs from their home country, the parental control over the "buy locally or import" decision was of more practical significance. In the early 1980s, U.S. affiliates were importing a higher proportion of their inputs than in the 1950s; but their main intragroup imports were more between themselves and their European subsidiaries than between the parent companies and their affiliates. None of the Japanese affiliates in the United Kingdom in 1982 imported any components and parts from their European sister affiliates; by the end of the 1980s, there was some modest intra–European trade between Japanese affiliates in the consumer electronics sector.

IMPACT ON LOCAL SUPPLIERS

The purchasing managers of both groups of subsidiaries asserted that they provided their local suppliers with more information and technical assistance than did their U.K. counterparts. While the Japanese like to stress that they treat their suppliers as part of their own family, in the 1950s at least one U.S. affiliate claimed a similar relationship. Dissatisfaction on quality of inputs, prices, and delivery dates were also voiced by both U.S. and Japanese affiliates. As a consequence, their reject rates tended to be greater than those of their U.K. competitors, and were only reduced by a much closer cooperation between suppliers and purchasers.

In the course of both surveys, the major suppliers of the affiliates were visited for their views. In both cases the story was similar; but there were a few important country-specific differences. Most suppliers agreed, for example, that their American and Japanese customers were stricter in their demands for close tolerances, adherence to specifications, and delivery dates. They were, also, uniformly more willing than the average U.K. firm to supply detailed information in the form of specifications, blueprints, drawings, designs, and the like. It also appears that contemporary Japanese firms are more prepared to give advice on product design, equipment and production methods, and work organization than their earlier (or, indeed, their current) U.S. counterparts, who were often afraid of being accused of interference. Moreover, compared with their dealings with their U.K. customers, domestic suppliers found the relationship with their Japanese counterparts less distant and more cooperative and stable. Country-specific cultural factors, for example, with respect to forming and fostering relationships, and the method by which decisions are made are again important influences on behavior. The Japanese, for example, believe in entering into close, long-term, yet often noncontractual, commitments with their suppliers. The Americans tend to prefer more formal and specific contractual relations with their subcontractors.

All but one of the twenty suppliers of Japanese affiliates contacted in the survey said that they were regularly visited by their Japanese firms and had the edge on their U.K. counterparts, especially in the frequency of visits by managers, design and production engineers, and technicians. Much more than in the case of their American counterparts, Japanese parent companies were brought in to advise on their suppliers' production problems. They were also universally regarded—and much more so than their U.S. counterparts—as extremely prompt payers of bills. Again, the practice of consulting suppliers is partly a culture-specific phenomenon.

On the other hand, there was some criticism that both U.S. and Japanese customers made insufficient allowance for differences in the supply conditions in the United Kingdom compared to the United States and Japan, and the fact that it was not always economical (because, among other things, of the size of the order placed) to install the equipment necessary to meet the standards and tolerances insisted upon by them. In the case of suppliers to Japanese affiliates in particular, purchasing requirements were regarded as unreasonably rigorous; while newly established U.S. subsidiaries were accused of being inconsistent in their orders and of treating the supplier as a stopgap until they could build up capacity to manufacture for themselves. This criticism was not directed at Japanese affiliates whose long-term commitment to their suppliers was generally appreciated. Indeed, 90 percent of the suppliers appeared to be satisfied with their dealings with Japanese firms.

Marketing Methods

Most of the Japanese manufacturing affiliates in the 1980s sold their output to their own marketing affiliates, unlike their U.S. predecessors who preferred to market the output of their factories directly. In the 1950s, U.K. marketing methods lagged noticeably behind those of the United States and it was in this area, along with product and process innovation, that U.S. affiliates made their most distinctive impact. In 1983, no fewer than 87 percent of the subsidiaries producing consumer goods and 43 percent of those supplying producer goods said that they assimilated sales and distribution techniques of their parent companies, though "some adaptation was often required to the particular circumstances at hand"; and, apart from the chief executive, the sales or marketing director was more likely to be a U.S. national than was any other departmental head.

By the early 1980s, most U.S.-originated marketing techniques had been assimilated by their U.K. competitors; and U.S. competitive advantages became less marked in this area. Relatively few marketing departments of U.S. affiliates are currently headed up by an American national;[11] and decisions relating to advertising and sales promotion, pricing policy, and distribution methods are largely decentralized. At the same time, the integration of corporate production and markets in the EC[12] has led to an increasing proportion of U.S. affiliates in the United Kingdom being "strongly or decisively" influenced by their parent companies, or, in some cases, by their European regional offices (Young, Hood, and Hamill 1985).

In contrast, Japanese subsidiaries tend to adapt their marketing methods much more closely to what they perceive to be the best of the European norm. There is nothing very distinctive about any aspect of their postproduction activities, except their insistence on the same attention to quality and detail in their after-sales maintenance and servicing facilities as in the manufacturing process. However, it is my impression that Japanese-trained salesmen are especially keen negotiators over price, and that they maintain rather closer contacts with their customers than is the normal practice. It appears that few marketing decisions have to be referred back to Japan for approval, except with respect to the markets that they are allowed to serve. Here, as in production policy, the Japanese affiliates follow a regional (i.e., European) strategy as dictated by their head offices.

Production Control, Budgetary Planning, and Costing

The distinctive contribution of U.S. subsidiaries in the areas of production control, budgetary planning, and costing in the 1950s was much greater than that of the Japanese in the 1980s. This fact largely reflects the greater similarity of accounting and financial methods, laws, and regulations between the United States and the United Kingdom than between Japan and the United Kingdom. At the same time, in the 1950s, the United Kingdom was well behind the United States in "best practice" techniques of production planning and budgetary control, and in the presentation of company reports. By the 1980s, the gap in best practice techniques had largely been closed—at least among the more progressive U.K. and U.S. multinational companies.

Very strict and regular control is exercised by the Japanese parent companies over accounting and financial practices in their affiliates, and these tend to follow Japanese rather than U.K. norms. Indeed, in about two thirds of affiliates, a Japanese expatriate is in charge of the finance department. Apart from meeting local accounting and financial reporting requirements, all the financial and operating data provided by Japanese affiliates is in pursuance of instructions by their parent companies; and all planning and budgetary control procedures are Japanese determined. The Japanese allow their affiliates no autonomy in decision making in this area, which they regard as critical to their success as is the quality and cost of the products they produced.

The Composition of the Board of Directors

Another indication of the extent to which decision making in foreign affiliates is likely to be controlled or influenced by their parent companies is the structure and composition of the affiliate's board of directors. In 30 percent of the U.S. manufacturing subsidiaries in the 1950s, at least one-half of the board consisted of U.S. nationals; the corresponding proportion of Japanese affiliates in the 1980s was 85 percent, and, in 7 affiliates, the entire board consisted of Japanese nationals. Of the 107 directors of Japanese affiliates in 1983, 81 (76 percent) were Japanese nationals, although 62 of these were absentee directors, that is, not resident in the United Kingdom. By the end of the decade, this proportion had most probably fallen.

Once again, it would be unwise to attribute these differences entirely, or even mainly, to the nationality of the parent companies. Other studies have revealed that the percentage of expatriates on subsidiary boards is directly related to the percentage of shareholding of the parent company, to the age of the affiliate and its size relative to the parent company, and to the extent to which the affiliate is part of a regional or global product or marketing strategy. Since the 1950s, the proportion of U.S. subsidiaries in the United Kingdom, which are fully owned, has increased as they have become part of an integrated product and production in Europe.[13] On the other hand, from the start, Japanese affiliates in the U.K. have been treated by their parent companies as a foothold for a full-scale penetration of the European market.

Conclusions

This chapter has sought to demonstrate that there are several important differences between the decision-making structures and processes of U.S. manufacturing subsidiaries in the United Kingdom in the 1950s and those in the early 1980s; but an even more marked difference between those of Japanese and U.S. firms in the early 1980s. In general, decisions tended to be less centralized in the former than in the latter group of affiliates and, where they were decentralized, it was more likely for a Japanese expatriate to be in charge than an American expatriate.

The chapter has also shown that the pattern and extent of these differences vary across functional groups according to the transaction costs of transferring intermediate goods and services (and especially technical knowledge and organization skills) from the United States and Japan to the United Kingdom; and those costs related to the delegation of decision making to local affiliates. These transaction costs are likely to be greater (a) the greater the difference between the normal operational practices of firms in the investing countries (i.e., United States or Japan) and those in the United Kingdom and (b) the greater the obstacles to successfully transferring or adapting these practices to and within a U.K. environment.

In essence, this conclusion about transaction costs supports the findings of other scholars who have found that new organizational practices, and particularly those that require a change in institutional structures, take longer to diffuse across national boundaries (especially between those of markedly different cultures) than do technological innovations.[14] But my research goes one step further, in that it suggests that, once transferred to a foreign country, not only are organizational advances more likely to be "internalized" within the transferring company, but that control over the way they are implemented is likely to be more centralized.

An earlier section argued that there were three reasons why decisions over the resource allocation within affiliates might be centralized, and I have shown that each of these is reflected in differences in the attitudes of American and Japanese MNEs to the management of their U.K. affiliates. Thus, to ensure maximum efficiency of their affiliates, the Japanese believe that they must have direct control over production management and planning, procurement policy, finance and accounting procedures, and work organization; they do this either by centralizing decision making or by ensuring that either Japanese expatriates are in charge of these functional areas or that local managers are inculcated with the Japanese philosophy and trained to meet the standards expected of them. By contrast, in the 1950s the Americans believed that the U.K. managerial weakness lay in its unprofessionalism, the lack of marketing expertise, and unfamiliarity with the more technically advanced products and production methods. Decisions relating to these matters then tended to be centralized or made by U.S. expatriates.

I have also asserted that the conflicts arising between the interests of U.K. affiliates and those of the organization of which they are a part, arise particularly in the case of MNEs pursuing a globally or regionally oriented product or marketing strategy. In the 1950s, very few U.S. affiliates in the United Kingdom were operating such a strategy and most subsidiaries were treated as self-contained profit centers. This is no longer the case—at least in the more globally or regionally integrated of industries—and in several strategic areas, notably R&D, recruitment of top executives, and sourcing policies, decision making in U.S. MNEs has become increasingly centralized. By contrast, the entry of Japanese MNEs into the United Kingdom is part of a long-term European development strategy; from the start, the tasks assigned to the affiliate have been designed to promote the goals rather than the welfare of the U.K. operation as such. With this vision in mind, it is then not surprising that most important decisions tend to be taken in Tokyo or Osaka rather than in Cardiff or Washington, Tyne & Wear.

At the same time, one must not neglect differences in cultures and ideologies between the two investing economies. The consensus approach to decision making by the Japanese makes for a good deal more discussion among the parties affected by any decision made than was (or is) practiced in U.S. subsidiaries, for all the emphasis in U.S. culture on industrial democracy. Among other things, this approach means the decision-making process is less formal but more protracted in the case of Japanese MNEs, although, in the last resort, there is an even clearer recognition of the role of the manager as a decision maker in Japanese than in U.S. enterprises.

On the third reason for decentralization of decision making, which has to do with the lower decision-making costs in the country of the affiliates rather than that of the parent company, there was considerably more pressure for U.S. enterprises to relocate managers in the 1950s than either these same enterprises or Japanese enterprises in the 1980s. However, in both cases, the costs of employing expatriates is (and was) between 50 and 150 percent higher than their domestic costs (due to differences in tax rates and costs of additional housing, education, travel, settlement, etc.).

In the 1950s, the average salaries of U.K. managers and management-related staff were about one-half of their U.S. counterparts; currently (1990) it is nearer three-fifths. By contrast, U.K. and Japanese managerial and related costs were about the same in the early 1980s and for this reason, Japanese MNEs had less incentive to decentralize the decision-making function. On the other hand, the greater unfamiliarity of the Japanese with the English language, business norms, and customs and their lack of knowledge about U.K. suppliers, laws and regulations, working customs, and ways of dealing with central and local government, make it more likely that they would favor decentralizing decision making to "on-the-spot" line managers.

Some of the other differences between the two groups of decision makers are those that cannot be attributed to their country of origin. In the following I discuss how these might react on the decision-making structures and procedures of the U.S. and Japanese affiliates.

Age of affiliate. This topic has been mentioned previously, so my comments here are brief. Since younger and less experienced affiliates are more likely to be subjugated to their parent companies, decision making is likely to be more strongly centralized in Japanese MNEs. However, while U.S. subsidiaries established in the 1950s were less autonomous in their decision making than those set up prior to the Second World War, they were considerably more autonomous than their Japanese counterparts in the 1980s. Exceptions include those that were part of an integrated network of value-added activities in the EC.

Size of affiliates. After taking age and industry differences into account, there appears to be no significant difference in the average size of U.S. affiliates in the 1950s as compared with that of their Japanese counterparts thirty years later.[15] However, relative to their parent companies, the Japanese affiliates were (and shall remain) considerably smaller; hence, their economic influence in the multinational hierarchy of which they are part may well be that much less.

Product diversification. I have indicated that in 1982, almost all Japanese affiliates were single-product firms, in contrast to U.S. firms in the 1950s—even those which had just been established. In the 1980s the perceived need to adapt products to local customer requirements had made for more local decision making. On the other hand, there is considerably more intraplant specialization among U.S. affiliates in the EC, particularly in the motor vehicle, earth moving equipment, computer, and electronics sectors.

Regional or Global Product Market Strategy. In my view, this variable is one of the most important factors leading to centralized decision making; even in the case of products customized to meet the specific needs of the local market.[16] Throughout this chapter, I have suggested that such a strategy (albeit in its infancy) is being practiced by Japanese MNEs with investments in the United Kingdom; in fairly marked contrast to the "controlled autonomy" allowed to U.S. subsidiaries in the 1950s. New U.S. subsidiaries now entering the United Kingdom to supply the European market might well be persuaded to follow the Japanese strategy, which is partly industry specific and partly a reflection of the United Kingdom's membership of the EC. Such a strategy affects the structure and process of decision making in almost all functional areas—especially where the MNE is promoting a world product—and is geocentric in its approach to resource management.

It would seem, then, while the general level of control exercised over decision making in U.S. and Japanese affiliates is associated more with firm or industry characteristics—particularly the degree of multinationalization of the parent company and the age of the subsidiary—the direction (or emphasis) of control and the manner in which it is exercised is strongly reflects the country of origin of the investing companies. In its turn, of course, this tendency may have a time dimension. As Japanese firms become more multinational, as they compete with U.S. and European MNEs on equal terms, as they become more immersed in different cultures, and as their competitors adopt their more successful managerial and other styles, they may lose some of their cultural idiosyncrasies, as indeed have U.S. affiliates in the United Kingdom since the 1950s. But, for the moment, these country-specific idiosyncrasies do help explain many of the differences in the structure and processes of the decision-making pattern of the two groups of firms studied in this paper.

Notes

1. In 1986, the foreign production of the world's largest industrial enterprises (as identified by *Fortune* magazine) accounted for about 30 percent of the total output of such enterprises. But, observe that in the late 1960s and early 1970s, Ray Vernon and his colleagues identified considerable differences in the industrial and organizational patterns of U.S., European and Japanese MNEs (Vernon 1974).

2. The results of these surveys are contained in Dunning (1958) and (1986a). An earlier analysis that compared and contrasted the industrial and geographical patterns of U.S. and Japanese manufacturing in the United Kingdom and their impact on the U.K. economy is contained in Dunning (1986b, 1988).

3. RTA is the proportion of the patents of the world's 729 largest industrial firms in a particular sector accounted for by a country, divided by the proportion of patents of the world's largest firms in all sectors accounted for by that country.

4. We are not arguing that any of these elements of efficiency are unimportant; simply that it would seem that, in the 1980s, U.S.-based firms were relatively better at performing some production and transaction functions than others; and that these functions generally were different from those in which Japanese-based firms are the most effective. Incidentally, some of the strengths of the Japanese firms in the 1980s were previously those of the U.S. firms in the 1950s.

5. For further examination of the differences in the industrial structure of foreign and indigenous firms in U.K. industries, see Dunning (1985). Since this paper was written, the United Kingdom's leading computer company, ICL, has been acquired by Fujitsu. This takeover immediately added another 20,000 to the employment roster of Japanese-owned firms in the fabricating industries.

6. Pages 21–34 of Dunning (1958) give examples of new products and production techniques originating in the United States in the forty years prior to the First World War, and suggest reasons for the tardiness of U.K. manufacturers to adopt and exploit the basic inventions of the period. U.K. firms were even slower to adopt the new organization structures pioneered by U.S. firms in the first decades of the twentieth century. See also Kogut (1990).

7. In the terminology of Vernon (1974), U.S.-owned MNEs investing in the United Kingdom were mainly innovation-based oligopolies while the Japanese investors, at least in the product are in which they were involved in the United Kingdom, are mature or even senescent oligopolies.

8. In 1981–1982, for example their R&D expenditure was 3.1 percent of their sales, a ratio nearly twice the average for all Japanese manufacturers.

9. Influence and control tend to increase with the number of countries in which a multinational operates; the degree of idiosyncrasy or importance of particular ownership-specific advantages; the younger the age of the affiliate; the smaller its relative size; and the greater the equity participation of the parent company.

10. Of course, Japanese firms may acquire R&D facilities when they purchase U.K. companies. Thus, Japanese owned R&D in the United Kingdom has risen sharply as a result of the acquisition of Britain's largest rubber tire and computer companies by Japanese MNEs.

11. Of a sample of 154 foreign affiliates replying to a postal questionnaire—75 percent of which were North American owned in 1984—only 6, or 4%, employed nationals from their parent country (Young, Hood, and Hamill 1985).

12. As witnessed, for example, by a very substantial increase in intrafirm trade between U.S. subsidiaries in the EC.

13. In the 1950s, most U.S. subsidiaries in the United Kingdom were part of a multidomestic strategy on the part of their parent companies; in the 1980s, an increased number were part of a regional or globally oriented strategy. Moreover, the proportion practicing such a strategy is likely to increase with the completion of Europe's internal market in 1992.

14. See Kogut (1990) for a discussion of these and related issues.

15. In 1953 the average number of employees of the 59 U.S. affiliates set up since 1940 was 361; the average number employed by Japanese affiliates in 1982 was 205 and in 1988, 290 (Dunning 1958, 1986a).

16. The balancing of the advantages of global integration and meeting the particular and specific needs of local customers is one of the most demanding tasks of the modern MNE. To achieve the right balance, a considerable exchange of information and ideas between local managers and central decision makers is necessary. However, while in practice, the division of decision-making responsibility may vary from firm to firm, in the last resort the local product and marketing strategy must be consistent with the global or regional strategy; and it is this latter strategy that is mapped out and coordinated centrally.

References

Archibugi, D., and M. Pianta. 1989. "The Technological Specialization of Advanced Countries." Report to the Commission of the European Communities. Mimeo.

Buckley, P. J., and P. Enderwick. 1985. *The Industrial Relations Priorities of Foreign Owned Firms in Britain.* London: Macmillan.

Cantwell, J., and C. Hodson. 1991. "Global Research and Development and U. K. Competitiveness," in M. C. Casson, ed., *Global Research Strategy and International Competitiveness.* ed. Oxford: Blackwell.

Doz, Y. 1986. *Strategic Management in Multinational Companies.* Oxford: Pergamon Press.

Dunning, J. H. 1958. *American Investment in British Manufacturing Industry.* London: Allen & Unwin. (Reprinted by Arno Press, New York, 1976.)

Dunning, J. H. 1981. *International Production and the Multinational Enterprise.* London: Allen & Unwin.

Dunning, J. H., ed. 1985. *Multinational Enterprises, Economic Structure and International Competitiveness.* Chichester: Wiley.

Dunning, J. H. 1986a. *Japanese Participation in British Industry.* London: Croom Helm.

Dunning, J. H. 1986b. *Decision-making Structures in U.S. and Japanese Manufacturing Affiliates in the U.K.: Some Similarities and Contrasts.* ILO Working Paper No. 41. Geneva: ILO (International Labor Office).

Dunning, J. H. 1988. *Explaining International Production.* London: Unwin Hyman.

Dunning, J. H. 1990. *The Globalization of Firms and the Competitiveness of Countries: Some Implications for the Theory of International Production.* The Crafoord Lectures, 1989. Lund, Sweden: University of Lund.

Hood, N., and S. Young. 1983. *Multinational Investment Strategies in the British Isles: A Study of MNEs in the Assisted Areas and in the Republic of Ireland.* London: HMSO.

JETRO. 1989. *Current Management Structure of Japanese Manufacturing Enterprises in Europe.* Fifth Survey Report. Tokyo: JETRO.

Kogut, B. 1983. "Foreign Direct Investment as a Sequential Process," C. P. Kindleberger and D. Andretsch, eds., *The Multinational Corporation in the 1980s,* pp. 38–55. Cambridge, Mass.: MIT Press.

Kogut, B. 1990. *The Permeability of Borders and the Speed of Learning Among Countries.* The Crafoord Lectures, 1989. Lund, Sweden: University of Lund.

Porter, M. 1990. *The Competitive Advantages of Nations.* New York: Basic Books.

U.S. Department of Commerce. 1984. *U.S. Direct Investment Abroad: Benchmark Survery 1982.* Washington: U.S. Department of Commerce.

Vernon, R. 1974. "The Location of Economic Activity," in J. H. Dunning, ed., *Economic Analysis and the Multinational Enterprise,* pp. 89–114. London: Allen & Unwin.

Young, S., N. Hood, and J. Hamill. 1985. *Decision-making in Foreign Owned Multinational Subsidiaries in the U. K.* ILO Working Paper No. 35. Geneva: ILO (International Labor Office).

Young, S., N. Hood, and J. Hamill. 1988. *Foreign Multinationals and the British Economy.* London: Routledge.

12

Supplying the Toyota Production System: Intercorporate Organizational Evolution and Supplier Subsystems

W. MARK FRUIN
TOSHIHIRO NISHIGUCHI

There is now overwhelming agreement that the Toyota Production System (TPS) represents the world's best practice for the manufacture of motor vehicles (Womack, Jones, and Roos 1990), though there is little evidence why the TPS works so well.[1] The surprisingly large yet strategically important number of suppliers to Toyota Motor Corporation is a particularly confounding aspect of this puzzle. Though a sizeable literature has appeared relating the postwar Japanese motor vehicle industry to issues of industrial structure, industrial relations, and economic growth (e.g., Ono and Odaka 1988; Cusumano 1985), little integration has been made between these themes, especially with regard to assembler–supplier relations.[2]

In this chapter, the size and strategic importance of Toyota's suppliers are examined regarding how organizational dynamics, contractual relations, economic conditions, and their interconnections have affected the development of Toyota's system of supply. We believe that large numbers of strategically important suppliers emerged in a process of *intercorporate* organizational evolution. This evolution, unfolding from the early 1950s through the 1980s, was characterized by a structuring of several tens of thousands of suppliers into tiered and clustered subsystems, distinguished by a transactional dynamic moving from bilateral/dualistic relations to multilateral/reciprocal ones. Also, the evolution of the TPS supply function was based on reciprocal learning between Toyota and its major suppliers.

The Organization Puzzle

According to a 1977 Ministry of International Trade and Industry (MITI) census on the division of labor supporting the auto industry, 47,308 independent, book-keeping entities supply Toyota Motor Corporation with parts, components, subassemblies, and services (see Table 12.1). Adjusting for double-counting drops the total to 36,468. Thus, depending on how one counts, between 36,000 and 47,000 organizations supply Toyota with about 70 percent of the manufacturing cost of Toyota-badge motor vehicles. The numbers are staggering, regardless of which figure is used.

How is it possible to coordinate and mobilize resources among 36,000 to 47,000 suppliers and still be, the world's "best-practice" producer? Conventionally, response to such an apparent contradiction is to claim that this policy optimizes a mix of hierarchies and markets, or, more generally, vertical integration as opposed to outsourcing. First, the institutional economic literature identified with the work of Oliver Williamson (1974, 1985) suggests that in order to minimize the hazards of opportunism and uncertainty, it is best to internalize factors of production; promote an internal division of labor; and coordinate, allocate, and plan effectively within unified and consistent corporate boundaries. This response is the transaction cost economizing solution or vertical integration on the basis of in-house hierarchies.[3] Evidence suggests, however, that Toyota is simply not taking this strategy.

Toyota is pursuing a buy rather than make strategy, maximizing the logic of market choice. On average, Toyota buys 70 percent of the value of the motor vehicles it assembles; the comparable figures for General Motors, Ford, and Chrysler are 30, 50, and 60 percent (and rising, apparently).[4] Hence, Toyota buys anywhere from 40 to 10 percent more of the value of its motor vehicles on average than do the "Big Three."

Yet, is such a heavy reliance compatible with Toyota's well-known ability to develop products quickly for the markets? Economies of speed (fast-to-market) are hard to achieve with "pure" buy rather than make strategies because information is not free and never perfect. The more one relies on market-based information, the more likely that response times will slow, especially when purchased items are not off-the-shelf (as is increasingly the case in the auto industry). Nevertheless, Toyota boasts among the shortest product development cycles, lowest inventory levels, and

TABLE 12.1 Division of Labor in the Automobile Industry (Toyota Motors' suppliers by level)

	First-level	Second-level	Third-level	Total
Engine parts	25	912	4,960	5,897
Electronical/electronics	1	34	352	387
Transmission, gears, steering	31	609	7,354	7,994
Brakes, suspension	18	792	6,204	7,014
Brake and suspension parts	18	926	5,936	6,880
Chassis and parts	3	27	85	115
Body and pressing	41	1,213	8,221	9,475
Other	31	924	8,591	9,546
Totals	168	5,437	41,703	47,308

Source: Small- and Medium-Sized Enterprise Agency, MITI, *An Investigation into the Current Level of the Division of Labor (Automobiles),* mimeographed, 1977.

quickest turnaround times in a global sample of representative motor vehicle companies.[5] In short, Toyota excels at cost- as well as time-based competition.

Thus, neither hierarchy nor market in their unadulterated forms seems to explain the role of suppliers in the TPS. Certainly, Toyota has financial leverage over some key suppliers. According to 1986 data, among seventy-seven of Toyota's largest, first-tier suppliers, the average level of Toyota's shareholding in affiliated, first-tier suppliers was 20.7 percent (Industry Research System 1986). Excluding the fifteen largest of these, either firms controlled directly by Toyota or firms that were spun out of Toyota, drops the figure to 13.7 percent.

Moving farther afield, outside the group of the largest 77 suppliers, Toyota's financial involvement falls dramatically and progressively to the point of insignificance. One reason for the progressive decline is the sheer number of suppliers; Toyota rarely holds shares outside of first-tier suppliers. If some 40,000 suppliers are used in the denominator, then the *average* level of Toyota shareholding in suppliers quickly drops below 1 percent.

It could be argued that Toyota surrogates, namely the largest first-tier suppliers controlled by Toyota, regulate lower tier suppliers so that financial power does in fact organize the system indirectly. But this interpretation is somewhat problematic. To be persuasive, one has to assume that an extremely dominant Toyota, and rather passive first-tier and lower-tier suppliers have conducted an informal conspiracy for at least four decades.

In contrast, the approach presented here argues for a dynamic, technology-based, organizational evolution of the TPS binding Toyota to its many suppliers by reciprocal long-term contracting. Reciprocity, profit sharing, and interdependent learning have come to describe the supply function while at earlier times, the 1950s for example, an extremely dominant Toyota and rather passive suppliers may have characterized the TPS. By this evolution, the supply system has become more than a simple sum of the parts as defined by firm-to-firm (supplier-to-Toyota) relations.[6]

The fundamental question is this: Given the exceedingly large number of Toyota suppliers how can the exacting cost, quality, and delivery standards of the TPS be exercised? Shareholding in two or three dozen firms, albeit core ones, does not appear to provide sufficient financial incentives to organize a division of labor as extreme as that sustaining the TPS. Just-in-time (JIT) purchase, delivery, or manufacture is manageable among a finite number of suppliers, but is too difficult to operate with suppliers in the tens of thousands as are currently supporting Toyota. As a consequence, confusion with regard to a definition of the TPS in the context of a diffuse, decentralized, and high performing supplier system may be warranted. Indeed, to our knowledge, no one has yet attempted to define the TPS in this way.

The Boundaries of Definition: The Traditional View of the TPS

Traditionally, the TPS has been assigned the following *single-site* characteristics in contrast to the mass production system. Instead of "push" production control under a master plan, TPS operates by a "pull" production system that flexibly adapts to changing market needs and manufacturing process requirements. Instead of a rigidly specialized workforce and dedicated equipment (e.g., as many as 200 job classifications and a large number of transfer machines at a traditional U. S. assembly plant), TPS seeks operational flexibility through multiskilled workers, running relatively flexible machines, in an autonomous fashion (e.g., three or four job classifications with workers responsible for the maintenance, inspection, and operation of perhaps a half-dozen machines per person where operator–machine systems incorporate "judgment" functions, such as auto-stoppers checking for abnormals).

JIT operations with minimum stock levels throughout the manufacturing process are in sharp contrast to the operations of mass production. Small-lot, ultimately one-piece-at-a-time, production with fast changeover times permits a large variety of goods to be manufactured in small volumes. On the other hand, large-lot production with long changeover times is typical of a mass production system. Zero defects are the target of the TPS. Its most successful performers are achieving 10–20 ppm (parts per million) defects at the level of components today, whereas several percent "acceptable" defects are characteristic of the mass production system.[8]

Finally, in its ultimate expression, the mass production system may seek to eliminate workers from the shopfloor because they are perceived to be a source of production problems. Instead, the Toyota Production System considers workers to be a source of problem solving, an infinite and irreplaceable reservoir of *kaizen* or continuous improvement.[9] In sum, the TPS is a production system that is pulled by final demand, that minimizes inventories and work in progress by close coordination with suppliers, and that relies on the initiative and development of human resources.

While a standard definition of the TPS hinges on the single-site, hardware-dependent factors as just described, there remain puzzling areas of inquiry, especially concerning organizational and behavioral features of the supplier system as a whole. If TPS represents best practice and if its hardware-based features are well understood, why is there so much variation in the degree of successful implementation? Why should TPS be a benefit to one manufacturer and a bane to another? How do some motor vehicle firms mobilize their resources in a TPS-like way while others cannot, even when they attempt to?

In what follows these issues are probed by offering two organizational models of the supplier system supporting the TPS: a dualist model and a network model.[10] A learning model, a dynamic variation on the network model, is also presented. The key concepts underlying these models are:

- A transition from residual to transaction-specific rights in the supply function.
- A change from unidirectional to multilateral flows of information and learning in an interfirm supplier network.
- A shifting emphasis from reciprocity (to equity) to distributive justice in the TPS supply function.

In sum, we propose that the TPS is an *interorganizational* matrix with certain embedded behavioral, institutional, and performance features. A definition of the TPS in the context of these characteristics suggests that the TPS may not be so widely diffused even in Japan.[11] Few manufacturing and supply systems can boast of TPS-like, systemwide advantages.

What Is the TPS?

The Dualist Model

Often, the TPS is presented as a dualist model of organization where Toyota induces (coerces?) many of its agents (workers, dealers, suppliers) to adopt certain organizational forms and practices. In this model, Toyota as the principal represents the interests of owners, managers, and shareholders against those of agents, either its nonmanagerial employees or other individuals and organizations cooperating with Toyota in the execution of the TPS.[12]

Structures and processes associated with the TPS include JIT operations; small-group activities—such as quality circles, training in statistical quality controls for supervisors and rank-and-file, training in multiple machine tool mastery (multis-killing), general flexibility in the use of plant, equipment, and personnel, reduction of waste (of energy, time, labor, resources in general), small lot manufacturing, and use of *kanban* (a system by which final demand pulls the production process from assembly back to suppliers).

Structures and processes such as these were generally worked out, evaluated, improved, and implemented within Toyota first and then transmitted to firms with which it closely cooperates.[13] In short, performance standards and parameters originated with Toyota and are supervised by Toyota.

The main features of this model are:

- Managerial prerogatives (what may be called residual rights of ownership to the physical equipment of production as well as rights to operate the plant and equipment) lie exclusively in the hands of Toyota managers.
- The flow of information about the structures and processes of the TPS is largely one-way, namely from Toyota management outward and downward.
- Regardless of the number and configuration of the organizational units in the TPS, the flow and control of transactions is predictable and managed.
- Power, rights, and information in the TPS are characterized by discrete, steplike functions in a hierarchy.

The assumptions of the dualist model may be illustrated as shown in Figure 12.1.

The Network Model

More recently, the TPS has been presented as a network model of organization emphasizing the number, configuration, and nature of interactions between many parts of an interconnected system. Managerial rights are not stressed, and, instead, a more symmetrical, multilateral model of reciprocal relations between Toyota and its many suppliers is offered.[14] A weakening of "residual ownership rights" may be a central feature of the network model.

The more easily others can affect the income flow from someone else's assets without bearing the full costs for doing so, the lower the value of the assets in question. For this reason, it is commonly thought that a firm will not rely on an outside contractor for a critical component or service that influences significantly the value of the final product, especially one that requires frequent coordination during the

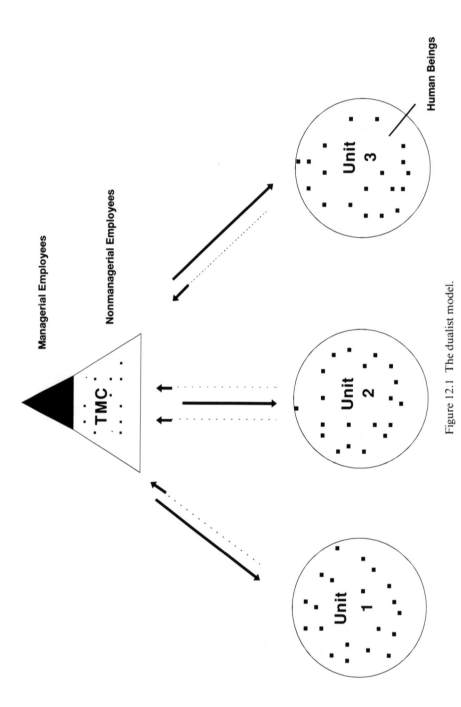

Figure 12.1 The dualist model.

production development cycle. Rather for such components and services, a firm should seek to maintain residual ownership rights as opposed to contracting out. Yet the TPS seems to defy this commonsense rule by allowing important automobile subsystems, such as engine control electronics, climate control systems, and brakes, to be designed and developed by outside vendors.

In network models where large numbers of organizational units are involved (hundreds instead of dozens), the network may be analyzed advantageously in terms of its organizational subsystems or "clusters" (for more details see Nishiguchi, 1993 [forthcoming]). Clustering refers to the grouping of subsystem providers that take responsibility for an entire subsystem, such as brakes, electronics, or climate control. Within clusters, interactions may tend either toward asymmetrical, bilateral relations (arms-length) as in the dualist model, or toward more symmetrical, multilateral relations (clustered) as in the network model (Figure 12.2).

In network models structures and processes of the earlier dualist model are not neglected. Instead they are viewed in light of an emerging multilateral system (the network as a whole) and its many bilateral parts. Credit for originating and improving structures and processes are not interpreted unilaterally but systemically. Symmetrical, bilateral, and multilateral dynamics characterized by reciprocity define the system. Further, mutuality of interests within the context of the network is emphasized, leading to an ethos of multilateral, reciprocal, collaborative bargaining, what is termed coexistence and coprosperity *(kyozon kyoei)* in Japanese.[15] Mutuality of interests appears related to an expanding volume of information (transactions), its multidirectional flows, and an increasingly large number of organizations (nodes) in the network.

Today, full-model changes come every four or five years, and meaningful, if minor, cosmetic changes occur every year in the Japanese auto industry. In these circumstances, transaction-specific rights of ownership provide suppliers with credible commitments sufficient to guarantee their pivotal involvement in design, development, and manufacturing activities not only of existing but also for new car production.

The features of the network model are:

- Specificities in transaction rights are separable from residual rights of ownership (for more detailed discussion, see Grossman and Hart 1986). Specificity in transaction rights refers to an expectation of (perhaps a guarantee to) a portion of the revenue stream generated by a product, process, or service over which one does not have final market power.
- System features, such as directional flow, velocity, frequency, and intensity of transactions, may be becoming more important than bilateral firm relations.
- Important behavioral and institutional characteristics of the TPS are more continuous than discrete in terms of their frequency and distribution within the network.

These features are illustrated in Figure 12.3.

The Learning Model: A Dynamic Extension of the Network Model

Most recently, the TPS has been seen as a form of manufacturing that embodies high degrees of system-specific learning (Hayes, Wheelwright, and Clark 1988). The

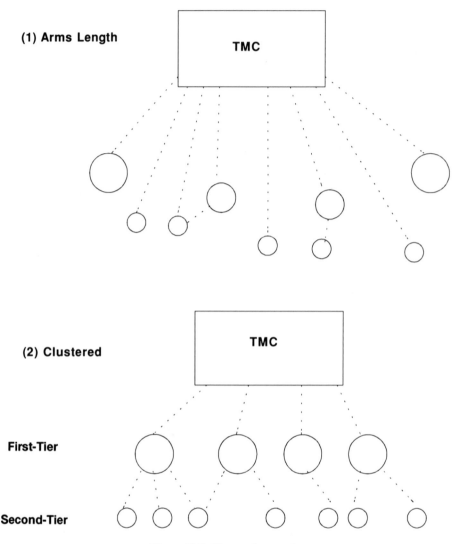

Figure 12.2 Clustered control.

learning model of the TPS represents a potentiality associated with the network model when certain crucial conditions are present. Among these, the most important are the full separation of transaction-specific ownership rights from residual rights of ownership and the further development of reciprocity and multilateral symmetry in information flow and exchange. The limited diffusion of the TPS, even in Japan, suggests the difficulties of attaining these conditions, as discussed in the following paragraphs.

Learning comes from many sources but, most important, from human beings involved in the TPS. Learning is of two sorts: the accumulated efforts of many individuals to improve, and the enhanced capabilities of organizations to harness those

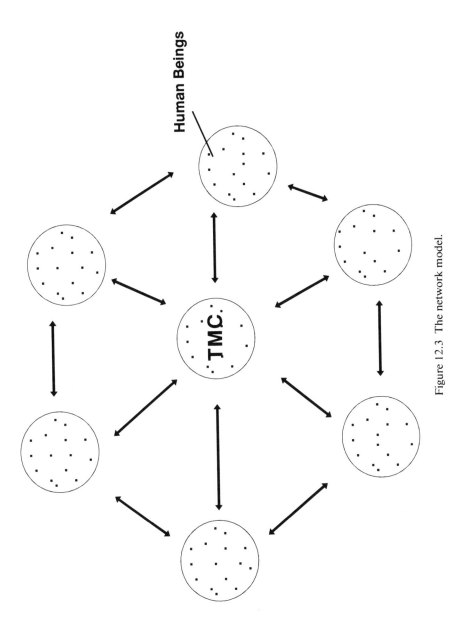

Human Beings

Figure 12.3　The network model.

improvements. In this perspective, experience—thoughtful, accumulated experience within the TPS, a behavioral transformation congruent with a strong shift in emphasis from residual to transaction-specific ownership rights, and the translation of experience into better ways of assessing and rewarding work—is stressed. Thus, individual experience and commitment are translated into organizational learning and this pushes system characteristics to new heights of performance.

In short, the structural process and transactional features of the dualist and less robust network models are not denied. Yet there are many kinds of learning, both general and local. What distinguishes the learning of this model are the higher rates of knowledge acquisition and application within as well as between organizations in the TPS. Higher levels of learning, more fully exploited, result in *qualitative* changes in employee attitudes, performance, and commitment.

Continuous improvements in the TPS depend on the accumulated efforts and insights of all the stakeholders in the TPS. Those efforts and insights are released by experiences of equity and distributive justice in the allotment of rewards and benefits derived from the TPS. Equity and distributive justice characterize economic relations in the TPS as there is a shift toward notions of transaction-specific rights of ownership and of diffuse rather than discrete bilateral relations (mutuality of interests). These notions include expectations that organizations and individuals without residual rights of ownership will benefit in some direct proportion to their contributions to the TPS.

The features of this extended network model are:

- Rights, interests, and inputs of stakeholders in the TPS are not separable; being inseparable, the benefits of lowering costs are distributed equitably.
- People are trustworthy (or can become so) and they are essential for continuous improvement of the TPS.
- Learning is more continuous than discontinuous, more diffused than concentrated.
- Learning is organic, self-reinforcing, growing from within and between rather than being transplanted from without.
- Organizational entities in the TPS are interdependent rather than independent; learning occurs within a highly integrated, interconnected context.

The learning model of the TPS may be represented as shown in Figure 12.4; the dots in the illustration are meant to suggest human beings and their increasingly important role in the TPS.

How to Reconcile the Different Views of the TPS

There are two ways to reconcile such different views of the Toyota Production System. In the first instance, the models may be different representations of the same phenomena even while this is not immediately apparent. In the second instance, an historical or evolutionary model that captures temporal aspects of the TPS as they evolve in structure and function over time may permit a reconciliation.

Some features of the two basic models represent different perspectives on the

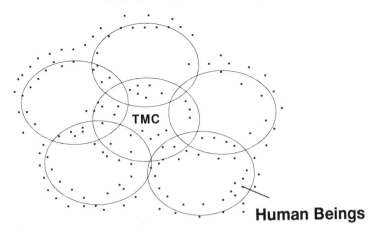

Figure 12.4 The learning model.

same reality, such as an agreement on hardware-based characteristics of the TPS, but other aspects of the two models highlight basic definitional differences, such as issues of ownership or managerial rights, the logic or dynamic of the TPS, and whether or not behavioral attributes are discrete or continuous. An evolutionary treatment of the TPS, however, allows for some features of the two models to be emphasized at certain times and for others at different times. Presumably, the timing and sequencing of these features may be especially critical, namely the temporal pattern of systemic evolution is significant. An important part of this interpretation is the concept of embeddedness.

The concept of embeddedness, as developed by Granovetter and others, refers to the progressive interrelation of persons, institutions, and institutional environments over time. Granovetter (1985) "stresses the role of concrete personal relations and structures of such relations in generating trust and discouraging malfeasance." Three aspects of this process of embeddedness may be especially important for understanding the nature of the TPS: (1) the sequence of adaptation (in what order the steps occurred), (2) when the steps occurred, and (3) when the effects of embeddeness were observed.

The Sequence of Adaptation

The dualist model appears most appropriate during the earliest days of experimentation with the TPS. Taiichi Ohno (1978) writes that trials having workers handle two or more machines in order to catch up with the larger output of American factories began in 1947 in the Number Two Machine Works in Toyota City, and that suppliers began to adopt JIT techniques in their deliveries with Toyota in 1963. So, during the period 1947–1963/64, major changes in the arrangement, use, and management of the physical assets associated with the TPS occurred. They were initiated on the prerogative and power of Toyota's top management. Between Toyota and its principal suppliers, the main elements of the hardware-dependent definition of the TPS began to be transferred toward the mid-1960s, on the initiatives of Toyota. The transfer of the TPS to first-tier suppliers, therefore, was largely conducted within the framework of the dualist model characterized by unequal rights and bilateral asymmetrical relations, a one-way transfer of know-how.

When the Steps Occurred

The network or interorganizational model emerges during a period from 1965 to the early 1980s. The network model focuses on a shift toward reciprocal, multilateral relations and a concern with specific rights of transaction rather than residual rights of ownership. So, this model assumes a fairly large number of organizational entities (at least hundreds, if not thousands), all cooperating in the implementation of the TPS. The network model assumes a period of transitional learning when the TPS was transferred outside Toyota, so that would be sometime after 1963/64 when Ohno (1978) says suppliers began to adopt JIT deliveries. More generally, the high volume of transactions associated with a network view of the TPS coincides with a phenomenal increase in output of Toyota-badge vehicles. Production, in fact, quintupled in a seven year period—from just 200,000 vehicles in 1961 to over 1,000,000 in 1968, and *doubled again* between 1968 and 1972! An increase in output associated with the transfer of the TPS to first-tier suppliers assumes an expansion of second- and third-tier suppliers to secure the inputs and outputs of first-tier suppliers.

When the Effects Were Observed

A learning model, as an extension of the network model, seems most appropriate for the decade or two since the mid-1970s when, initially, the oil crises forced Toyota to cope with a much more demanding technical market for automobile design and manufacture in terms of fuel efficiency, environmental protection, safety, price, and quality, and when, later, a much more rigorous financial market with a dramatic reevaluation of the yen in 1985 and constant political pressures affected export market pricing and penetration strategies.

At the same time, the maturation (not saturation) of the motor vehicle industry in Japan led consumers to demand variety, choice, and style in the purchase of automobiles.[16] The consecutive, nearly simultaneous, occurrence of these developments (increasing technical requirements, financial discipline, political pressures, and consumer demand) largely shifted the burden for product development and flexible manufacturing away from Toyota as the primary party responsible for the organization and management of the TPS.

Along with diminution of Toyota's control, time to market shortened, product variety increased, technical complexity climbed, and financial exposure widened. Toyota was forced to rely increasingly and in notably more interdependent ways on firms to which it had diffused of the TPS. A learning emphasis came to imbue Toyota and TPS suppliers as a result.

During the 1970s, we argue that Toyota became a large and efficient firm by buying more so than by making. However, Toyota's success was not found in a simple buying of more and cheaper parts but in a complex buying of higher value-added parts. Toyota's success was tied to a diffusion of the TPS among suppliers. The buying of high value-added, supplier (or jointly) designed parts, components, and subassemblies is rather different from that of sourcing Toyota designed parts from subcontractors.

The asset specificity of make or buy decisions hinges largely on who bears most of the design, development, and production costs associated with those things of value purchased by Toyota. If the costs of product development and, therefore, of the underlying asset specificity of the transaction lie more with one side than the other, that party has clear ownership rights. It may elect to sell or to retain them. But, if the value of the product hinges largely on its purchase by a party other than the one responsible for its design and development, then ownership rights become clouded. The cost of product development is borne by one party but the value of the product lies in its purchase by another. How should profits be distributed in such transactions?

In the shift from the dualist model of the TPS to the network model, there is an emerging shift in the burden and nature of asset specificity. The transition is from residual rights of ownership toward an emphasis on transaction specific ownership rights. This parallels a shift from bilateral asymmetry to bilateral and multilateral symmetry in information flows, followed by a corresponding shift from unilateral to bilateral purchasing agreements.

Reduced concern for property rights and enhanced flow of technical information unlock possibilities for collaborative product development and self-developed technologies. Network-embedded interactions grow, and become recognized and rewarded (see Figure 12.5). Such developments occurred in Japan, especially among Toyota suppliers and more generally among industrial equipment suppliers, from the late 1960s and early 1970s as shown in the figure.

The learning model as an extension of the network model implies a certain degree of spontaneity and mutuality of interests as to when, where, and how improvements to the TPS occur. Hence, it is obvious that the network and learning models of the TPS must have come after the dualist model, that is, after the hard-edged definition of the TPS had been transferred to major suppliers by the 1970s.

What is less clear is the developmental relationship between the network model of TPS and its extension, the learning model. The emphasis on building good bilateral relations within the network model is the key. Organizational development from a network-based entity into a learning paradigm requires the appearance of a new organizational culture, interpreting culture as "learned ways of coping with experience" (Gregory 1983), and this learning would undoubtedly take time. There is an argument in the organizational learning literature that asserts a progression from reciprocity to equity to distributive justice (Ring and Van de Ven). This argument is congruent with a shift in behavioral emphasis from control to commitment (Walton 1985). But for a new organizational culture to coalesce, emerge, and grow around the themes of equity, commitment, trust, and distributive justice, a decade or two were needed.

To move to a full-fledged learning model, however, there should be a role shift

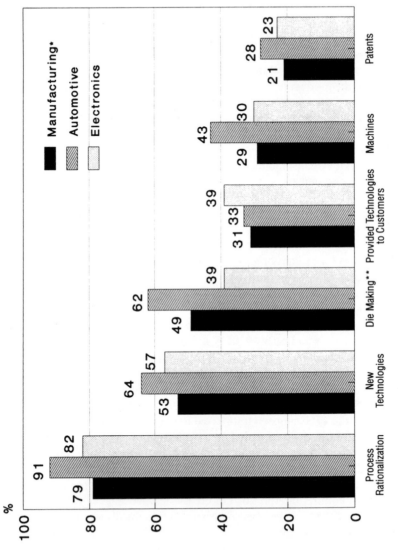

Figure 12.5 Percentages of subcontractors who possessed self-developed technologies in use and who provided them to customers in manufacturing industries (1983). Notes: *Sample size = 1,592 subcontractors; **percentages of those who were using self-made dies among those whose processes included the use of dies. *Source:* Data from *Shitauke Chusho Kigyo no Shin Kyokumen* (New Facets of Subcontracting Small and Medium Enterprises), Central Bank for Commercial and Industrial Cooperatives, Survey Department, 1983, pp. 61–8; compiled by Toshihiro Nishiguchi.

within the TPS. Coexistence and coprosperity imply that Toyota assumes more of a coordinating than commanding role and that role becomes more of a strategic than operational hub of the TPS. It is just this sort of a progression that would allow improvements to occur more spontaneously and autonomously in the TPS. Furthermore, as the TPS moved to a less centralized system of ownership rights, a tendency to favor mutual problem solving would lead to a situation where reciprocity and equity became general principles of diffuse, multilateral transactions. In short, the combined shift from (a) bilateral asymmetry to multilateral symmetry, and from (b) residual rights of ownership to transaction-specific rights of ownership creates an organizational system where localized learning is enhanced and shared.

Thus, a "multiplier effect" distinguishes the learning from the network model. Learning and profit sharing diffuse rapidly because organizations supplying the TPS experience coexistence and coprosperity based on multilateral, future-oriented, collaborative activity. Learning is multiplied throughout the system by the creation of countless pathways for enhancing the performance of the TPS without an attendant requirement that these pathways culminate in or even intersect with Toyota.

The Diffusion of the TPS in Japan

Accepting an historical or developmental approach to reconciling different models of the TPS results in combined hardware-dependent and software-dependent definitions of the TPS. Physical, behavioral, organizational, and systemic characteristics and capabilities have become enmeshed in an evolving interdependent way of working. Using this matured definition of the TPS as a standard, what can be said about the spread of the TPS in Japan? Here, a critical distinction must be made regarding whether or not firms practicing the TPS are in regular contact with Toyota Motor Corporation. We distinguish between a group of companies that are and another set that are not.

In the case of firms engaged in recurring transactions with Toyota (mostly members of the *first-tier* of Toyota suppliers or, for our purposes, the Toyota transaction group), the adaptation of the TPS corresponds neatly with the chronology previously outlined for explaining the evolution of the TPS. However, the diffusion of the TPS to the Toyota transaction group must be considered in light of two factors.

First, there is an inevitable time lag in the transfer of the TPS depending on the organizational capabilities and managerial skills of those firms wishing to learn the TPS; also, the intensity and scope of transactions with Toyota will affect the speed and degree with which the TPS is learned. Second, there is also a spatial factor in addition to the developmental one affecting the diffusion of the TPS within the Toyota transaction group. The network model of the TPS is an aggregation of various subsystems. Subsystems are defined as zones of transaction between first-tier companies and other, lower-tier, companies in the group. The nature of these transactions, like those between Toyota and first-tier companies, may be defined by information flow characteristics such as intensity, density, and duration of transactions.

However, spatial dimensions affect the spread of the TPS in several ways. A fully elaborated network model of the TPS is multitiered, multihierarchical, and multinodal. Obviously, Toyota's involvement in these many tiers, hierarchies, and nodes is not equal, and this inequality may affect the diffusion of the TPS by the creation of differential transacting and learning opportunities.

The principle of "clustered control" describes the key organizational mechanism for managing transactions in subsystems of the TPS. In effect, lower-tier suppliers cluster under higher-tier suppliers. While the transfer of the TPS between Toyota and first-tier suppliers can be assumed to have followed the chronology detailed earlier, it is less certain when and to what extent the TPS was diffused to lower-tier firms.[17] While the TPS spread beyond the first-tier of Toyota suppliers since the late 1970s and early 1980s, it seems that some of this diffusion occurred as a result of burden-shifting, that is, as a result of lower-tier firms holding inventories to satisfy the JIT directives of higher-tier firms. Stories abound of delivery trucks of lower-tier suppliers lining up for hours in advance of their scheduled deliveries at higher-tier factories.

The evaluation of burden-shifting is pivotal for assessing the spread of the TPS. If burden-shifting represents a transitional stage on the way to a full implementation of the TPS (where burden-sharing rather than burden-shifting is the rule), then this shifting should be accepted as evidence of the spread of the TPS to lower-tiers of the network. This shift occurred perhaps as much as ten years ago (the late 1970s to early 1980s) inside the group.

Outside the Toyota transaction group, however, the methods of adapting to the TPS, and the timing, clustering, and evaluation of the fullness of that transfer are not at all clear. As indicated already, the TPS is not merely a structure of production, a hardware-oriented solution to increasing manufacturing throughout. The TPS is a dynamic of intra- and interfirm relations, a philosophy of human resource management, an insistence on method as well as on attitude, and a manufacturing system that perhaps cannot be disentangled from (inter)organizational characteristics, industry structure, macroeconomic conditions, and institutional experience. All of these features make imitation and, therefore, diffusion difficult.

Nevertheless, certain points can be mentioned concerning the spread of the TPS outside the Toyota transaction group. First, there appear to be few production sites or managers in Japan that have *not* been affected by the advent of the TPS. The periodical literature on the TPS is huge, and lectures and training courses are readily available. Second, employing our full-scale model of the TPS, however, few manufacturing organizations outside the Toyota transaction group seem to be fully implementing the TPS. Many are trying to move in that direction, nevertheless. Third, only by confining the TPS definition to its hardware-dependent version—emphasizing minimum stock and the use of *kanban*, "autonomous" machines, and so on—has the TPS diffused widely.

The difficulties in diffusing the full-scale version of the TPS lie in building *systemwide incentives* for mutual problem solving and profit sharing. In the case of firms that have not enjoyed as profitable an expansion of output, it may be rather difficult to convert and transfer hundreds and thousands of suppliers to an extremely exacting and demanding production system like Toyota's. Two case studies illustrate why this may be so.

Nissan

Although a limited *kanban* system (called the "action plate" system) was introduced at Nissan during the late 1970s in an endeavor to emulate the TPS, it did not achieve as much as was hoped. Nissan's inventory turnover did not approach Toyota's (Cusumano 1985). Even though JIT delivery from suppliers was much encouraged, buffer stocks tended to increase rather than decrease in various production sites and stages. On occasion, materials needed for production and arranged through Nissan or its affiliates failed to reach suppliers just in time, while suppliers were nevertheless expected to deliver finished components to Nissan on a JIT basis.[18]

Nissan and Toyota are similar in their pursuit of a full product-line strategy and in their reliance on an extensive infrastructure of suppliers. However, they are very different in the perception and execution of basic production principles and in supplier management practices. In between the terrain framed by the dualist and network models of the TPS, Nissan is struggling in-house with production management problems. As of the late 1970s, Nissan's suppliers appeared relatively less effective in adapting to the stringent performance standards equivalent to those of the TPS.

Toshiba

In the case of Toshiba, a specific and focused effort to transfer the TPS was initiated from the mid-1970s, coinciding with the oil crises and with what Toshiba called "senbetsu no jidai," or the age of selectivity. Among other things, selectivity referred to the need to reduce the number of Toshiba suppliers and to upgrade their performance. Upgrading their performance included more stress on JIT, multiskilling, layout flexibility, and small lot production. (To its credit, Toshiba emphasized these improvements as much internally as it did externally with suppliers.)

Nevertheless, Toshiba managers admit that the company has not been so successful in implementing the hard-edged definition of the TPS. Two reasons are usually given for this circumstance. First, the characteristics of the electronics industry make it rather more difficult to identify best practice: electronics technology is highly fungible and consumer electronics markets are rapidly changing. Second, product characteristics are exceedingly varied: short product life cycles, wide variation in product sizes and length of production runs, and variable asset specificities in production know-how (making it difficult, for example, to reach agreement on the apportionment of residual and specific transaction rights, as in the cases of producing nuclear power equipment or ATM machines where software and hardware rights may be hard to disentangle).

Being between a dualist model and a network model of the TPS has certain consequences for Toshiba. It is not able to achieve nearly synchronized production throughout the manufacturing process and an unusual, perhaps unequal, burden for implementing the TPS falls on suppliers' and affiliates' shoulders. It is difficult in some product lines to move beyond the confrontation of dualist, asymmetrical bargaining relations. Nonetheless, *when product characteristics allow for a TPS-like evolution in the electronics industry,* the power of the TPS model is likely to convince industry managers that they should encourage an evolution of production systems by deemphasizing residual rights and by sharing information.[19]

The Reality

As the examples suggest, it is doubtful whether the full-scale model of the TPS has spread as far in Japan as is widely believed. Other cases involving reputable, first-line firms, such as Hitachi, Honda, and Sony, could be cited. Even in the case of Toyota, the diffusion of the TPS is mostly confined to the Toyota transaction group although some second- and third-tier companies are adopting the TPS. Hence, when a full-blown definition of the TPS is employed, there is some question how far the TPS has diffused beyond Toyota's first-tier suppliers.

Conclusions

This paper has sought to define and interpret the large numbers, central importance, and functional interdependence of suppliers in the Toyota Production System. Our proposed definition is a two-part one, referring to a number of traditional hardware-based characteristics associated with the TPS on the one hand, and with a range of behavioral and organizational features linking Toyota and its suppliers on the other. The most important of the latter include:

- An extremely large number of suppliers that are neither financially dependent on nor technically independent of Toyota.
- A decentralization of key design and technology development activities to numerous suppliers.
- The separation of residual rights from transaction-specific rights of ownership; this separation is seen as pivotal for encouraging the development of the high value-added, self-developed technologies and products that are increasingly traded within the Toyota supplier system.
- A shift toward multilateral symmetry in information flows among suppliers and between suppliers and Toyota.
- A progression from simple reciprocity in bilateral and multilateral relations to equity and distributive justice among key members of the supplier network.

The full elaboration of these features transpired over a forty year or longer period from 1947 to the 1990s, during which time the Japanese automobile industry and general economy grew enormously, more rapidly in fact than have ever been witnessed in world history. We emphasize the coincidence of these micro- and macroeconomic and organizational conditions leading to the fully matured TPS supplier system. Obviously, creating trust is easier for firms facing rapid economic growth compared with firms experiencing stable or declining demand (Klein, Crawford, and Alchian 1978).

In general, we suggest that the TPS supplier system in its organizationally embedded, fully elaborated sense has not spread as far as is widely believed. Nevertheless, the "success" of the TPS has already been widely studied and discussed in Japan and elsewhere.[20] Paradoxically, therefore, even without a clear-cut organizational definition and understanding of the supply function in the TPS, the Toyota Production System has become an example and vision of what is possible in the world of motor vehicle production and supply. Workers, engineers, managers, and academics, along with millions of Toyota motor vehicle owners can attest to the workings of that vision.

Notes

The authors would like to thank the members of PRISM (Pacific Roundtable on Industry, Society and Management) for their insightful and helpful comments on earlier drafts of this essay.

1. While anecdotal, a good story can be told concerning the TPS and its acknowledged founder, Mr. Taiichi Ohno. Mark Fruin recalls a conversation with Mr. Norihiko Shimizu, former director of the Boston Consulting Group in Japan. On a number of occasions, Shimizu sat on panels or participated in workshops with Ohno. Shimizu reports that Ohno once said, "We know that the TPS works but we don't know why it works so well."

2. Banri Asanuma (1988; 1989), perhaps the leading authority on the contractual relations binding suppliers to assemblers in Japan, is a rare exception, though he has little to say concerning the organizational dynamics of the supplier system as a whole in contrast to its firm-to-firm, bilateral relations.

3. As early as 1972, and some would say even earlier, beginning with R. H. Coase (1937), economists have chafed and belabored the dichotomy between markets and hierarchies in economic relations. G. B. Richardson (1972) pivots on this issue.

4. Interview with John Eby, Director of Strategic Planning, Ford Motor Company, Detroit, August 10, 1990. It might be noted that these figures are contradicted by other evidence that suggests various procurement levels depending on the source and the method of measurement for GM, Ford, and Chrysler. Some of the confusion comes from the efforts of U.S. auto companies to buy more in recent years thus raising the overall totals in question, and some of it may spring from variations within car model lines. The new Saturn affiliate of GM, for example, has a higher level of outsourcing than traditional GM lines.

5. This assertion can be sustained on the basis of data published in Womack, Jones, and Roos (1990). The background data for this book, as well as for other materials, will be published by members of the International Motor Vehicle Program, and they will document beyond a doubt the greater efficiency and speed of the Toyota Production System. See also Marvin B. Lieberman, Lawrence J. Lau, and Mark D. Williams (1990); and a recent special issue of the Japanese language periodical *Economisuto* (Feb. 1991), especially three articles by Professors Sei, Nishiguchi, and Omura that treat the nature of the auto parts supply system in Japan.

6. For a thorough historical account of this evolution, see Toshihiro Nishiguchi (forthcoming, 1993), especially chapter 4.

8. Based on our recent field research in Japan covering nine assemblers and ten first-tier suppliers; interviews conducted from November 13–28, 1990.

9. There is a considerable literature that deals with the basic notions of the TPS. Among the most useful are Ohno (1978; 1988), Monden (1983; 1985), Schonberger (1982), and Cusumano (1985).

10. While this essay treats only two models of the Toyota Production System—dualist and network—undoubtedly there are finer gradations.

11. In consequence of these features, the competitive advantages associated with the TPS seem less country-specific than organization-specific. Nonetheless, the principles and practices of the TPS are well understood in Japan. As a result, the TPS may be becoming a general model of how best to organize in industries characterized by high-volume production, multiple-year product life-cycles, and considerable product variety. In these industries, the spread of TPS-like production systems may be culminating in country-specific competitive advantages.

12. The dualist argument, when applied in the extreme, can result in treatments that are highly critical of Toyota, such as that of Satoshi Kamata (1982).

13. Michael A. Cusumano (1988) argues that the history of innovations supporting the development of the TPS was one of moving from an emphasis on process improvement to product improvement within Toyota and then transferring these improvements to suppliers.

14. This is the model of the TPS explored in W. Mark Fruin (1991).

15. The characters for this phrase can be read equally correctly in two ways: *kyozon kyoei* or *kyoson kyoei.*

16. There is a major interpretative difference between maturation and saturation of markets. *Maturation* of markets, the more common term, refers to the matching of demand with available products. *Saturation,* on the other hand, implies a surfeit of products relative to demand. If you like, maturation is "demand-driven" and saturation is "supply-driven." The best known recent statement of the saturation thesis relative to modern production is Michael Piore and Charles Sabel (1984).

17. An examination of the evolution of Daihatsu and Nippondenso's relations with Toyota is contained in Fruin (1992). Similar discussions abound in Japanese language materials.

18. Drawn from Toshihiro Nishiguchi's field research and comparative observations of Nissan and Toyota supplier networks in Japan from 1986 to 1990.

19. Information on Toshiba is drawn from Mark Fruin's fieldwork and observations in a Toshiba factory in Japan from 1985 to 1990.

20. Comparative data gathered and analyzed by Toshihiro Nishiguchi and John Krafcik document the considerable differences found in motor vehicle and component production facilities worldwide. See, for example, John Krafcik and James P. Womack (1987) and Toshihiro Nishiguchi (1987).

References

Asanuma, Banri. 1988. "Japanese Manufacturer-Supplier Relationships in International Perspective: The Automobile Case," Working Paper Number 8, Faculty of Economics, Kyoto University.

Asanuma, Banri. 1989. "Manufacturer-Supplier Relationships in Japan and the Concept of Relation-Specific Skill," *Journal of the Japanese and International Economies* 3:2–4.

Coase, R. H. 1937. "The Nature of the Firm," *Economica,* pp. 386–405.

Cusumano, Michael A. 1985. *The Automobile Industry in Japan.* Cambridge, Mass.: Harvard Council on East Asian Studies, Harvard University Press.

Cusumano, Michael A. 1988. "Manufacturing Innovation: Lessons from the Japanese Auto Industry," *Sloan Management Review* **29**(fall):29–39.

Fruin, Mark W. 1992. *The Japanese Enterprise System: Competitive Strategies and Cooperative Structures.* New York: Oxford University Press.

Granovetter, Mark. 1985. "Economic Action and Social Structure: The Problem of Embeddedness," *American Journal of Sociology* **91**:491.

Gregory, Kathleen L. 1983. "Native-View Paradigms: Multiple Cultures and Culture Conflicts in Organizations," *Administrative Science Quarterly* **28**:364.

Grossman, Sanford J., and Oliver D. Hart. 1986. "The Costs and Benefits of Ownership: A Theory of Vertical and Lateral Integration," *Journal of Political Economy* **94**(Aug.):691–719.

Hayes, Robert H., Steven C. Wheelright, and Kim B. Clark. 1988. *Dynamic Manufacturing.* New York: The Free Press.

Industry Research System. 1986. *Toyota Jidosha.* Nagoya: Industry Research System.

Kamata, Satoshi. 1982. *Japan in the Passing Lane.* New York: Penguin.

Klein, Benjamin, Robert G. Crawford, and Armen A. Alchian. 1978. "Vertical Integration, Appropriable Rents, and the Competitive Contracting Process," *Journal of Law and Economics* **21**:297–326.

Krafcik, John, and James P. Womack. 1987. "Comparative Manufacturing Practice: Imbalances and Implications." Paper presented at the First Policy Forum, International Motor Vehicle Program, M.I.T., May.

Lieberman, Marvin B., Lawrence J. Lau, and Mark D. Williams. 1990. "Firm-Level Productivity and Management Influence: A Comparison of U.S. and Japanese Automobile Producers," *Management Science* **36**:1–21.

Monden, Yasuhiro. 1983. *Toyota Production System: Practical Approach to Production Management.* Atlanta: Industrial Engineering & Management Press.

Monden, Yasuhiro. 1985. *Toyota Shisutemu.* Tokyo: Kodansha.

Nishiguchi, Toshihiro. 1987. "Competing Systems of Automotive Components Supply." Paper presented at the First Policy Forum, International Motor Vehicle Program, M.I.T., May.

Nishiguchi, Toshihiro. 1993, forthcoming. *Strategic Industrial Sourcing: The Japanese Advantage.* New York: Oxford University Press.

Ohno, Taiichi. 1978. *Toyota Seisan Hoshiki (The Toyota Production System).* Tokyo: Daiyamondo.

Ohno, Taiichi. 1988. *Toyota Production System: Beyond Large-Scale Production.* Cambridge, Mass.: Productivity Press.

Ono, Keinosuke, and Konosuke Odaka. 1988. *The Automobile Industry in Japan—A Study in Ancillary Firm Development.* Tokyo: Kinokuniya.

Piore, Michael, and Charles Sabel. 1984. *The Second Industrial Divide.* New York: Basic Books.

Richardson, G. B. 1972. "The Organization of Industry," *Economic Journal* September, pp. 883–96.

Ring, Peter Smith, and Andrew H. Van de Ven. 1988. "Structures and Processes of Transaction," Discussion Paper 86 (May), Strategic Management Research Center, University of Minnesota.

Schonberger, Richard J. 1982. *Japanese Manufacturing Techniques: Nine Hidden Lessons in Simplicity.* New York: The Free Press.

Walton, Richard E. 1985. "From Control to Commitment: Transforming Work Force Management in the United States," in Kim B. Clark, Robert H. Hayes, and Christopher Lorenz, eds., *The Uneasy Alliance.* Boston: Harvard Business School.

Williamson, Oliver. 1975. *Markets of Heirarchies.* New York: The Free Press, and London: Collier Macmillan.

Williamson, Oliver. 1985. *The Economic Institutions of Capitalism: Firms, Markets, Relational Contracting.* New York: The Free Press, and London: Collier Macmillan.

Womack, James, Daniel Jones, and Daniel Roos. 1990. *The Machine That Changed the World: The Triumph of Lean Production.* New York: Rawson Associates.

IV

CONCLUDING
NOTES

13

National Specificities and the Context of Change: The Coevolution of Organization and Technology

GIOVANNI DOSI
BRUCE KOGUT

The chapters in this book present a wide range of evidence that the organizing of work varies considerably among countries. Country variations are historically persistent; in the language of Midler and Charue (Chap. 9), they have the characteristic of "irreversibility." The challenge posed by these studies is to understand to what extent the historical persistence in the variation of national organizing principles explains the long-term differentials in the income and growth of countries.

Whereas differences in organizing principles among countries tend to persist for long periods of time, economic leadership has proven to be historically cyclical. To a large extent, the chapters in this book are a discussion of the relative decline of the United States and the organizing principles of mass production, and the rise of Japan and Germany that are advancing on the strengths of quality production. The historical record suggests a cycle of divergence in the performance of countries due to the introduction of new organizing heuristics, followed by a gradual convergence due to the diffusion of these heuristics across borders (Boyer 1988; Kogut 1991).

What we are currently witnessing is a period of divergence resulting from the expansion of new techniques of organization in a few countries. These new techniques do not spring up uniformly from the soil of a nation. Rather, as the chapters by Midler and Charue (Chap. 9) and Kern and Schumann (Chap. 5) show, there is substantial variation within a country. Certain sectors, such as machine-tools or autos, may lead in advance of other industries. The study by Fruin and Nishiguchi (Chap. 12) suggests that many new practices in Japan are still in development and that their diffusion across sectors, and even within the lead automobile industry, is still very much in progress. Despite the discussion in the chapters by Webster

(Chap. 8), Jürgens (Chap. 6), and Dunning (Chap. 11) on the diffusion of Japanese techniques, the impression left by these studies is that the adoption of flexible work roles and subcontracting systems is substantially slower in the United States, the United Kingdom, France, and, perhaps to a lesser extent, Germany.

One way to understand national patterns in organizing is to identify, along the lines of Herrigel (Chap. 1), Lincoln (Chap. 3), and Westney (Chap. 2), the roles that larger institutions play inside a country. Since schools, technical training facilities, unions, and government agencies are regional and national institutions, they generate what Dimaggio and Powell (1983) have labelled "isomorphic pressures" that drive firms toward adopting similar practices. Firms in the same country draw, for example, from a pool of workers who have been trained in similar educational institutions and whose responsibilities and rights are defined under a common body of law.

It is the absence of international institutions, on the other hand, that accounts for why these pressures do not act similarly on firms located in different countries. Unions do not effectively span borders. Though the education of white-collar workers has been influenced by an international ideology of business education (witness the diffusion of American business schools among countries), workers are, by and large, trained in uniquely different educational systems.

If there is a factor that cuts across countries, it is the role played by competition in international markets. The reason why national variations in the organizing of work become important at particular historical junctions is because international competition is, at these times, driven by technological and organizational innovations that have not diffused across the borders of countries. International competition causes not only a fundamental challenge to firms losing market share, but to the very educational, labor, and legal institutions prevailing among countries.

The force of international competition drives the nature of adjustment to four distinct, though not exclusive, outcomes. The first is that a country with inferior practices may simply withdraw from the world market; autarkic policies, such as raising tariffs or forbidding trade, are historically quite significant. Indeed, the current era of relatively free flows of international trade and investment is the exception, but the longevity of this political order is clearly in question.

Second, the inferiority of organizing practices, which is revealed in relative productivity rates, is compensated by lower wages. According to numerous recent estimates, wage rates in the United States relative to Japan and Germany have rapidly deteriorated since the 1980s. Whittaker's description (Chap. 7) of the inability of British firms to match the Japanese practice of using a single employee for the integration of programming and operating tasks subtly suggests that lower efficiency is offset by the significantly lower wage rates in the United Kingdom.

Third, the analysis by Sorge and Maurice of the machine-tool industry in France and Germany (Chap. 4) shows that adjustment may also occur through market differentiation. Over time, French producers lost market share to both Japanese and German firms, with the surviving French firms focusing on specialized markets. Even with the expansion of mass produced automobiles in the first half of this century, there remained many producers of cars who specialized in low volume, customized production. Whether this outcome generates similar levels of income and wealth across countries is problematic, but it would seem to be an unlikely event.

The fourth mechanism of adjustment is the international diffusion and adoption of best practices. Many of the chapters in this book are analyses of the process by which new principles of organization are adopted. The composition of these practices, as the divergent cases of Japan and Germany suggest, need not be the same, but the direction of development should reflect a basic convergence in the design of tasks and organizing principles.

A comparison of these alternatives would certainly imply, from an economic perspective, that the fourth outcome of adopting a variant on new organizing principles would be the most appealing. Yet, the historical record, as outlined for Taylorism in the chapter by Kogut and Parkinson (Chap. 10), indicates that convergence is slow and only approximate. Moreover, the degree of convergence varies substantially by country.

These considerations raise a few fundamental questions. Can one identify a unifying and historical logic that shapes the development of distinct national technological and organizational trajectories? If different organizational features of firms matter in terms of national economic performance, why should particular countries "lock-in" within seemingly "inferior" organizational forms? The first question is a more general way of investigating why certain countries display historically bounded leadership. The second directs attention to why such leadership appears to be cyclical; convergence is not rapid, but economic leadership is also not enduring.

The kind of unified explanation required to address these diverse observations should provide an account of (1) the coevolution of firm-specific and country-specific technological and organizational capabilities, and (2) the implications for economic performance regarding trade, investment, and growth. To be historically realistic, this explanation must provide an argument by which firms and countries reproduce over time particular technological and organizing characteristics, even when these characteristics are inferior, in terms of efficiency, to existing forms of best practice.

Though these are large questions, there has been considerable agreement that their answers require a formulation sensitive to historical events, social institutions, and the cumulative growth of knowledge specific to firms and countries. No existing theory is near the full realization of the task of combining these elements to explain why firms and countries reproduce over time particular organizational and technological characteristics. But we can suggest, as a way of commenting on the contributions to this book, an outline of what such a theory would look like.

Coevolution of Organization and Technology

There are, in our view, three central elements to the sort of story of the coevolution of organization and technology we would like to develop regarding country cycles in economic leadership. These elements are expressions, in the language of Campbell (1969), of the three fundamental social processes of variation, retention, and selection (see also Aldrich 1979). The first element is that major innovations evolve at particular periods of time that alter, fundamentally, the way work is organized in specific locations. The second element is that firms and organizations retain new knowledge in the form of institutionalized rules and heuristics of search and decision. Because new knowledge builds on old knowledge embedded in institutionalized patterns of social action, innovations evolve and diffuse in a cumulative manner, with incremental learning being a driving factor in growth. Finally, these new practices must be in some sense selected by the environment; governments may subsidize their use, or consumers may favor the derived goods for reasons of price and quality (Nelson and Winter 1982; Dosi 1982, 1988; Silverberg, Dosi, and Orsenigo 1988).

The consequence of these three processes is that economic change is spatially and temporally bounded and is evolutionary. There are many ways to explore these issues, from historical and social analysis to more formal models. Yet, the underlying ideas are the same. The economic and social history shows that change tends to be ordered, complex, and irreversible. There are, in effect, self-organizing forces capable of generating multiple but finite number of historical outcomes.

Let us take a concrete example. The decision to organize a factory by mass production has several immediate effects. First, it is a destruction of the existing knowledge on how to organize a factory by alternative methods; a return to the old organization cannot instantaneously recover previous levels of productivity. Second, the knowledge gained in organizing a mass production system in one factory may suggest the application of similar methods (that is, problem-solving heuristics) to other factories or activities. Some of these activities may be quite distant from a manufacturing facility; witness the growth of mass production in higher educational systems. Third, the change in organization makes it more attractive to develop new capital equipment and technologies to facilitate mass production. Some of the new capital equipment may be bought from outside of the firm.

Technology and organization tend to coevolve with each other. Adam Smith noted this relationship when he attributed the organizing principle of the division of labor as linked to the invention of specialized machinery (Smith 1970, p. 112). Over time, the reciprocal effect of technology and organizing principles on each other creates what Hughes (1983) has called a technological system in which the efficiency of individual parts and firms depend on the whole.

To continue the example, the diffusion of mass production is, in principle, the ordered replication of a method of organization that progressively diffuses in an economy. This process of diffusion is self-reinforcing due to the accumulation of learning on how to do such mass production in better ways and due to the coevolution of technologies. As long as the social environment favors the relative growth of mass production, these techniques, once they have begun to expand, will diffuse either by the elimination of, or their imitation by, firms using older techniques.

This process of coevolution of technology and organization is described by a variant on the schema used in sociobiology (Durham 1991, pp. 182, 186). Initially, there are a finite number of types of technologies and ways by which work is organized that approximate the role played by genes in biological evolution.[1] By the tendency of firms to search locally for new ways of doing things that are similar to current practice, these technologies and organizing principles may be incrementally and interactively adapted and changed. Simultaneously, the technological and organizational attributes of a firm are subject to selection pressures. The joint process of learning and selection generates, in turn, a new frequency of technologies and organizing principles.

There are two important complications in this process by which new techniques of production and technology coevolve within an economy. The first is that the evolution of a new heuristic is characterized initially by increasing benefit. Eventually, however, declining gains from further development sets in. The early decades of mass production showed considerable investment in exploring new methods, but as the most fertile ground for incremental innovation is explored and exhausted, the benefits of further search decline.

Second, the new techniques will not fully diffuse in an environment. A residual demand may persist for products built on alternative systems. But also the heterogeneity in social institutions will maintain a heterogeneity in organization; factories in the American south differed substantially from the factories in Philadelphia and Boston regions where Taylorism was first introduced.

Nevertheless, competition within a fairly homogeneous national environment favors over time the expansion of particular techniques. From the perspective of history, these techniques are unlikely to be the "best." By the accident of war or social conflict, one technique may have been initially favored, which, due to learning and coevolutionary economies, locked a country into a particular and irreversible developmental path.[2] In all European countries, the demand of military production in World War I was a major impetus toward the introduction of principles of standardization of work. This change caused an irreversible departure from the old system in many of these countries. The impact of the war on the organization of work varied by nation.

Of course, these abstract statements do not do justice to the institutional richness of the social process of change and development. The decision to introduce mass production is itself embedded in a wider social context. Many suggestions (e.g., Lazonick 1990) have been made for the leadership of the United States in the development of systems of standardization and mass production, from the scarcity of labor and the task of training immigrant workers, to the pull of a mass market for the new household and construction goods to build the new frontier. As suggested by Kogut and Parkinson (Chap. 10), the absence of an embedded craft and guild tradition certainly abetted the diffusion of Taylorist ideas in the United States, while these very traditions slowed the adoption of work changes in the United Kingdom.

In this sense, coevolution takes on a wider meaning than just the positive externalities between certain kinds of organization and technologies. Rather, coevolution also tends to promote the mutual expansion of complementary social institutions.[3] A system of mass production and standardization of work encourages the development of labor unions concerned about job definitions and rules by which workers are laid off in cyclical downswings. Social institutions tend to coalesce around the principles by which work and human activities are organized.

These issues are old, but unsettled, themes in organizational theory. Webster's description of the incompatibility of the new technology with the existing organization (Chap. 8) shares many concerns of social-technical theory. The sociotechnical concept was initially worked out in the course of several field studies conducted by the Tavistock Institute in the British coal mining industry. For example, the classic study by Trist and Bamforth (1951) found that the introduction of a new kind of mining technology required a change in organization that conflicted with social and psychological norms. Technology cannot simply determine the organization, it was found, because its implementation is conditioned by the prevailing social system.

Since that basic study, there has been a bounty of research on the relationship of technology and organization. The findings have tended to fall into four camps: the primacy of technology (e.g., Woodward 1965); bureaucratic processes associated with size (Pugh, Hickson, and Hinings 1969); the contingency of the environment (Lawrence and Lorsch 1967; Pennings 1992; Sorge and Maurice, Chap. 4); and strategy (Child 1972). Yet, it is fair to say that despite the considerable research, the search for the factors that determine a mapping of a specific technology to a specific organizational structure has proved elusive.

Consider the chapters in this volume. Lincoln (Chap. 3) details how American and Japanese firms, after controlling for technology, differ in their practices by which decisions are reached and authority is exercised. Sorge and Maurice (Chap. 4) describe at length different organizing modes for German and French machine-tool firms. Midler and Charue (Chap. 9) found that even within the same country, two firms evolved different organizational structures by which to adopt flexible manufacturing methods.

The difficulty of identifying a connection between technology and organization is surprising, for common sense suggests that such a relationship should exist. It cannot be expected, for example, that the processing of high-speed steel could be carried out by the factory organization of the nineteenth century. Chandler (1977), in particular, has strenuously argued that the economies of speed demanded the development of new organizational capabilities at the turn of the century.

One way to reconcile common sense with the confusing findings on the relationship between technology and organization is to think of the problem as identifying a correspondence between sets as opposed to between elements. The study by Whittaker (Chap. 7), as noted earlier, showed that the introduction of computer controlled numerical machinery in Japan changed the task responsibilities of the operator to include programming. In the United Kingdom, the lower skill level of the operator ruled out this design; instead, an engineer was assigned the task of programming. These two solutions differ substantially, and there is no unique matching of the technology of flexible manufacturing to a single organizational design.

Still, there clearly is a set-to-set correspondence in organizing principles and technology. The chapters by Whittaker, Webster, and Midler and Charue (Chaps. 7, 8, and 9) provide careful documentation that organizational practices were altered by the introduction of new technologies. As Jürgens shows in his chapter (Chap. 6), throughout the world's auto industry, several new and fundamental practices, such as multiple manning of machinery, are being adopted, but with large differences in adaptation. The history of industrial relations, firm strategy, and social context strongly conditions the nature of the relationship of technology and organization, but this relationship must still conform to the broad technical constraints discovered in implementation.

Specificities in national principles of organization are sensitive, consequently, to the coincidence of unique historical events and the prevailing social order. In a broad sense, the coevolution of technologies and organization are constrained to reveal a pattern of convergence among countries. International competition, among other forces, motivates countries toward adopting the apparent best practices by which technology and organization are structured. Yet, the specific structures revealed over time are tempered by the national contexts and initial conditions.

Costs of Change

To complete the analysis of why coevolution carries significant implications for the economic performance of countries, it is essential to examine why these country-specific principles of organizing may be reproduced despite the selective pressures of international competition. The difficulty with the question is not the lack but, rather, the plethora of answers. The challenge to the existing economic and political order, the inability to identify the need for change, or the noncomprehension of the changes required are all viable candidates for explaining why new practices are not quickly diffused across the borders of a country.

Despite this embarrassment of riches, the condition of being locked into inferior practices even when better practices are identified can be explained in terms of three kinds of three factors that influence costs: switching, learning, and hysteretic. We abstract from two important considerations. First, the process by which organizations and institutions in one country come to make comparisons between the existing order and new ways of organizing differs substantially from this stylized description of these three factors that determine a condition of "lock-in." Second, these costs are not the same for all actors in a country; entrenched powers (e.g., incumbent firms or organized labor) may attach a greater cost to switching to a new system than might start-up companies or workers entering the labor force.[4]

In Figure 13.1, these three kinds of costs are described. There are two distinct ways of organizing activities, A and B. In each case, B is revealed as a less costly way of accomplishing a given task.

Figure 13.1*A* depicts the simple case where the costs of switching between organizing principles A and B are greater than the benefits. An obvious example is the continued use of a nonmetric system of measurement in the United States. The incremental benefits of using a metric system are offset by the large costs of changing all the existing standards and measurements.

One of the most complex considerations is that the desirability of switching increases with the number of institutions and firms who find it advantageous to adopt the metric system. The dependence of any one firm in a larger technological system means that the costs of switching vary depending on the decisions of other actors in the country. Overcoming the effects of history requires a collective choice.

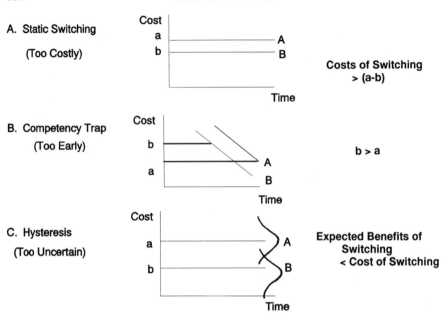

Figure 13.1 Three cases of lock-in. A and B represent technologies; a and b represent the current cost of using a given technology.

For this reason, switching to a new technique is not simply a decision for the firm, but rather, is a question of the organization of the national industrial system.

In Figure 13.1*B,* the effect of history is seen to result in a competency trap; learning to be good at an inferior technique has advanced so far as to make switching to better organizing principles unattractive. Even though technique B is better than A, a country has built up a cumulative experience in using the latter technique. To switch to B means that it must scrap the value of this gained learning. At the same time, it will be forced to begin the learning process again. A static comparison shows that the costs of producing with B are greater than those with A.

It is easy to conclude that the decision to stay with A is myopic. With proper foresight, it should be clear that with new learning, technique B is superior. The actual calculation is complicated by such factors as the discount rate (i.e., how important is the future relative to the present) and the usefulness of technique B to new endeavors.

A more complicated consideration is that a firm and country may be locked into a vicious circle. If a firm switches to technique B, it will incur losses if it faces international competitors that have already gained experience using these organizing principles and are operating at lower costs. The ability to sustain these losses is a question of whether a country and its resident firms have access to the necessary capital funding. With insufficient funding, the firm may be unable to switch to the better technique, or, if it does switch, it may become bankrupt. In the meantime, its competitors will be in a virtuous cycle by enjoying decreasing costs with further experience in the superior technique.

One way to break out of the vicious circle is to adopt technique B and finance the losses by lower returns to either capital or labor. If capital is mobile and can easily flow to foreign countries, then the costs of adjustment will fall on workers' wages. Of course, by staying with technique A, wages also will eventually fall in any event as competitors gain further experience with the superior technique. The flexibility in labor and social institutions that will govern this period of adjustment rests largely on the strength of the political order in managing this critical juncture.

Given the complexity of these issues, the benefits of switching are clearly uncertain. This uncertainty itself has fundamental consequences for why a social system should, on rational grounds, persist in its prevailing form. The sources of the uncertainty are several; the degree of social unrest and the costs of investing in the new technology are two sources previously stressed. But there may even be doubts about the benefits of the technology. Flexible manufacturing is less valuable in a stable environment regarding the value of flexibility in the future.

The implications of uncertainty on the decision to switch results in what is described as hysteresis. In Figure 13.1C the costs of techniques A and B are probabilistic. Though the mean costs differ, there remains the possibility that A may prove to be better than B. If there were no costs to switching, then a firm and country could simply switch from technique A to B, and back again. As shown earlier, one-time (or static) switching costs may render such change economically unattractive. These static costs understate, however, the unattractiveness of switching once uncertainty has been considered. Since costs are incurred and since the future best technique is uncertain, switching will not occur as frequently. After all, it may be adviseable to switch back in the near future. The effect of uncertainty is to increase the perceived dynamic (i.e., over-time) costs of switching compared to the static costs described in Figure 13.2A. Only a large disparity in the benefits of A and B will induce a switch.

The impact of uncertainty, therefore, is to heighten the persistence of history. It is easy to underestimate the importance of hysteresis. And yet rather small degrees of uncertainty over the future benefits can result in a substantial tendency toward inertia (see, e.g., Dixit 1989, and Kogut and Kulatilaka 1992). In retrospect, it is obvious to conclude that one way of doing something is superior to another. At prevailing prices of petroleum, the era of gas guzzling autos is clearly at an end, but the volatility in oil prices in the 1970s rendered such forecasting more hazardous. The costs of scrapping decades of experience in the production of large car manufacture and of investment in new plants and tooling for fuel efficient cars have proven to be astronomical. Small amounts of uncertainty over the direction of future demand can have a powerful influence on sustaining current capabilities and methods of organization.

Some Theoretical and Normative Conclusions

There is a troubling conclusion to this consideration of the costs of switching to new practices. No matter what choice a country makes, a fall in wages relative to foreign wages would appear to be avoidable. If best practices are not adopted, lower wages is a permanent state; if a decision is made to switch, the costs incurred during the transition period would require a reduction in relative wages by which to amortize the adjustment investment. However, even in the case where a country initially persists in its old practices, the desirability of switching would increase over time if the new practices should reveal greater dynamism and learning economies.

The implications of these observations is that country cycles in economic leadership are tied to the arrival of innovations in a lagging country and the high costs of the leader country to switch to the new practices. As per the argument advanced by Kogut and Parkinson (Chap. 10), the costs of adopting new innovations should be higher for new organizing principles (e.g., subcontracting systems) than for new technologies. Contrary to the belief that the decline of the United States derives from a fall in the *appropriability* of American technologies, we would suggest that this decline is linked to the diffusion of American organizing practices to other countries; at the same time, new and better practices are being introduced and worked out in other countries. But whereas the consequences of diffusion and the introduction of rival organizing principles force a decline in relative American wages, the historical process over the past century has generated substantial levels of wealth and capital accumulation by U.S. residents and corporations.

A reasonable deduction from this argument is that, in general, national specificities in organizing principles are only short-term phenomena without any long-lasting consequences on performance. Indeed, the long-term irrelevance of organizational forms can be argued from quite different theoretical points of view. Take, for example, an extreme version of a transaction-cost model of corporate organization. This model would suggest that observed institutional set-ups are the organizational responses to the requirement of efficient governance of exchanges. Hence, any observed international difference in the typical modes of organizing transactions would be primarily attributed to lags and leads in diffusion of more efficient forms of organization (assuming transaction costs to be similar across countries). In the long term, an extreme version of a transaction-cost theory of organization would suggest a convergence in institutional structures as determined by the differential efficiency of various organizational modes. There is some point where the fall in relative wages in the United States is sufficient to justify the costs of adopting better practices.

While this explanation is plausible, it need not be compelling if we are to take historical and institutional context seriously. We suggest that national specificities persist because the micro rules that generate differences in country performances are poorly understood and are difficult to change.[5] Better practices are not easily adopted because decision makers do not identify and calibrate the full set of opportunities. As suggested by many of the contributions to this book, an efficient governance approach fails to recognize the strong inertial forces that cause social institutions to be reproduced over time. Environments are complex and nonstationary, so that an understanding of the causal links between alternative organizational forms and outcomes is very opaque. The mapping between information, actions, and outcomes is, at best, imprecise, and undertaken on the grounds of available decision heuristics and untested expectations. It is not that firms and policymakers do not make choices, but, rather, that their choices are made in reference to a limited understanding of opportunities.

The variations in the micro rules that prevail in a society can generate significant differences in the macro performance of an economy. In this respect, Aoki's comparison between two "ideal" types—the "Japanese firm" and the "American firm"—is a good example: different internal governance structures affect learning and performance, despite identical economic opportunities (Aoki 1988). In an exploratory attempt to model and simulate the relationship between behavioral norms and patterns of growth, Chiaromonte, Dosi, and Orsenigo (1992) have shown how economic dynamics widely differ when simple alterations are made to behavioral rules (e.g., how adjustment occurs in labor markets), even when other system parameters, such as technological opportunities, are left unchanged.

It would follow from this discussion that the influence of history on restricting an economy's ability to transform itself radically can only be overcome by changing the expectations that inform the choices of firms, workers, and institutions. These expectations, or what can be called "notional" possibilities, concern the identity of available technologies and organizing heuristics (i.e., micro rules).[6] Because of the dependency of parts on the whole, however, these expectations consist also of anticipations regarding what other actors in the system will decide.

Several of the chapters in this volume comment directly on the process by which explicit public policies have influenced the notional set of technological and organizational opportunities. Herrigel (Chap. 1), in particular, describes the success of the government and public institutions of Baden Württemberg in providing institutional support by which new practices were diffused in the region. Similarly, Sorge and Maurice (Chap. 4) find French government policies to have been far less successful than the German in reorienting the machine-tool industry toward more flexible manufacturing technologies.

Kern and Schumann (Chap. 5) suggest a far more subtle dynamic in their study. The German economy, as argued by their original studies, was at a crossroad in the late 1960s. Rising wages threatened the export viability of mass production, and the importation of competing goods, when not prohibited by quotas or tariffs, rose in a number of sectors. Indeed, one would have been hard pressed to predict the high performance of the German economy in the 1980s in the context of the high unemployment of the 1970s. But what eventually caused a few sectors in the German economy to switch to new practices stressing flexibility and worker autonomy was the combination of a highly trained work force *and* the severe restraints on German firms to cut wages or to move production outside of the country. In other words, German firms were forced to search for new practices because the wage constraints ruled out persisting with traditional work methods.

Is there a lesson, then, in the ability of German firms to adapt to the pressures of international competition? Herrigel (Chap. 1) intimates that leaders have the capacity to lead by changing the notional possibilities understood by workers and managers. Kern and Schumann (Chap. 5) suggest that, by placing severe constraints on management and by empowering workers at the workplace, firms are forced to invest in searching and implementing new methods of organizing. Better practices evolve, they appear to suggest, when the attractiveness of short-term adjustment by cutting wages is eliminated.

But the complexity of the interdependence of institutional elements makes it difficult to extrapolate from one country's experience. Would raising minimum wages in the United States also evoke a similar response given high heterogeneity in labor training and skills? Should restrictions on outward flows of direct investment also be required, or should laws require the representation of labor on boards of directors and the formation of work councils?

These are difficult questions to address, and this difficulty is, in fact, the clue to the answers. The causality between action and outcome is highly dependent on the institutional context. National specificities in organization persist because knowledge of the causal relationships between practice and performance is gained only incrementally. The chapters in this book, by and large, agree that the direction of change is toward greater worker autonomy and reliance on skilled employees. Within this broad notion of convergence, there remains considerable play for the persistence in the variations of national principles by which work is organized.

Notes

1. There has been a growing literature in sociobiology on how to analyze culture in ways analogous to genes. See the discussion in Winter (1990) who identifies the genetic analogue with methods of organization.

2. For a discussion of historical accident and lock-in, see David (1985) and Arthur (1988).

3. This meaning is closer to the original use of coevolution in biology as the coadaptation of two species. The growth of the school stressing the population dynamics of genes, best known through the popular writings of Richard Dawkins, is closer to our discussion of the evolution of techniques. See Durham (1991, 166n.).

4. These concerns raise important issues of public choice and property rights. For applications to understanding cycles in country leadership, see Olson (1982) and North (1981).

5. See the discussion in Kogut (1990) on why practices may be more difficult to identify and adopt across borders.

6. See Dosi (1982, 1988) for a discussion.

References

Aldrich, Howard. 1979. *Organizations and Environments.* Englewood Cliffs, N.J.: Prentice Hall.

Aoki, M. 1988. *Information, Incentives and Bargaining in the Japanese Economy.* Cambridge, U.K.: Cambridge University Press

Arthur, Brian. 1988. "Competing Technologies: An Overview," in G. Dosi, C. Freeman, R. Nelson, G. Silverberg, and L. Soete, eds., *Technical Change and Economic Theory,* pp. 590–607. London and New York: Printer Publishers.

Boyer, Robert. 1988. "Technical Change and the Theory of 'Regulation'," in G. Dosi, C. Freeman, R. Nelson, G. Silverberg, and L. Soete, eds., *Technical Change and Economic Theory,* pp. 67–94. London and New York: Printer Publishers.

Campbell, Donald T. 1969. "Variation and Selective Retention in Socio-Cultural Evolution," *General Systems* **14**:69–85.

Chandler, Alfred. 1977. *The Visible Hand: The Managerial Revolution in American Business.* Cambridge, Mass.: Harvard University Press.

Chiaramonte, Francesca, Giovanni Dosi, and Luigi Orsenigo. 1992. "Innovative Learning and Institutions in the Process of Development: On the Microfoundations of Growth Regimes," in R. Thompson, ed., *Learning and Technological Change,* London: Macmillan.

Child, John. 1972. "Organization Structure, Environment and Performance: The Role of Strategic Choice," *Sociology* 6:2–22.

David, Paul. 1985. "Clio and the Economics of QWERTY," *American Economic Review* 75:332–37.

Dimaggio, Paul, and Walter Powell. 1983. "The Iron Cage Revisited: Institutional Isomorphism and Collective Rationality in Organizational Fields," *American Sociological Review* 48:147–60.

Dixit, Avinash. 1989. "Entry and Exit Decisions Under Uncertainty," *Journal of Political Economy* 97:620–38.

Dosi, Giovanni. 1982. "Technological Paradigms and Technological Trajectories: A Suggested Interpretation of the Determinants and Directions of Technical Change," *Research Policy* 11:147–63.

Dosi, Giovanni. 1988. "Sources, Procedures, and Microeconomic Effects of Innovation," *Journal of Economic Literature* 26:1120–71.

Durham, William. 1991. *Coevolution. Geneses, Culture, and Human Diversity,* Stanford, Calif.: Stanford University Press.

Hughes, Thomas. 1983. *Networks of Power: Electrification in Western Society. 1880–1930,* Baltimore: John Hopkins University Press.

Kogut, B. 1990. "The Permeability of Borders and the Speed of Learning Among Countries," in *Globalization of Firms and the Competitiveness of Nations,* Crawford Lecture. Lund, Sweden: University of Lund.

Kogut, Bruce. 1991. "Country Capabilities and the Permeability of Borders," *Strategic Management Journal* 12:33–47.

Kogut, Bruce, and Nalin Kulatilaka. 1993 (forthcoming). "Operating Flexibility, Global Manufacturing, and the Benefits of a Multinational Network," *Management Science.*

Lawrence, Paul, and Jay Lorsch. 1967. *Organization and Environment: Managing Differentiation and Integration.* Boston: Division of Research, Graduate School of Business and Administration, Harvard University.

Lazonick, William. 1990. *Competitive Advantage on the Shop Floor.* Cambridge, Mass: Harvard University Press.

Nelson, Richard, and Sidney Winter. 1982. *An Evolutionary Theory of Economic Change.* Cambridge, Mass.:: Belknap Press.

North, Douglass C. 1981. *Structure and Change in Economic History.* New York: W. W. Norton.

Olson, Mancur. 1982. *The Rise and Decline of Nations: Economic Growth, Stagflation, and Social Ridigities.* New Haven, Conn.: Yale University Press.

Pennings, Johannes. 1992. *Structural Contingency Theory: A Reappraisal,* vol. 14, Research in Organizational Behavior. San Francisco: JAI Press.

Pugh, Derek, David Hickson, and Robert Hinings. 1969. "The Context of Organizational Structures," *Administrative Science Quarterly* 14:91–114.

Silverberg, Gerald, Giovanni Dosi, and Luigi Orsenigo. 1988. "Innovation, Diversity, and Diffusion: A Self-Organizing Model," *Economic Journal* 98:1032–54.

Smith, Adam. 1970. *The Wealth of Nations.* Harmondsworth, Middlesex, U.K.: Penguin.

Trist, Eric, and Kenneth Bamforth. 1951. "Some Social and Psychological Consequences of the Longwall Method of Coal-getting," *Human Relations* **4**:6–38.

Winter, Sidney. 1990. "Survival, Selection, and Inheritance in Evolutionary Theories of Organization," in *Organizational Evolution: New Directions,* J. Singh, ed, pp. 269–297. Newbury Park, Calif.: Sage.

Woodward, Joan. 1965. *Industrial Organization: Behavior and Control.* London: Oxford University Press.

Index

Aix Group, 75–76
American organizing principles in Europe, 179–99
  American organizing principles, 181–87
  multidivisional structure, 187–96
American organizing principles of work, 181–87
  American system of manufactures, 181–82
  diffusion to continental Europe, 184–86
  diffusion to United Kingdom, 183–84
American Production and Inventory Control Society (APICS), 143
Assembly line, 109, 115, 161, 184
  cycle times, 118
Aston centralization scale, 60, 63–64
Asymmetrical, bilateral relations (arms-length), 231
Autarkic policies, 250
Automated transfer lines, 116
Automation in car industry, 113–16
  substitution of human labor with, 109
Automobile body shop robotization, 156–74
  automatic line control, 162
  chain of command hierarchy, 164
  design of organizational objectives, 163
  diversity as result of irreversible learning processes, 167–68
  diversity of production patterns, 163–64
  flexibility and production capacities, 160–61
  importance of technological obsolescence, 172–73
  inadequacy of traditional working systems, 162
  labor organizations and, 170–71
  line controller, 163–65
  management models, 166
  new industrial doctrine, 164–65
  plant layout and human-machine relationships, 160
  production flow constraints, 160
  restructuring labor force, 168–70
  role of management in, 171–72
  stability of organized models versus dynamic process of job development, 173–74
  stabilization via increased production volume, 173
  three typical robotization models, 165–67
  transformation of production supervisors, 170
Automobile industry. *See* Car industry

Babbage principles, 129
Baden Württemberg, 15–32
  banks in, 19
  chambers of commerce in, 18–19
  decentralization in, 22–24
  decentralized production among small and medium-size firms, 16–22
  education institutions in, 17–18
  industrial adjustment in, 15
  large firms and capital mobility, 28–32
  large firms and decentralized small and medium-sized production, 25–32
  mutual convergence, 16
  number of small and medium-size firms, 16
  openness in, 20–22
  organizations, 17–20
  origins of decentralized system and role of large firms, 22–25
  partible inheritance in, 22–23
  power imbalances in contracting in, 26–28
  redundancy in, 20
  regional government and, 19–20, 29–30
  risk socializing system in, 22
  role of large firms in, 23–25
  self-policing through fear in, 21–22
  small and medium-sized firms and mass production in post-war Germany, 24–25
  success of small and medium-size firms, 16–17
  technology subsidy programs in, 20
  trade associations in, 18–19
Banks, in Baden Württemberg, 19
Bedaux system, 184, 185, 186
"Best practice"
  techniques, 218
  as term, 111
Bicycle industry, 183

263